Norma Jean Profitt, DSW

Women Survivors, Psychological Trauma, and the Politics of Resistance

Pre-publication
REVIEWS,
COMMENTARIES,
EVALUATIONS . . .

"Through the stories and experiences of women survivors of abuse, Norma Jean Profitt presents a compelling argument on the importance of political and collective action as a means of resisting oppression. She questions current practice with its emphasis on treatment for survivors of abuse over the active involvement of survivors in the violence-against-women movement. She also asserts that the channeling of action by service providers into community-based committees does not produce any real change. She calls for the revitilization of the spirit and struggle of the violence-against-women movement through the re-politicization of women's shelters and collective struggle for social change that involves survivors in the work. This book should be read by survivors, services providers, and activists in the violence-against-women movement."

Gloria Geller, PhD
Faculty of Social Work,
University of Regina,
Saskatchewan, Canada

More pre-publication
REVIEWS, COMMENTARIES, EVALUATIONS . . .

"**T**his is a daring book, in which Norma Jean Profitt first encourages us to more fully understand the courageous process of women with abusive partners confronting and working through the contradictions in their lives. She then challenges us to face the contradictions and struggles we also experience as activists in our feminist/antioppressive work. By addressing both of these sets of contradictions, Profitt calls on us to reassess our assumptions regarding 'survivors,' our organizational shifts away from political action in the past decade, as well as our investment in the status quo.

While challenging us, Profitt does not demonize or simplify. Instead, she gives voice to the expertise of women who have survived abuse and become politically active, highlights connections between their personal healing and collective work, explores the complexities and struggles of feminist/antioppressive organizations working to support such healing and political action, and invites us all to 'forge a new configuration of collaboration among feminists, activists, survivors, and community-based professionals.' It is a call worthy of our response."

Sue McKenzie-Mohr, MSW
Counselor,
University of New Brunswick,
Canada

The Haworth Press, Inc.

Women Survivors, Psychological Trauma, and the Politics of Resistance

Women Survivors, Psychological Trauma, and the Politics of Resistance

Norma Jean Profitt, DSW

The Haworth Press®
New York • London • Oxford

The Haworth Press, Inc., 10 Alice Street, Binghamton, NY 13904-1580

Excerpts from Teresa de Lauretis's "Eccentric Subjects: Feminist Theory and Historical Consciousness" are reprinted from *Feminist Studies*, 16(1), Fall 1990, by permission of the publisher, Feminist Studies, Inc.

Cover design by Jennifer M. Gaska.

Library of Congress Cataloging-in-Publication Data

Profitt, Norma Jean.
   Women survivors, psychological trauma, and the politics of resistance / Norma Jean Profitt.
      p.   cm.
   Includes bibliographical references and index.
   ISBN 0-7890-0890-4 (alk. paper) — ISBN 0-7890-1113-1 (pbk. : alk. paper)
   1. Abused wives—Canada—Interviews. 2. Abused women—Canada—Interviews. 3. Feminism—Canada. I. Title.

HV6626.23.C2 P76 2000
362.82′920971—dc21

99-462147

CONTENTS

ABOUT THE AUTHOR

Norma Jean Profitt, DSW, is a feminist social worker who has worked for many years in the fields of women's issues and violence against women. She was a board member, program committee member, and director of a transition house in Nova Scotia, and a member of the provincial coalition of transition houses. She also had a small private practice with women in Halifax, Nova Scotia.

For five years she worked in Costa Rica with a rural women's organization and a feminist collective engaged in community organization and education. With colleagues, she developed a theoretical framework and methodology for addressing that issue, facilitating a mutual support group in a small, semirural community, designing popular education materials for women, and carrying out workshops for collective members and grassroots women's groups.

Dr. Profitt is currently Assistant Professor in the Department of Social Work at St. Thomas University in Fredericton, New Brunswick, Canada, and is conducting research on the relation between woman abuse and child abuse. She looks forward to becoming involved again in international work with women.

Acknowledgments

I would like to express my solidarity with the women who participated in this research, particularly those who shared their stories with me, and to Patricia Elliot, Department of Sociology and Anthropology, Wilfrid Laurier University, Waterloo, Ontario, for her continuing wisdom and support. I dedicate this work to Lucie Marion and her spirit in recognition of the instrumental part she played in deposing Judge Raymond Bartlett from the Family Court of the Province of Nova Scotia in 1987, during my tenure as director of Bryony House, Halifax, Nova Scotia. Finally, I gratefully acknowledge the support I received in the form of National Welfare Fellowships from Health and Welfare, Canada, a program that, while still very much needed, unfortunately no longer exists under the current liberal government.

Chapter 1

Introduction

A RETROSPECTIVE

What are the processes through which women who have been beaten or otherwise abused by their male partners become involved in collective action for social change? How do survivors of woman abuse make connections between their experiences of abuse and oppressive social arrangements, develop a critical consciousness about their situation, and act on that knowledge to engage in collective action to resist violence against women?

This book critically explores these questions through the stories of survivors of woman abuse who are engaged in collective action, and interviews with educators and activists in the antiviolence movement. As a feminist social worker who has been involved in the transition house movement in Canada and in feminist community organizing on gender violence with poor women in Costa Rica, the issue of women's movement from individual survival to collective action is important to me for three reasons. First, feminism has been fundamentally concerned with the relation of individual and social change in attempting to theorize and practice a politics of transformation (Henriques et al., 1984). For feminism, questions of subjectivity, consciousness, identity, and agency have been central to social change. Chris Weedon (1987) defines subjectivity as "the conscious and unconscious thoughts and emotions of the individual, her sense of herself and her ways of understanding her relation to the world" (p. 32). Consciousness, a component of subjectivity, refers to the conscious emotional and cognitive ways in which we make sense of ourselves and our world. Consciousness and experience are inextricably intertwined, and consciousness is intimately linked to our sense of self or identity—our definition of who we are. Therefore, transforming subjectivity—the ways in which we experience and define ourselves—is key to contesting oppression, a necessary and significant component in socially transformative struggle.

Second, as a feminist social worker concerned with social work's insertion in social relations of ruling, I have an ethical and political commitment to exposing and challenging social work's complicity with the status quo and the contradictions within its theoretical base, professional values and ethics, and practices.[1] My commitment includes uncovering ways in which I reproduce oppressive norms, images, and practices that limit women and make them "Other" (Lazreg, 1990; Mohanty, Russo, and Torres, 1991). By Other, I mean that we make people whom we perceive as different from us into something other than we think we are, by objectifying them, creating knowledge about them, and establishing their worth as less than ours. Adopting a position of self-scrutiny, I continually search for more respectful ways of practicing feminist social work with women.

Third, upon my return to Canada in 1992 after a rich and vibrant organizing experience in Costa Rica, I was disenchanted by the prevalent professional, social service approaches to working with abused women in the transition house movement. As a member of the feminist collective Pancha Carrasco (Colectivo de Mujeres Pancha Carrasco), with headquarters in San José, Costa Rica, a co-worker and I facilitated a mutual support group for women in a small, poor, semirural community who wished to confront the multiple expressions of violence and disrespect they experienced in their daily lives. Our involvement with this group formed part of the collective's feminist political project and organized work with women of the popular sector in urban and rural areas of Costa Rica.[2] The collective's grassroots organization of work with women was linked with the organizing efforts of both the Costa Rican women's movement and the popular movement. It was against the background of this spirited and invigorating experience that I initiated my research on survivors and the transition house movement.

The struggle of the Canadian women's movement to end woman abuse has been called the battered women's movement, the transition house or shelter movement, and, most recently, the antiviolence movement. The movement includes transition houses, related services such as battered women's advocacy clinics, coalitions, sexual assault centers, women's organizations and groups, survivor self-help and social action groups, political advocacy organizations, and second-stage housing (longer-term housing specifically intended for women who are leaving a shelter and seeking a safe and supportive housing environment in which to rebuild their lives). My exploration of the transition house movement began with a review of the literature on woman abuse and the shelter movement, informal conversations with workers in the movement, and volunteer work with a women's shelter. The literature suggested that while feminist shelters and political organizations in the movement were endeavoring to maintain a structural analysis of violence against women and a progressive politics, they were doing so in the face of the professionalization of services and chronic underfunding of, and cutbacks to funding for, women's organizations and services. Several authors have analyzed and documented the processes through which feminist analyses of women's oppression and demands for fundamental social change have been diluted by apolitical frameworks for understanding violence toward women and by individualized remedies for addressing it (Currie, 1990; Fraser, 1989; Hilton, 1989; Walker, 1990). Recognizing that the efforts of feminist shelters and organizations to develop a broad-based, feminist antiviolence movement have become fragmented, different authors have called for a critical reevaluation of the movement and its struggle for social transformation (Timmins, 1995; Walker, 1990).

Specifically, Gillian Walker (1990) documented the ways in which feminist analyses of the role of violence in women's oppression were absorbed into a professionalized and depoliticized family violence framework. The discourse of family violence treats men's abuse of female partners as simply one instance of family violence in the larger context of family dynamics and social norms. Whereas gender may be recognized as a factor in woman abuse, the most salient concept is violence in family relationships rather than an emphasis on unequal social relations of power. I use the term "discourse" to point to the relationship between language and social reality. Discourse can be defined as a regulated system of statements and set of assumptions, socially shared, often unconscious and reflected in language, that position people who speak within it and delimit what can be said by framing knowledge within certain bounds. Feminist and antioppressive discourses challenge and subvert dominant understandings of the world, such as common sense notions that women are to blame for men's violence or that racism is mainly rooted in individual biased attitudes and ideas. These discourses are "competing ways of giving meaning to the world, which imply differences in the organization of social power" (Weedon, 1987, p. 24). As Walker (1990) persuasively argues, from each discourse or way of making sense of woman abuse follows a particular set of implications for action and practice with abused women.

CONTEXTUAL FRAMEWORK

I identified two key interrelated issues in the political struggle over the needs of abused women as particularly relevant to the context of my inquiry into survivors' activism in southern Ontario. The first issue concerns the depoliticization of shelters and women's organizations in the movement as sites of resistance against violence toward women. The adoption of apolitical theoretical frameworks for understanding woman abuse, professional language, and hierarchical organizational structures dilute feminist structural analyses of woman abuse, weaken feminist political advocacy, and marginalize the voices of survivors in the movement. As early as the mid-1980s, woman abuse became perceived primarily as a matter of systemic discrimination by the police and courts, lack of access to current institutions, public misperceptions, and the need for public education rather than a question of social power, structural dependency, and unequal gender relations (Andrew et al., 1986). As the efforts of the transition house movement to fundamentally alter women's subordination were absorbed into a family violence framework, the work of the movement comprised services to women beaten and abused, rather than a movement of women beaten and abused (Walker, 1990). As clients and social service recipients, abused women have fewer opportunities to actively interpret their own needs, identify the kinds of community changes that would improve their lives, and define themselves as survivors, advocates, and activists.

The second issue in "the politics of need interpretation" concerns the influence of dominant family violence discourse on shelters and the work of the transition house movement.[3] In the course of the movement's interaction with the ideologies and structures of the Canadian state, social institutions, and professionals of all types, feminist political analyses were weakened, neutralized, and contained by family violence discourse. Apolitical understandings of woman abuse, rooted in therapeutic ideology, focus on individualized solutions to the exclusion of efforts to change the social and material conditions of women's lives. Although feminist shelters and organizations have resisted therapeutic perspectives to differing degrees, family violence discourse has permeated and shaped shelter discourse and practice with survivors. Feminist consciousness-raising and self-help models have given way to treating women as individualized victims with the ubiquitous problem of low self-esteem.[4] Although an individualized social service approach addresses individual, psychological needs, survivors again have little access to the ways of understanding woman abuse that would facilitate self-descriptions and constructions of their experience as advocates and activists for social change.

This is the context in which I situate my exploratory study of survivors' processes of conscientization and movement from individual survival to collective action. Survivor is a political term that recognizes women's oppression and takes into account the ways in which women have coped with, survived, and resisted abuse and violence by male partners. Kathleen Barry (1984) was perhaps the first person to use the term survivor in the feminist literature. She employs survivor to counter what she calls the practice of "victimism" (p. 44), in which women are assigned the role of victim, a label that becomes a defining feature of their identity. Countering this false portrayal of women, she emphasizes women's efforts to survive and make changes in their situations: "Surviving is the other side of being a victim. It involves will, action, initiative on the victim's part. Any woman caught in sexual violence must make moment-by-moment decisions about her survival" (pp. 46-47). Survivor recognizes women's agency—their ability to act and make decisions for themselves in the context of structural inequalities and social relations of power that limit individual action.

Conscientization or conscientizaçaõ (Freire, 1994) is a process that involves learning to perceive social, political, and economic contradictions, analyze and uncover the largely invisible ways in which social structures, processes, and practices organize the operation of power and act against oppressive elements of reality (Freire, 1994; Lather, 1991).[5] In progressive social work literature, empowerment describes a similar process encompassing psychological, educational, cultural, and spiritual dimensions in which people understand their oppression and take steps to overcome it psychically, and in different spheres, for example, in organizations and institutions that affect their lives (Mullaly, 1997; Simon, 1990). I prefer conscientization, which translates as "critical consciousness," because it poses the world and women's relation to it as a problem (Freire, 1994; Mann, 1987).[6] The terms collective action, resistance, and struggle are used interchangeably to refer to the various forms of collective work to end violence against women. Collective action encompasses the social actions of a collectivity that through pressure, influence, and education, challenge and seek to change, either directly or indirectly, aspects of the dominant social order that produce and sustain women's oppression.

One of the aims of the feminist antiviolence movement is to eradicate systemic violence and the abuse of women and girls. This aim is part of a larger goal of feminist political practice to eliminate the material and negative effects of gender on women's lives. Although women individually resist multiple forms of oppression, these acts of resistance are often stigmatized or contained by social control mechanisms in the family and community, thus lessening the social change implications of individual acts of resistance (Chaftez and Dworkin, 1986; Young, 1992). Both individual and collective forms of resistance are necessary to eliminate acts of discrimination against women, change structural modes of social organization, and transform social representations and images of "woman" (Grosz, 1990). Women's resistance to abuse includes a range of efforts that oppose, modify, refuse to cooperate with, or submit to the exercise of different forms of social and individual power over them, and the immediate circumstances in which they live. Resistance can encompass daily practices and routines, the use of language, habits of being, and actions. Women resist in many places and forms, such as refusing to accept certain attitudes and behaviors, expressing anger or dissatisfaction and demanding change, practicing self-care and reciprocity with others, and building alternatives to the status quo. Resistance signals opposition to domination and the potential for personal and collective social change.

Despite the fact that survivors now have a more limited role in feminist theorizing and activism in the antiviolence movement than in its earlier phases, women who have been beaten and abused have always been part of this struggle. Our knowledge of oppositional social movements clearly demonstrates how oppressed peoples have individually and collectively resisted their oppression, joined by allies in solidarity with their struggles for social justice (Findlay, 1994; Mostern, 1994). However, the responsibility for theorizing, initiating, and working for social transformation does not lie exclusively with women who have suffered violence and abuse. To assign exclusive or greater responsibility to any oppressed group for their own liberation perpetuates victim blaming (Crosby et al., 1989). We all have a responsibility to work for social justice, transforming social relations of power and the material conditions of our lives (Brittan and Maynard, 1984). Survivors and their knowledge about oppression, situated within social relations of power and privilege, must, however, play a pivotal role in knowledge production about woman abuse and in political decision making and action for change.

I hope that my focus on survivors' stories of activism will provide deeper insight into the ways in which they transform their sense of self and identity, construct new meaning from their experiences of violation, and act on their understanding to resist violence against women. I am challenging feminist social workers, professionals, and others in the antiviolence movement to critically reflect on how their discourses about and practices with survivors limit or expand the possibilities available to them as social actors. By extension, the opportunities available to all of us are closely linked with the ways in which we work with survivors of woman abuse. My work will contribute to broadening the ways of seeing survivors, finding new ways of animating survivors' participation in social change processes, and building new models of feminist social work with survivors of woman abuse.

My critical look at the transition house movement is intended to encourage reflection about it, its potential for resistance and social change, and the place of survivors in the struggle rather than to evaluate or criticize it or the efforts of the many committed women in the movement. I want to openly acknowledge the incredible efforts that women have made to effect social change and provide services for abused women, efforts that have been undertaken in difficult and often overwhelming circumstances. Cognizant of the hopes and dreams that we all have for our work with survivors and the movement, I suspect that the issues I raise in this book will strike us on an emotional as well as intellectual level. Although at times during my research I felt inundated by what I uncovered, and less than hopeful about the ability of the antiviolence movement to continue to forge progressive, radical change, my faith has been fortified by my interviews with survivors, educators, and activists in the movement. I have an even greater faith that we will use our knowledge, experience, and wisdom to expand our transformative visions for ourselves and society, and cultivate new and creative ways to work through the issues, challenges, and possibilities that we face.

SITUATING THIS STUDY

Feminist social work and the related literature on abused women neglected the important question of survivors' participation in collective action. However, this literature, primarily comprising material on feminist educational groups for survivors (Brown and Dickey, 1992; Pâquet-Deehy and Robin, 1991; Pence and Burns, 1985; Poels and Berger, 1992; Wood and Middleman, 1992) and qualitative research studies (Hoff, 1990; Kelly, 1988; Mills, 1985; Riessman, 1989), provided valuable insights into women's transformative processes and the factors that facilitate them. Feminist educational groups for survivors emphasize the social and political conditions affecting women's lives rather than focusing narrowly or exclusively on self-esteem or personal limitations. They point to the material and negative effects of gender on women's lives and the importance of women's experiences of oppression for defining strategies for social change.[7] Survivors' processes of empowerment included challenging disempowering self-perceptions, developing assertiveness and affirmative capacities, questioning the sacrifice of personal desires and well-being to meet the needs of others, and knowing that they are not alone in experiencing woman abuse and not responsible for men's violence (Brown and Dickey, 1992; Pâquet-Deehy and Robin, 1991; Poels and Berger, 1992; Wood and Middleman, 1992).Women gain tremendously from their participation in these groups, exercising their agency by taking up study, self-development, and employment opportunities, confronting not only partners but family members and service providers (Brown and Dickey, 1992; Poels and Berger, 1992), and gaining skills to access community resources and support outside the group (Wood and Middleman, 1992).

Research studies emphasized several factors in women's empowerment: the importance of naming experiences of abuse, through access to feminist discourse, in ways that differ from dominant interpretations of social reality (Kelly, 1988; Riessman, 1989); the role of insights, contradictions, and turning points in facilitating a reassessment of one's relationship and life (Kelly, 1988; Mills, 1985); and the significance of support networks in helping women assume and maintain a "survivor" identity (Hoff, 1990; Mills, 1985). Several authors have suggested that abused women's empowerment entails making the transition from "victim" to "survivor" (Hoff, 1990; Mills, 1985; Riessman, 1989). Lee Anne Hoff (1990) claims that becoming a survivor involves leaving the abusive relationship and learning to avoid further victimization. While women may leave abusive partners and come to recognize their self-worth, the notion that we can learn to avoid further victimization is problematic. It obscures the fact that women are most at risk of being killed by their partners after they have taken steps to end the relationship (Timmins, 1995). The home continues to be the most dangerous place for women and girls (Radford and Russell, 1992), and social relations of inequality place women and girls in subordinate positions, exposing them to forms of violence such as sexual harassment, incest, and rape. In addition, this position does not recognize that women who choose to remain with their partners seek ways to end abuse, and sometimes their strategies are successful.

FOCUS AND METHODOLOGY OF STUDY

Based on my assessment of the feminist social work and related literature, I identified four key areas to explore with survivors in my study: first, the processes through which they named and made sense of their lived experience of abuse and violence, thus transforming their understanding of their victimization; second, the ways in which they made connections between their experience as gendered, raced, and classed subjects and the oppressive social conditions in which they lived; third, women's own understanding of their personal journey, including the difficulties and contradictions they faced, their desires for change, and the discursive and material conditions that facilitated change; and fourth, the relation between changes in women's subjectivity and their participation in different forms of collective action.

These specific areas were important for me to explore for other reasons that are rooted in my personal history. Of Scottish, English, and French heritage, I grew up on a farm and later in a working-class home on Prince Edward Island. At an early age I knew that I was treated differently than my brother, and I observed that certain groups of people, such as aboriginal people, were shunned and held in disdain on our small island. It was not until I was a social worker-in-training in 1980 in a transition house that I encountered feminism and a language with which to speak about my keen sense of injustice and personal experience of oppression. For me, feminist theories provided wonderfully liberating ways of understanding the world, its effects on us as women, and our responses to it.

During my work in a transition house in the mid-1980s, I grappled with all kinds of questions concerning how shelter residents understood abuse in our male-dominated society, how they began to interpret their experiences through a different lens, and the mystery of simultaneous conformity and resistance to gender norms. My desire to learn about how women across cultures understood and resisted woman abuse propelled me to Costa Rica. Through my relationships with co-workers and women with whom we, the collective, worked, I realized that my search and their search—a search for understanding about our lives, our strengths, joys, and dreams, and our experiences of pain, subordination, and resistance—were delicately interwoven. The solidity of our relationships enabled us to grapple with difficult issues, including issues concerning working across differences. My experience with the feminist collective in feminist organizing and political advocacy in Costa Rica transformed me in a fundamental way. It shifted my political and analytical framework, not only for understanding other women's oppression, but also my own. Because the areas that I chose to explore with survivors are part of my journey, I am more comfortable with making my research public.

I chose the practice of storytelling and *testimonio* as feminist qualitative research methods because they allowed survivors to talk about what they had lived and interpreted as significant and meaningful in their journey to collective action (Acker, Barry, and Esseveld, 1991; Beverley, 1992; Chanfrault-Duchet, 1991; Patai, 1988; Sommer, 1988). Storytelling refers to the accounts constructed by women within the framework of the interview situation (Patai, 1988). Testimonio is a narrative form in which people document their struggle and resistance (Beverley, 1992; Sommer, 1988).[8] It encompasses political and social as well as subjective, spiritual, and private aspects of struggle, unites within its structure the private and the political (Agger, 1994), and crosses the borders between the public and private spheres of life (Beverley, 1992). Both storytelling and testimonio illuminate the unfolding of personal histories as well as the broader social discourses that shape women's understandings of their lives.

Storytelling and testimonio reveal the ways in which we become aware of how our experiences and understandings of self and identity have been shaped and influenced by dominant culture. They also expose how we create new and liberating meaning from our experiences and memories of violation, not simply as actors who follow ideological scripts but as agents who read them in order to insert ourselves into them (Smith, 1988). As moments of articulation, women's stories and testimonios recount the process of "rewriting the self" (Freeman, 1993, p. 3). As accounts of meaning making, they reveal how we come to understand ourselves and our world in ways that differ from what had existed earlier. Reflecting upon the past and recounting it through a different lens involves a process of critical remembering (McLaren and Tadeu da Silva,

1993). Memories of the past can be rendered politically and psychically useful when forms of oppression are unmasked and critically appropriated into the fabric of the self (Gunn, 1992). As an attempt to understand the past differently, critical remembering carries conflict and pain but also the possibility of freedom, hope, and resistance (McLaren and Tadeu da Silva, 1993). Critical remembering and rewriting "the elusive being we call the 'self'" (Freeman, 1993, p. 5) need not, however, blind us to the relation between telling and living, or to the social realities in which lives are lived and the stories women tell about them.

In my work I draw on multiple feminist theories, most notably feminist poststructuralist, feminist psychoanalytic, and socialist feminist theories. The feminist theoretical framework, methodology, and analytical and interpretative approach that I use in this study are anchored in three premises. First, feminist research on women's lived experience has been a cornerstone in the production of feminist knowledge and the feminist reconstruction of our understanding of our social world (Personal Narratives Group, 1989; Reinharz, 1992). Lived experience is a rich source of knowledge about the ideological and social processes that constitute subjectivity (Haug et al., 1987). Through analysis of personal experience, one can learn about the general from the particular since individual experience is only possible within the domain of the social. According to Chris Weedon (1987), the subjective is significant "since the ways in which people make sense of their lives is a necessary starting point for understanding how power relations structure society" (p. 8). Critical analysis of lived experience illuminates the ways in which dominant social messages limit our vision of what is possible for ourselves, the material conditions that circumscribe our life chances and opportunities, the power of individual agency in negotiating courses of action amid social constraints, and the ways in which particular courses of action undermine or reproduce inequality and domination.

Second, feminist theories value and build on women's everyday experience. The notion that the personal is political, which is foundational to feminist theory, emphasizes the authority of experience in knowledge production and social change (Fuss, 1989; Haug et al., 1987). Magda Lewis (1993) affirms that "the importance of the feminist focus on 'the story' born of experience is . . . to emphasize that subordinate groups live subordination and marginality through our subjectivity, that we live it through social relations which are inscribed in personal practices which are, in turn, reflective and constitutive of our social organizations" (pp. 9-10). Understanding subjectivity as something produced does not signify a seamless or noncontradictory unity. Individuals are "a mixture of subjectivities, locked in common sense understandings and played out in social practices" (Henriques et al., 1984, p. 94). Everyday consciousness with its common sense understandings contains an amalgam of unexamined assumptions, internalized rules, moral codes, and partial insights (Weiler, 1988), an amalgam that contains possibilities for self-consciousness and critique. Subjective transformation and engagement in collective struggle are possible outcomes of critical self-awareness and social and political consciousness.[9]

"Experience," by itself, is not the end point of knowledge, the sole guarantor of truth, or the meaning of "reality" (Haug et al., 1987; Bannerji, 1995). Recent debates about the nature and place of experience in feminist theory, analysis, and political strategizing have called into question experience as the source of ultimate truth as well as the basis for political action (Fuss, 1989; Scott, 1992). As Chris Weedon (1987) points out, "the meaning of experience is perhaps the most crucial site of political struggle over meaning since it involves personal, psychic and emotional investment on the part of the individual" (p. 79). Women of color, women of the "third world," and lesbian women have called attention to different forms of socially constructed disadvantage, and the ways in which oppressions such as racism, sexism, and ableism are simultaneously experienced by women. These critiques, which emphasize the interconnectedness of all forms of oppression, have challenged fundamental assumptions underpinning feminist theories, such as the notion that women as a group have a common experience of oppression or possess a unique, innate female nature. Therefore, feminist theories and the politics that follow from them must recognize the complexity and diversity of women's experiences within historically and culturally specific contexts (Mohanty, 1992).

Third, my reading of the role of experience in meaning making suggests that "experience" must be analyzed and interpreted in order to uncover how it is socially organized and the ideological, discursive, and material conditions that produce it. Given that "the political becomes personal by way of its subjective effects through the subject's experience" (de Lauretis, 1990, p. 115), we need to reflect critically on the ways in which we experience our subordinate social positions as women. This reflection is the starting point for exploration and analyses of the relation between the personal and the social. Himani Bannerji (1995) describes this task as a process of meaning making that validates the ways in which we experience and define ourselves, and exercise our agency. This process also illuminates the historically constructed patterns of power that shape our experience.

> "Experience" . . . is the originating point of knowledge, an interpretation, a relational sense-making, which incorporates social meaning. This "experience" creates and transforms. It is a continuous process of relating with the world as "our world." . . . Experience, therefore, is that crucible in which the self and the world enter into a creative union called "social subjectivity." . . . Since political agency, experience and knowledge are transformatively connected, where but in ourselves and lives can we begin our explanatory and analytical activities? (pp. 86-88)

From the starting point of experience, we can unravel the politics of our subordination, the ways in which our social being and knowing contain internalized oppression and domination, contradictions, and potentially revolutionary knowledge. The subjective is important since, through sense-making of their lived reality, women produce the knowledge and social analysis they need for personal and social change.

The primary source of data for this study consisted of interviews with eleven survivors who self-identified as women who had been abused by a male partner in a live-in relationship and as participants in some form of collective action to end violence against women. Self-identification was critical to the quality and integrity of women's stories (Reinharz, 1992). My criterion "women who have been abused by a male partner," which omitted women who had been abused by lesbian partners, was not intended to discount or marginalize abuse in lesbian relationships. For me, this important issue merits a separate study, one which would require analyses of misogyny, heterosexism, and homophobia as factors shaping both lesbian abuse and the transition house movement's responses to this issue (Ristock, 1991).

This research was conducted in southern Ontario, Canada, between 1995 and 1998. I used a purposeful sampling approach with the goal of reaching a specific but diverse group of participants (Cannon, Higginbotham, and Leung, 1991; Merriam, 1988; Patton, 1990). Participants came from different backgrounds (an aboriginal woman, two women of Latin American origin, and nine women of European descent). The majority were from poor and working-class families. One woman identified as lesbian, and all were mothers. Participants had been involved in their respective collective action from two to nine years. Biographical information about participants and a brief sketch of the chronological and formative events in each participant's story is presented in the appendix.

I reached the participants in this study through contact with organizations that reflected diverse forms of collective struggle against violence toward women. These contacts included shelters, a Latin American working group against violence toward women, sexual assault and rape crisis centers, multicultural community organizations and health centers, social action and advocacy groups, community development initiatives, and second-stage housing. I reached ten of the eleven participants in this study through these contacts. One woman was referred to me by another participant. My sole interview with the participant whose country of origin was El Salvador was conducted in Spanish. Of the eleven participants, ten had sought assistance from educational, support, or self-help groups, shelters, and second-stage housing in the course of dealing with their experiences of abuse (the participant from Chile was the exception). Since most women who are abused do not contact or stay in a transition house (Rodgers, 1994), the processes of politicization for survivors outside the sphere of the transition house movement might differ in meaningful ways from those of survivors who reached out for help and remained connected to these sources of politicization.

In my initial interview with participants, I shared my personal and professional investment in listening to their stories and asked them to tell me their story or testimonio of how they became active in the work they were doing. I encouraged their storytelling process by suggesting: "Please start your story anywhere you wish. What has been important to you in your journey? What were critical moments and turning points for you? What do you feel is important for me to know about how you became involved in your work?" I interviewed nine of the eleven participants twice, with each interview averaging two hours, and continued contact with half of the participants for two years, discussing my interpretations and sharing various chapters with them. While issues of class, "race," ethnicity, and sexuality were significant in women's lives, my reading of women's stories focuses predominantly on gender and its intersection with other structuring forces shaping survivors' processes of conscientization.

Interviews with fourteen educators, activists, community workers, and counselors working in various facets of the antiviolence movement constituted a second source of data. I defined a key informant as someone who was woman-centered, committed to ending violence against women, and highly recommended by others as possessing valuable knowledge and expertise about my research subject. I identified them through telephone contacts, the women I interviewed, and other key informants. Seven of the fourteen had been or were active in other social justice movements. Key informants included a feminist educator/activist/shelter worker who had extensive experience working with Latin American women, a community worker/antiracism educator with years of experience in community-based organizations and teaching about violence against women, and a feminist educator/activist with many years' experience in lobbying, advocacy, and organizing. An informal interview guide served as a starting point for these interviews.

Although the interviews were initially intended to serve as a secondary source of data about survivors' journey to collective action, they yielded valuable insights into the range and depth of issues, tensions, and dilemmas in the transition house movement. The themes and issues from these conversations inform my analysis of survivors' stories and the antiviolence movement as well as my discussion of the implications of this study for all of us in the movement. Interviews with key informants were supplemented by a comprehensive review of government documents and a national

newsletter on family violence. This review increased my understanding of the history and evolution of the transition house movement, its relation to the state, and the ways in which the state and
professionals viewed survivors, their agency and needs, and the
issue of woman abuse.[10]

Fieldwork was also a significant component of my study. I spent
considerable time at a vibrant second-stage housing program with
which several research participants were connected, talking with
both staff and survivors. I joined staff and participants in public
protests against the Ontario government's funding cuts to second-
stage housing and services for abused women. I also spoke publicly
with activists, some of whom self-identified as survivors, at a community rally organized by second-stage housing. This fieldwork
provided rich opportunities for situating and understanding survivors' stories and their work for change, and the kinds of environments and worker-survivor relations that foster their participation.

My own subjectivity as a researcher and as a former worker/fem-
inist in the transition house movement in Nova Scotia constituted
another critical source of data for this book. As previously men-
tioned, my experience in Costa Rica shifted my sense of myself as a
feminist and a professional, encouraging me to think more critically
about professionalism and its effects on women, and the ways in
which the women with whom we work challenge us personally and
professionally. What are the contradictions between feminism and
professionalism? How are women's stories connected with our
own? How does professionalism exclude women's voices, including our own? What are my investments in particular ways of thinking about issues and how do they undermine my feminism and its
radical roots of solidarity with women? How have I ignored
women's knowledge and awareness about their lives, and in doing
so, denied my own?

For me, utilizing my subjectivity as a source of data also meant
analyzing the conscious and unconscious psychic and political dimensions of conducting this research. As researchers, it is impossible to separate ourselves from what we experience and feel while
doing research, or to remain untouched by the research we do.
Feminist researchers have long emphasized the role of affect in
knowledge production (Fonow and Cook, 1991; Mies, 1983; Stan-

ley and Wise, 1993). Despite the fact that we are the medium through which inquiry is conducted, general counsel among mainstream social science researchers is that emotional involvement is taboo and preventable (Stanley and Wise, 1993). Academics may even consider self-reflexivity as a form of navel-gazing (Ristock and Pennell, 1996).

The splitting of the subjective from the rational (Rockhill, 1987b) and the omission of the self as a significant component in shaping professional practice has been reinforced by my professional education and practice in the field of violence against women and children. Under the guise of professionalism, we often disregard our subjectivity since it falls outside the professional discourse of helping. The expression and dissection of emotions, psychic dynamics, and defenses is usually reserved for clients subjected to the scrutiny of the state and other helping apparatuses. Writing my subjectivity into, rather than out of, my work illuminated my relations with survivors as a feminist, researcher, and professional and the changes that are needed in our relations and modes of working with survivors. In Chapter 6, I explore my subjectivity as a researcher and how my research with survivors brought me back to myself.

ORGANIZATION OF THE BOOK

This book is organized in the following way. In Chapter 2, I situate my study by discussing two key issues in the transition house movement that affect survivors' transformative processes. In Chapter 3, I present June's story to illustrate one woman's process of meaning making. The significance of June's story for understanding processes of conscientization is discussed in Chapter 4. Chapter 5 focuses on the voices of survivors, conveying the diversity and complexity of their change processes. My interpretation of women's voices is organized according to the key processes and themes that I located in their accounts. My reflection about the psychic dynamics and emotions that I experienced in the research process constitutes Chapter 6. The issues, themes, dilemmas, and tensions raised by key informants in the transition house movement are considered in Chapter 7. Finally, in Chapter 8, I discuss the implications of this study for all of us in the antiviolence movement, and for feminist social work theory and practice with survivors of woman abuse. I suggest directions for future thought and action in the continuing struggle against violence toward women.

In my analysis and interpretation of participants' stories, I identified six major themes concerning women's transformative processes and engagement in collective action. The first theme captures the complexities involved in naming experiences of violation as violence or abuse. The second concerns women's struggle with contradiction and conflict in shifting their consciousness about themselves and the current social order. The psychic dynamics evoked in change processes and in learning about woman abuse and oppression is the third theme. The fourth relates to participants' development of a critical social analysis of their personal experience and encounters with social institutions, and the kinds of knowledge and communities that fostered this. The fifth theme encompasses changes in women's sense of self, including the uncovering of internalized oppression. The sixth theme concerns the relation between changes in women's consciousness and subjectivity and their participation in collective action for social change.

In presenting these themes, I will argue that women's movement from individual survival to collective action involves significant changes in consciousness and subjectivity. Women's processes of conscientization were often complex, contradictory, and painful for several reasons. First, survivors' struggles to resolve the contradiction and conflict that they faced in their lives were protracted and fraught with ambivalence. Second, the tasks of working through experiences of abuse and identifying the social and material factors that limited their lives involved both political and psychic dimensions of subjectivity. Third, making sense of their lives sometimes evoked resistance to knowledge and information that threatened to unsettle their relatively stable notions of self and identity. Changes in women's consciousness and subjectivity are closely linked to access to feminist and antioppressive discourses about women's inequality and to social spaces and connections with other women. These spaces included support groups for abused women, self-help groups for incest survivors, educational programs and groups in transition houses and second-stage housing, and other communities of women. Feminist and antioppressive ways of making sense and survivors' connections with other women enabled them to challenge dominant interpretations of their realities and understand their lives differently.

In our work with abused women, then, we need to acknowledge the multifaceted and difficult nature of women's journey in recognizing and naming abuse, making sense of their experiences, and acting on this knowledge to work for change. We must also take into account the social, material, and psychic costs that women face in their growth processes as well as the discursive and material conditions that facilitate their understanding of themselves and their social world. Feminist social work theory and practice with survivors of woman abuse must recognize survivors' work for social change, and develop new, more inclusive models that provide opportunities for survivors to make sense of their experience, develop a critical consciousness, and belong to community as they undertake personal change and make explicit commitments to strive for a more just world.

Chapter 2

Shaping the Practices
of the Transition House Movement:
From a Discourse of Agency
Toward a Discourse of Self-Esteem

BRIEF OVERVIEW
OF THE BATTERED WOMEN'S MOVEMENT

In the early 1970s the feminist movement introduced the issue of wife battering into public consciousness (Beaudry, 1985; Gilman, 1988; Hilton, 1989), fundamentally challenging the social structures, norms, and practices that had created and maintained violence by men against women and girls. Writing about the battered women's movement in the United States, Susan Schechter (1982) concurs that "society did not recognize battered women, feminists and grassroots activists did" (p. 3). Feminist activists and women working in local rape crisis centers and women's centers became cognizant of the difficult situations facing abused women and organized the first responses to wife battering (Walker, 1990). Residential shelters for battered women emerged as a response to the numbers of women who sought refuge at volunteer support services run by community-based women's groups (Currie, 1990; Gilman, 1988). In her history of the shelter movement in Canada, Susan Thomas Gilman (1988) notes that the movement appears to have begun in Vancouver and Toronto, where shelters opened in 1973.[1] The first shelter in Quebec was established in 1975. Shelters were intended to provide women with a safe place to escape physical assault and make whatever decisions they felt were necessary in their lives. As part of local feminist movements, transition houses served as the physical anchor of the battered women's movement, from which networks of women's groups organized (Hilton, 1989; Pennell, 1987; Walker, 1990).[2]

Feminist analyses of women's oppression set the social and political groundwork for the radical act of articulating painful, personal, and private experiences and naming them as social. Grounded in a radical feminist perspective, rape crisis centers viewed violence by men against women as an integral part of women's oppression and a mode of domination rooted in unequal gender relations. Shelters reclaimed the home as a place of action, reconstituting it as a political space (Beaudry, 1985). Feminist principles such as collectivity, consciousness-raising, the primacy of women's experience, and respect for women's strengths, resilience, and power guided the work of shelters and related support services. Utilizing a women-helping-women self-help approach, staff and volunteers acted as educators and organizers, providing abused women with practical assistance, information, peer support, and a political understanding of men's violence. Consciousness-raising about patriarchal social arrangements challenged women's self-blame and guilt, helping them make sense of their experiences, overcome isolation, and transform powerlessness into strength and anger.

Consciousness-raising also served as a method of building a political movement to challenge women's social subordination and alter the social and material conditions that denied women power and control over their lives (Walker, 1990). Women's everyday experiences were the starting point for analysis and action and the ground from which to challenge "privatized patriarchal authority" (Currie, 1990, p. 89). The battered women's movement initially set out to organize and mobilize initiatives that would change women's structural position of dependency as well as provide emotional and practical assistance to women who were abused. Tension between the political goal of calling attention to the socially structured power inequities between women and men in capitalist patriarchy, and the humanist goal of providing practical help to women and facilitating political consciousness and independence among women, has existed since the very beginning of the movement (Morgan, 1981; Schechter, 1982).

As feminists, grassroots activists, women's groups, and transition houses consistently identified woman abuse as a matter requiring redress, the women's movement took up the issue, placing it on the political agenda of the state. The movement demanded that the federal government and society as a whole share responsibility for eliminating wife battering. As a result, the federal government began its involvement with the issue in the late 1970s (MacLeod, 1987; Walker, 1990). By the early 1980s, the women's movement had succeeded in locating the issue of woman abuse in the public sphere of action. Feminist demands such as state funding of shelters, legal protection for abused women, and the prosecution of wife assault as a criminal act rather than a family matter necessarily brought feminists into a struggle with the state, professionals, social services, and legal advocacy groups to define the issue and propose strategies to address it.

THE STRUGGLE OVER DEFINITION OF THE NEEDS OF BATTERED WOMEN

Gillian Walker (1990) eloquently and compellingly maps out the women's movement's organizing work and struggle for change, and the processes through which the issue was taken up and absorbed by the state.[3] According to Walker, the transmutation of the women's movement's political concern about woman abuse into a "social problem" requiring appropriate administrative, professional, and institutional responses constituted a process of "absorption and control of the struggles undertaken by the women's movement" (p. 6). Dawn Currie (1990) frames this knowledge/power struggle as one in which feminist discourse and practice has been transformed from "a critique of patriarchal power to demands for protection from male power" (p. 88). Although protection from male power remains a real need, the expansion of current patriarchal institutions to satisfy this need cannot be equated with social justice for women (Currie, 1990).[4] In her analysis of the battered women's movement in Canada, Zoe Hilton (1989) interprets the mainstreaming of the movement and the institutionalization of feminist services as the effects of government co-optation, made possible both by the range of positions within the feminist coalition and by government control of funding to the movement. She concurs that the shift toward professionalization occurred with government involvement in the issue.[5]

THE PROFESSIONALIZATION
AND REPOLITICIZATION OF SHELTERS

I identified two interrelated issues in the political struggle over the needs of abused women that have implications for survivors' engagement in collective action in southern Ontario. I will discuss these issues and the ways in which they shape survivors' processes of conscientization. The first issue concerns the shift toward the professionalization of shelters and women's service organizations, and the corresponding resurgence of apolitical frameworks for understanding woman abuse.

As feminist analyses of woman abuse and radical demands for social change were absorbed by the social problem apparatus, the feminist struggle for a redistribution of social power was reorganized into an expansion of existing patriarchal institutions (Currie, 1990) and efforts to fix the "malfunctioning of the social problem apparatus" (Walker, 1990, p. 193).[6] Concurrently, government funding of shelters dictated the use of these funds for the residential and crisis components of shelter services, and introduced bureaucratic practices and the hiring of staff with professional qualifications. For already underfunded shelters, the labor of providing ongoing service usually meant that social action, by necessity, became a lesser priority due to the overwhelming and chronic struggle for survival (Pennell, 1987). Consequently, shelters were forced to place more emphasis on service provision and the professionalization and expansion of services to the detriment of feminist political education, advocacy, outreach, follow-up, and public education, all of which are components of a political movement (Walker, 1990). Hilton (1989) frames this outcome as the replacement of a social action and lobbying function by a reform philosophy that supports the goal of conserving the family unit and challenges neither class nor patriarchal structures.

Although some shelters struggled, and continue to struggle, against this shift, significant changes in shelter philosophy and practice accompanied government sponsorship of and involvement in the transition house movement. Shelters shifted from an ideology of feminism and empowerment to a professional service delivery model; from an acceptance of funds from like-minded sources to the acceptance of funds from varied sources that required compliance with specific dictates; from collective models of working to a hierarchical organization; and from a philosophy of self-help among women to the hiring of primarily white, middle-class professionals (MacLeod, 1987). Abused women who, according to feminist ideals of the battered women's movement, were viewed as experts on their own lives, became "clients" in need of professional expertise and intervention.

The profound changes in shelter philosophy and practice altered the relation between workers and abused women. Shelters were gradually absorbed into a system that reproduces class and racial oppression by subjecting residents to increasing scrutiny and social control. Transition house workers' anguish and sense of inadequacy about meeting women's needs (decent housing, child care, and employment) (Pennell, 1987) are exacerbated by social controls of shelter residents under government sponsorship and professionalization. Workers witness how women have been charged with contempt of court for refusing to testify against their partners; abused women who call the police subsequently find out that they cannot drop the charges against their partners; and under the law children can be removed from mothers whose partners assault them (MacLeod, 1987). Women of color, aboriginal women, and women who have immigrated to Canada find it difficult to accept the advocacy of arrest and imprisonment that is characteristic of many shelters (McGrath, 1979; MacLeod, 1987). Power inequities between workers and clients are intensified by social controls that revictimize shelter residents, the majority of whom are young and poor.[7]

Within the transition house movement, divisions emerged between community-based and professional feminists; white, middle-class professionals, and women of color and working-class women using shelter services; and academics and grassroots women. Although some feminist shelters and organizations have diligently worked to develop a broad-based inclusive movement and analysis of violence against women, oppressive attitudes and practices such as classism, ableism, racism, and heterosexism within mainstream and feminist organizations and services have hindered the development of shared visions, coalitions, and political alliances. Government funding has also led to the establishment of nonfeminist and related support services, further complicating the tasks of working together for change and listening to the voices of abused women. Those shelters and services that are committed to forging radical, progressive change, to exposing misogyny and abuse as a logical extension of unequal social relations, and to making their services accessible to all women are often in danger of being declared redundant to mainstream services and called upon to justify their existence (Currie, 1990).

These changes have reverberated in many different directions throughout the transition house movement as a whole, fundamentally altering the relationship between transition houses and battered women. In the early shelter movement, abused women who used shelters often became counselors and movement activists (Gilman, 1988; Hilton, 1989; MacLeod, 1987; Walker, 1990). Nancy Fraser (1989) points out that when feminists first constructed a discourse naming wife beating as a systemic, political matter, battered women were addressed as "potential feminist activists, members of a politically constituted collectivity" and not as individualized victims (p. 176). Rather than see themselves as to blame for what had happened to them, they adopted new self-descriptions that offered them new models of human agency (Fraser, 1989). The trend toward counseling and "the language game of therapy" (p. 176) designed to treat victims' low self-esteem has supplanted consciousness-raising and the affirmation of political agency as radical ways of working with survivors.

Although some feminist shelters and organizations continue to struggle to implement and maintain processes and practices that embrace the voices of abused women, survivors have been marginalized in organizational structures and decision-making processes. Particularly where dominant theoretical frameworks and professional language prevail, survivors often do not have opportunities to speak and represent themselves. Furthermore, the language of educated, professional, white, middle-class women frequently has the effect of silencing survivors' voices. Abused women thus have little access to spaces where they can fully participate and influence policy development, service provision, and directions for political advocacy. The development of political strategies apart from or on behalf of battered women isolates them, defines them as recipients of action, and limits their role as actors in the social sphere.

DOMINANT DISCOURSE AND THE POSITIONING
OF ABUSED WOMEN AS CLIENTS

The second issue in "the politics of need interpretation" concerns the influence of dominant family violence discourse on the transition house movement and the ways in which it situates abused women as "clients." In the struggle over definition and control of the issue of woman abuse, Walker (1990) asserts that feminists sought to establish woman abuse as a manifestation of male dominance and women's structural position of dependency and subordination, particularly in the family. In contrast, in the family violence framework, woman abuse was seen as an issue of violence among family members, a subset of family violence, "both a product and a reflection of a violent society" (Walker, 1995, p. 72). The concept of "violence," then, provided the common ground on which to unite the male violence framework with the family violence framework, thus organizing the work to be done against wife battering.

The view of wife battering as "violence" enabled woman abuse to be reformulated as "wife assault." The efforts of both activists and professionals converged, resulting in the redefining of wife battering as criminal assault. Wife battering, reconceived as wife assault, was still tenuously linked to the feminist framework of male violence against women and to the political mobilizing intent of the feminist movement. However, once conceptualized as assault, feminist efforts to treat wife battering as a crime were more easily absorbed into the family violence discourse. Its reformulation as wife assault induced feminists into working with state institutions responsible for criminal justice and law and order, turning "women's need for protection into campaigns for law and order" (Findlay, 1988, p. 9). Unfortunately, the law has been limited in its ability to either protect women or deter woman abuse, and, furthermore, has reproduced systemic inequalities of class and "race" by jailing working-class, aboriginal, or men of color for wife assault (MacLeod, 1987; Walker, 1995).

As Walker (1990) points out, a framework that defines men's violence toward female partners as assault presents these violent actions as an infringement of women's individual rights under the law. Furthermore, it suggests that male violence is the result of socialization into violent roles. Once wife battering was understood as a problem of "uncontrolled and unmitigated violence" (Walker, 1990, p. 71), the law's tentacles reached into the family, situating abused women as "victims" of assault. Male violence, perceived as either pathology or faulty gender socialization, encouraged clinical and legal initiatives focusing on "helping the 'violent family' handle 'its' violence" (Walker, 1990, p. 193). As Gillian Walker (1995) clarifies, the family violence framework provided the bridge between the criminal justice and welfare systems, linking justice and social service jurisdictions and criminal with clinical correlates. The strategy of assault located the issue of woman abuse and responses to it within these particular institutions of the social problem apparatus. Professionals became involved in regulating men's abuse of their authority in the family by focusing on "the treatment of men to 'cure' the individual of his violence or for the removal of men who 'abuse their authority in the family,'" and by supporting a newer family form made up of women and children dependent upon the state (Walker, 1990, p. 108). Treatment for batterers and counseling for women constituted legitimate interventions into the family unit. Women who are beaten are thus viewed and treated as a welfare problem and men who batter are criminals (Walker, 1995).

The idea that individual therapy is the intervention most appropriate for individual cases of family violence underpins the family violence framework. In promoting individual therapy as the primary response, this approach is intimately tied up with the state and the governance of clients, many of whom are women (Epstein, 1994). As woman abuse was remade into an issue concerning the assault of individual female victims by individual male perpetrators within the family unit, wife battering was reduced to a series of violent acts by a man against a woman (MacLeod, 1987). At the same time, the issue of woman abuse was reconstructed as a phenomenon affecting individual women and men, not an issue concerning socially structured power inequities between women and men. The different forms and locations of women's oppression as well as the structural inequities that create dependence were thus obscured from view. In this framework encompassing both family violence and assault, the occurrence of violence against women within the family was effectively severed from any connection to women's social status outside the family as well as from any alternative ideas about how social relations between men and women might be reorganized (Walker, 1990).

Consequently, even though feminist shelters and organizations have struggled against this apolitical understanding of woman abuse, the gender-political and political-economic needs of abused women have increasingly been redefined and recast as individual, psychological problems requiring individual intervention (Fraser, 1989). Despite feminist resistance to therapeutic perspectives, family violence discourse and practice has gained substantial ground, obscuring political advocacy work and alternative nonhierarchical and co-operative ways of working with survivors. In such an individualized service approach, abused women become clients while solutions to woman abuse are framed as therapeutic services designed to meet women's psychological needs for counseling and support. Expert needs discourses redefine abused women as "individual 'cases' rather than members of social groups or participants in social movements" (Fraser, 1989, p. 174). As needs are reorganized into "cases," the class, "race," and gender specificity of women's needs are erased, as well as any oppositional meanings that these needs may have in the context of a social movement (Fraser, 1989).

Early in the shelter movement, women were viewed as capable and resilient, requiring peer support and practical assistance. With the resurgence of apolitical frameworks for addressing woman abuse, survivors have long ceased to be equal participants in the struggle against woman abuse. As Gillian Walker (1990) attests, as social service recipients, abused women had little real participation in defining and responding to an issue that paradoxically most affected them. In summary, this state of affairs has had significant implications for survivors' engagement in collective action for social change. One effect is that survivors have been denied access to avenues of action for their justified rage.

Chapter 3

June's Story

In this chapter, I present an uninterrupted narrative account of June's story. This account poignantly illustrates many of the multifaceted, complex, and contradictory processes contained in participants' stories. It also highlights the discursive and material conditions that both facilitate and thwart processes of conscientization. In Chapter 4, I discuss June's journey and its meaning in relation to her work for social change.

June began her story by stating that she had always been aware that her life as a girl differed from the life her brother had as a boy. She recalled that, growing up, her mother had called upon her and not her brother to do housework and serve family meals. Something else had also stuck in her mind: her mother had waited on her father "hand and foot" while her "father never did anything" around the house. But, June reflected, it was really during adolescence that she became aware of the difference between the lives of girls and boys and what life held in store for her as a woman.

> Your whole life seemed to go toward that goal of being a married woman and then waiting on your husband for the rest of your life . . . and I never thought that was a good idea. But everything that I was taught to do always revolved around men . . . looking nice for men, doing things to make men more comfortable. . . . Everything was geared toward men, keeping them happy, yeah. And they were the ones that knew what was right and what should be done.

June distinctly recalled that she had never liked the idea of getting married and doing all those "things" that women do. As an adolescent she aspired to be a lawyer, but, despite her parents' great respect for education, they urged her to become a nurse or some other "girl-type thing." In reality, no one ever bothered to ask her what she wanted to do with her life, and so she simply went along with "what she was supposed to do." June confided that, paradoxically, even if women's liberation had provided an alternative script for her then, she would have vigorously affirmed her identity as a "normal woman," saying, "Oh no, not me; I'm going to grow up and get married and have kids and do all those things that normal women do."

June's conflicting desires played themselves out during her adolescent years. In high school, she felt that she didn't fit in, that she was different from other young women her age:

> I hated school 'cause I could not fit with what everybody else was doing . . . into the social circles, of doing all this makeup stuff with all the other girls. I just didn't fit. . . . It just couldn't be me that was different but it was wrong for me to be different. I should be like them; I should want to do what they want to do 'cause that's normal, so I'm not normal. . . . Every time I sort of acted against the status quo, that feeling that there was something wrong with me was reinforced because my parents . . . my teachers would come down on me, my friends would reject me. They told me that, yes, there was something wrong with me and in their eyes there was something wrong with me . . . . That I couldn't fit into this mold that everybody including me was trying to push me into. . . . I was a square peg trying to fit into a round hole.

Following this assertion of her misfit status, June stated: "I just couldn't do it [fit into the mold], so I just moved from one man to the next to the next, and it got progressively worse and then Ivan came along," the last man with whom she lived. Even though she had rebelled against gendered expectations of her, at the same time she had pushed herself to fit into the mold.

In beginning her story with an account of her contradictory desires and feelings, June set the stage for talking about her life with Ivan. She situated her relationship with him in the context of a contradiction that was central to her story of transformation: how she could have questioned her own and women's place in the world and yet have considered Ivan's treatment of her as just part of "the way it was."

June then described how she came to see that she was being physically and psychologically abused by Ivan. He was a formidable man, "very violent and . . . extremely physically abusive, emotionally abusive, a very, very violent, horrible man." Early in their relationship when she was being beaten and verbally degraded, she did not identify what was happening to her as violence or abuse:

> Even when I was first with him and I was getting beaten up, I would say, "Well, I don't know why women stay with abusive men—they must like it," but I never equated it with myself. . . . I would read in the newspaper about battered women and I would say, "Oh, [that] doesn't happen to anybody I know." . . . I knew it wasn't right for men to hit women, but the reasoning for it was that men were bigger and stronger, and they shouldn't do that, but there was no questioning about control or what they would do . . . but I guess I justified it too. I would say, "Well, she's a real bitch, maybe you should smack her," and—never even looking at what was really happening 'cause it was never a part of my life. I didn't know anybody, I thought. I mean, I'm sure I knew lots but I thought I'd never met anybody, and probably it was only poor people or drunk people or people on welfare that it happened to.

Although June was being beaten and knew that other women were being beaten by their male partners too, it was something "out there," external to her situation. Furthermore, she justified men's abuse of women and their presumed right to discipline women when they stepped out of line. Ivan's circle of friends and his family firmly supported his status as head of the household and his right to control and discipline "his woman" by whatever means necessary.

After describing how she had failed to equate the situation of other battered women with her own, June juxtaposed the fact that she had always questioned why she and other women could not apply for, or were denied certain jobs, because they were women:

> I always had, I mean I always questioned why things were different for women than they were for men . . . why I didn't get jobs, why I couldn't apply for certain jobs and why women didn't get certain jobs because maybe sometime in the future they might get pregnant. It never made sense to me but I didn't . . . it just didn't make sense.

As she told her story, June was still amazed that she could have questioned women's place and yet have understood Ivan's mistreatment of her as "just the way it was." How had such a thing been possible? She concluded that she had implicitly accepted the legitimacy of prevailing social arrangements between men and women despite the fact that she had questioned employment discrimination based on gender. In her judgment, she had not truly challenged this discrimination, only feebly questioned it. She pondered the processes through which she had learned to see certain ideas and practices as "normal," to "accept things without question," and to cling to those ideas and practices even when she was being hurt by them:

> I did not grow up in a family where my mother was . . . beaten or physically abused. . . . but I still thought that that was the way it was. . . . But nobody sits you down and teaches you that . . . tells you, "Listen, you're gonna spend the rest of your life catering to some man." You don't learn it that way, you learn it more by osmosis. . . . You learn it from everywhere because it is everywhere, so you kinda just soak it up as a kid even though nobody sits [you] down. In a way sometimes they do sit down and tell you that's the way it's supposed to be, because they tell you, "Well, that's not a ladylike thing to do— cross your legs, don't sit like that! Girls don't do that!"

After expressing her amazement at the coexistence of such opposing thoughts within her consciousness, June related her ordeal with Sheila, the partner of Ivan's brother, Gary, and how she eventually came to see that Sheila was being unjustly treated. One day, Sheila asked June to pick her up at her apartment because Gary was beating and harassing her. June did so and brought Sheila back to the house she shared with Ivan. At that time, June saw no evidence that Gary had beaten Sheila. Several hours later, June drove Sheila, who was drunk, to the apartment that Sheila shared with Gary. The following day, June found out that Sheila had called the police to charge Gary with assault. Gary called Ivan and demanded to know what had happened to Sheila while she had been with June, all the while protesting that he had not laid a hand on her. Gary, released on bail, stayed with June and Ivan. When he continued to harass Sheila, June told him that she did not want any more trouble and kicked him out.

The day finally arrived when June went to court to testify as a witness in the matter. She testified that she did not know what had taken place after she had dropped Sheila off at her apartment. What happened next in court affected June profoundly and unequivocally:

> [The Crown prosecutor] showed me these pictures from the police station. This poor woman—this woman was like four foot nine and he was six foot three—was just covered in bruises and cuts and big bite marks on her arm. It was horrible; it was really horrible, and I looked at these pictures and all of a sudden I thought, oh my God. . . . And she said, "Do you think it's okay for men to beat up women?" and I said, "Ach." I didn't know what to say. And I looked over at Gary, and I just didn't know what to say. My whole life changed right then 'cause all of a sudden there it was right in front of me and I didn't know what to do. I'd never seen anything like this before and I thought, oh my God, how can anybody do that to somebody?

June was so shocked and confused that she could not answer the Crown prosecutor's question. She insisted that Sheila had not looked like that when she left her. She immediately became angry at Gary because he had convinced her to believe his version of events. Even though she had responded to Sheila's plea to intervene precisely because Gary was beating her, June had believed Gary's claim that Sheila, intoxicated, had fallen down the stairs leading to the basement apartment. The stark and horrifying reality of the photographs forced June to face and recognize Gary's brutal and unjustifiable assault on Sheila and the fact that she, in believing Gary's version of events and testifying for him, had denied that reality.

June accentuated the fact that "from one minute to the next my life changed." How could something like that happen to someone that she knew "hadn't done anything to deserve it"?

> All of a sudden it became real—it all of a sudden became something that really happened. It didn't just become something that happened to someone I didn't know for reasons that I could rationalize in my head. It became something that happened in my life because it was something that I knew.

Confronted with this horrible reality, June could no longer distance herself by rationalizing that Sheila was poor, deserving, or a bitch. This was not about some stranger for whom she could fashion some justification for a beating. The source of her knowledge was herself and what she had witnessed in the photographs. Suddenly she was seeing things differently from the way she was supposed to see them: it was supposed to be Sheila's fault, wasn't it? And wasn't Sheila out to get Gary, anyway? June realized that Sheila was one of those battered women and what Gary had done was wrong.

However, while June did recognize Gary's assault on Sheila, her recognition of the brutal beating did not crack open, once and for all, the naturalization and justification of men's violence toward women. Just because she knew that what Gary had done was wrong did not mean that every instance of a man beating a woman was wrong; it was only that particular situation that was wrong. "Just because Sheila wasn't to blame for this didn't mean that Mary next door, who's an absolute bitch anyway, didn't deserve it, right?" June did not challenge the social power accorded to men to exercise authority over women.

Moreover, June recalled that even though Gary's attitude and behavior toward Sheila paralleled Ivan's treatment of her, she did not immediately see that everything that Ivan was doing to her was wrong. Nevertheless, Sheila's brutal beating did prompt June to question in some fundamental way her interpretation of Ivan's behavior. When Ivan beat her even more severely than he had done in the past, she began to look at her situation differently:

> All of a sudden, it was different . . . it wasn't all right. It was still my fault, but it wasn't okay any more—it was just differ-

ent. I still blamed myself because it was always, well, if you didn't piss me off so much. . . . It was if you didn't do this, if you didn't do that, I wouldn't have to do this. So I bought into all that, but there was something in the back of my head—that this wasn't right anymore. . . . That was the first thing that made me start to question, but I didn't question too much. I knew it wasn't okay, that there was something wrong that didn't fit with the way that I had been thinking, but I didn't put it together.

Phallocentric discourse naturalizes and justifies men's violence toward women, constructing women as responsible for "provoking" men's assaults or "asking" to be raped. Although June still blamed herself for Ivan's violent actions, now something chafed at her consciousness, something that did not fit with the way she had been thinking. This disjuncture between her previous understanding that men's beating of women was justifiable and her insight that all instances of woman beating were not okay indicated that perhaps what Ivan was doing to her was . . . what?

Even while this disjuncture nagged at her consciousness, June still could not let herself admit that her situation might be similar to Sheila's and that what Ivan was doing was wrong:

I couldn't let myself think it was the same. Like, as soon as I admitted to myself that it was the same then I had to do something about it. It was happening to me but I wasn't admitting that it was happening to me. . . . When it was Gary and Sheila I could say, "Gary's an asshole, he shouldn't be doing that . . . she was right to charge him, she was right to leave him." But that wasn't the same as me. . . . It didn't apply to me; mine was different . . . I didn't get hit for no reason, I got hit because I did something wrong.

Some of the social messages with which June had grown up worked against recognizing that what Ivan was doing was wrong and that she did not merit such treatment. She had been brought up to place her man at the center of her life, direct her efforts at ensuring his happiness, and "be there" for him. She recalled these messages that admonished her to accept her lot with fortitude and be content with what was handed to her:

> What the hell do you want? Do you want the world to hand you things on a silver platter? That's not the way it's gonna happen. Don't ask—you don't ask for anything—I mean, you don't even ask for contentment. You take what's given to you and be satisfied with your lot in life because there's a whole lot of people out there that are worse off than you. . . . I was convinced that what was happening to me was not that bad, that a lot of women had it a lot worse. . . . I should just stop being such a wuss and just take what I got, and if I hadn't started it, I wouldn't [have gotten] it anyway.

Paradoxically, while June wished for happiness in her relationship, she knew that she was not to complain if things were not as she had hoped. Ivan reinforced this message by taunting her, saying that she was a wimp for not being able to take what he dished out to her.

June first went to a shelter about two and a half years after her court experience with Gary and Sheila. Her first and only child, Amelia, was just three months old. Afraid for Amelia's well-being, June stated that when Amelia was born she knew she just had to get out [of the relationship]. Propelling her flight to the shelter was an assault in which Ivan had knocked her unconscious while she held Amelia in her arms. He had also threatened to take Amelia and "dump her somewhere." Ironically, it was Ivan himself who unwittingly supplied information about shelters. When June was pregnant with Amelia, Ivan had come home from work one day to announce that, yes, that house across the street was a shelter for "those battered women," and why didn't she go over there someday?

Although she felt safe in a shelter in another town, she remained anxious and terrified of what Ivan might do to her. She decided not to press charges against him because he had threatened to make it "worth his while" to go to jail if she ever did so. June was also unsettled by all the questions shelter staff asked during her initial intake interview, which lasted over two hours. For example, did he kick, punch, slap, or bite you? How many times? When? Where?

I thought, how did you know this? . . . I just didn't have a clue what was happening out there to women. I had no idea of what was going on and I really thought, how the hell did they know that this was happening to me? . . . that he was doing all these things? And how did they know that he was saying this? And they knew that he was blaming me for it and that I was blaming myself—how'd they know all that? I stayed up all that night and I'm thinking, something's wrong here, I don't know what's happening. I was so confused—my mind was just spinning with all this. . . . I went down in the middle of the night and I said, "Why did you ask me all these questions? How did you know that he does that?" . . . They said, "Well, it's pretty common." I said, "No way." And they said, "Well, just about every woman who comes in says the same thing." I said, "Ah, no way." I just couldn't deal with that.

June, shocked that what she considered to be the private details of her life were so well known to others, felt vulnerable, scared, and exposed. Despite this, she posed some questions for herself that contained the seeds for understanding the gendered, social dimensions of her personal experience of woman abuse (Breines and Gordon, 1983). However, she was unequipped to tackle them at this juncture:

I just couldn't accept it. I couldn't think about it anymore, you know, it just opened up too much. It was like looking into this great big hole and I'm not going in there, that's too much for me right now, and I just refused to think about it. . . . It was just too big. . . . I thought, how many of these places [shelters] are there? . . . It was just too many questions that I didn't have any answers for and I was just so scared. . . . I was so scared that I just couldn't deal with all these questions. I couldn't come up with any answers . . . yeah, I didn't want to ask them. . . . If I was being hit because I was doing something wrong . . . were all these women out there doing the wrong thing, you know? Whoa! Scary question! . . . Was it women that were wrong or was it men that were wrong? I mean, it didn't feel right, what was happening, but that's what everybody told me . . . it was my job to keep him happy, right? . . . to make sure that life

> went smoothly. . . . I could face it if it was just me because I had been wrong forever—I never did do anything right—but was nobody doing it right? . . . It was like my whole world wasn't what I thought it was. For thirty-six years I'd been living somewhere else. . . . I thought I was quite aware of what was going on in the world and I questioned women's place in the world. . . . Why is this whole world out there that I didn't know about? . . . There were just too many questions and if I opened that door, it just would [have] been too overwhelming.

June reflected that she just could not deal with all of the questions that were welling up inside her then. She was struggling to survive with a new baby and had few reserves to summon in seeking answers to them. At the same time, closing off these questions prevented a clear and conscious awareness of the contradictions that were coming up: if she was the sole author of her misfortunes, then how could so many battered women exist? If so many other women were not wrong, would that mean that she was really okay, that it was not her job to keep Ivan happy and make life go smoothly?

June left the shelter determined to make a life of her own. She moved into a tiny, grossly overpriced basement apartment complete with cockroaches. Continuing to work as a secretary, her daily routine consisted of dropping Amelia off at the home of the woman who cared for her, commuting over two hours a day, and arranging for Ivan to visit Amelia. One evening, when he arrived at her apartment and began to scream obscenities at her, her exhaustion from coping with an infant, unstable child care arrangements, substandard housing, no family support, and daily commuting gave way to feelings of futility and despair. Feeling that she was being punished for trying to make a better life, and envisioning an exhausting routine stretching out endlessly in front of her while Ivan lived in the comfort of their townhouse free of child care responsibilities, she felt trapped:

> It just seemed almost like I was being punished. Am I going to be able to cope with living like this forever? . . . Having no family support, my family and friends telling me what to do constantly—everything I was doing was wrong. It got too much for me and I just felt, this is it, I can't get away from him. . . . Every day

there was something . . . I just felt like this is it, I'm trapped in this relationship with this guy, it's either him or all this other stuff . . . he was showing up at the house . . . and I hadn't really gotten away from him anyway. . . . It felt like a trap.

The social realities materially organizing June's life stared her in the face, creating very real barriers for her. As a mother she was expected to assume total responsibility for Amelia's care, and no assistance was forthcoming from anyone. When she returned to work, she was refused the position that she had had before her maternity leave. June felt that Ivan had a right to visit Amelia and thus found that even though she had her own apartment, she had not really gotten away from him after all. That men should have access to their children even when they are abusive to the children and/or their mothers, is a common belief and actual practice in mainstream society (Vancouver Custody and Access Support and Advocacy Association, 1995).

June returned to live with Ivan. Several months later, following a severe beating, she fled to another shelter, refusing to return home unless Ivan moved out of the house. One night after he arrived to get some belongings, she agreed to work on the relationship one more time because, as June pointed out, Ivan could be very convincing and charming, "promising the moon." As it turned out, working on the relationship meant that she alone worked on it. Within a week Ivan beat her again, and she sought shelter for the third time. During this time she began to look more closely at her life and reconsider some of the questions that she had refused to think about during her first shelter respite:

I really just started to look at my own life, the process of getting up to where I was and all the relationships I'd had with men and how bad they were. . . . I started thinking, something's wrong here . . . and why is this happening, and I can't get myself out of this, and I was listening to women in the shelter tell me that it wasn't my fault. . . . I started to see what was happening in a different light, that if it was happening to other women so parallel to my experience, then how could it be just because there was something wrong with me? There'd have to be something wrong with them as well and they seemed perfectly fine to me, so maybe it wasn't me after all. So I guess that's how I started thinking. . . . I started really seeing how much everybody's story was the same and how much . . . men all used the same—like right down to the same words. It was almost like a script, I used to think. . . . Two men who come from two different life backgrounds and they use the exact same words. . . . I was just amazed by that, so I thought, if they're so much alike and this woman and I are so much different but our experience has been the same, then maybe it's them—maybe it's them that's wrong, not us. Maybe they're the ones who are doing it; maybe we don't have to have this; maybe this isn't just the way it's supposed to be.

Until this point, June had resisted considering the possibility that she was not to blame for Ivan's violence toward her. She now contemplated this and more, questioning her self-blame for his violent behavior and also why all her previous relationships with men had been so unsatisfactory. Challenging the pattern of assigning fault to women, she concluded that it was really quite improbable that so many women could be "wrong." If women were not to blame for abuse, then what exactly was happening? And what did this have to do with the fact that she had not found the happiness, joy, contentment, and everything else she was told she would find for "doing her womanly duty"? What if she had not been the sole author of her bad relationships and limited life opportunities? Could her own life be something other than what she lived with Ivan?

Around this time June had another experience that hastened the reevaluation of her relationship with Ivan and furnished an insight into the social value accorded to women. As a condition of returning home, Ivan agreed to attend Turning Point, a program for men who abuse their female partners. She recounted how he became even more proficient at psychological games during his participation in this program. Using "social-worky words," he accused June of being abusive to him! When he was "losing control," he called time out and demanded that she shut up! He rationalized that he acted as he did because his parents had abused him as a child. In a program interview designed to elicit feedback from female partners, June became furious, voicing her anger to program staff:

> I thought, this is ridiculous. This [men's abuse of women] is everywhere. All these women I'm meeting and they're all telling me exactly the same things I'm telling them and I just couldn't believe it, I was so angry! . . . They [program staff] were telling me about the cycle of violence. I said, "You tell me about the cycle of violence—I'll tell you about the cycle of violence." And I was so angry there and I remember that's the very first time I think that I was ever really angry about it, and I was just so angry that they were making this pretense that they were doing something for me and they weren't doing shit for me.

She was furious that a program that purported to help her provided men with even more ammunition and justification for their actions, ultimately reproducing women's disadvantage. If the staff were unable to see men's manipulation, then how was the program going to help her? June's anger galvanized around Turning Point because she intuited that "something bigger" was happening, something bigger than just isolated individual men beating isolated individual women.

June emphasized that every shelter stay (five within approximately one and a half years) provided her with the opportunity to listen to other women talk about their lives. The knowledge that she garnered in shelters illuminated and reinforced her insights into Turning Point and Ivan's behavior. She became less and less accepting not only of Ivan's violent acts but of all of his attempts to control her. During this time June wove together an interpretation of his behavior that challenged his claim of "losing control" of himself in a fit of anger:

> I would go back to him, but I wouldn't hear the things he was saying the same way. And I was saying, I know exactly what you're gonna say now. I know how this is going to proceed from here . . . what he was going to do and what he was going to say . . . the things I would do that he would use as an excuse to start on his path. . . . That's how I started looking at things differently. . . . I started thinking: Hmm, this is true; this isn't about uncontrollable anger. Hmm, makes sense, you know.

June's analogy for her process of conscientization was that of putting together the pieces of a puzzle. This process was a gradual and painstaking one in which she fit one piece at a time. Shelters played a pivotal role in this process, stimulating her critical questioning, reinforcing her insights, supporting her desire to know, and validating her growing sense of self. Upon leaving a shelter she had a host of questions which, by the time she returned again, would either have been answered or have mushroomed into many more. She also left shelters armed with information about her legal and human rights as well as community resources and organizations.

When June left Ivan for the fourth time, she had just found new employment as a secretary and new day care for Amelia. Fearing that she would lose her job because she could not get to work on time from the shelter, she spoke with her boss, albeit with much embarrassment, about her situation. Given her difficulties getting to work, she decided to return home with a plan to survive there until she could save some money. She hid some clothes for herself and Amelia in the trunk of the car and, not long afterward, she left Ivan for good.

June related that shortly after leaving him for the last time, her boiling anger that had erupted at Turning Point appeared "more on the surface," propelling her to make a life for herself and Amelia.

> By that time I was really angry. I didn't know what I was angry at—I was angry at everything, everybody. There was something wrong here and why didn't everybody see this? And why didn't everybody know? And why wasn't there anything I could do about this? And I was just so aware of this seething anger and I guess this anger must have been building for years. I was just bubbling and boiling. . . . Why did I have to be afraid? This was so unfair and it was just anger, just really becoming angry, and so when I got into second-stage housing I was just ripe for anybody who had any answers for me at all and I started listening to women talk. . . . So why isn't anybody doing anything about this! . . . Why is it only women that are talking about it? And why is it being allowed to happen?

June was unable to articulate the exact source of her anger, but she knew from experience that she was the one who had to leave her home, live in fear, work, and care for Amelia while Ivan sat at home with impunity. She was outraged. Her anger generated a desire to know even more and when she moved into second-stage housing after her shelter residency, she was "ripe for answers":

> I just got to this point where I just wanted to learn everything there was to learn . . . read everything there was to read . . . talk to every woman there was to talk to. I just wanted to learn why this was happening and how . . . and who knew . . . and who didn't . . . and who was doing anything about it and who wasn't. I just had to know everything there was. . . . I guess that was the hand that was behind me—the goddess hand— and I guess that's what was pushing me to keep going on and on and on and on.

June had already learned a great deal from shelter residents and staff, and in second-stage housing she realized that she could learn even more by listening closely to women's stories. Before doing that, however, she had to refute lessons she had learned about women: "Women are untrustworthy! They'll backstab you! They'll steal your man!" June had never made real friendships with women, but she decided to take the risk. After all, she reasoned, the women in second-stage housing had something in common: they had over- come many obstacles and were trying to rebuild their lives. These friendships formed a web of support as she sought to understand and reconstruct her life.

June credits the staff and structure of second-stage housing with saving her life. Its rules and constancy provided not only physical safety from Ivan's threats and violence but emotional safety from being "sucked in" by him again:

> [Second-stage housing] was safe because I was safe from my- self, because he couldn't come over. No matter what I did he couldn't come over. I couldn't get sucked in by him again. . . . I felt like a fish that he was playing with, that he would let me run for a while and then all of a sudden the hook in my mouth, he'd pull on it. I never got that hook out of my mouth. He always could reel me back in. . . . They helped me take that hook out of my mouth . . . took control of a part of my life for

me until I had the strength to take care of that myself and that's when I could leave, you know, you can't do that in six weeks . . . . You need longer than six weeks to rebuild your life, to build your strength again because you have nothing. You're powerless when you're in an abusive relationship. You're powerless because you see yourself as powerless, not because you necessarily are but because that's how you view yourself.

Second-stage housing provided a secure space in which June could take the hook out of her mouth. Notwithstanding all the efforts that she had made to cut her bonds with Ivan, she still felt vulnerable to him. During this time she continued to take Amelia to visit him. Following a visit during which he railed at her, she refused him further visitation. Insisting on his right to see his daughter, Ivan stepped up his attempts to control her, making death threats and harassing her by telephone. June had considered seeking legal custody of Amelia on many occasions, and now the time had come. When the judge awarded June interim custody, he granted Ivan a restraining order against her based on Ivan's claim that she was harassing and stalking him. Assuming the role of the victimized man, he demanded to know why she was punishing him by seeking custody. Plagued by guilt over her decision, June considered backing out of the court date to settle long-term custody but instead persevered. Against her lawyer's advice, June conceded to supervised access at Ivan's parents' house rather than at a custody and access center. While they were in the waiting room and judge's chambers at Family Court, Ivan imitated putting a gun to her head and shooting her. Particularly distressing to her was the fact that this occurred in full view of the police and the judge, and no one said a single word to him.

During subsequent access visits, June became attuned to the nature of the interactions between members of Ivan's family. One particular interaction between Ivan's mother and Amelia, now sixteen months old, had such an effect on her that she refused to take Amelia there again. Ivan's mother was swatting Amelia on her behind, teaching her to hit her doll in the face, and instructing her that everyone needed to know how to fight. Shocked that such a thing was happening in front of her very eyes, June finally "woke up" and told Ivan's mother to stop.

By this time June was living on social assistance, since she had lost her job when her employer went bankrupt. With only the shelter and second-stage housing concerned with her well-being, she still wondered whether she would ever be able to really get away from Ivan. She became acutely aware of her physical and emotional vulnerability to Ivan and people's general unwillingness to help women in need of protection. Despite this, she persisted, albeit unconsciously, in taking bigger and bigger steps to distance herself from him:

> It was all planned, not consciously at the time, but each step kind of came along and as I got through each step, it was sort of, well, let's go a little bit farther. Like it was not just a one-day thing—okay that's it, I'm never going to speak to this guy as long as I live, and I never for a second, thought that it would work. I never, not for a second at that time, thought that I would actually go four years without hearing the sound of that man's voice. At that time [I] thought that he would get to me one way or another.

Given the unhealthy environment at Ivan's parents' house for supervised visits, June took yet another step to protect herself and her daughter by arranging supervised access through a children's center. After this was done, Ivan never contacted the center to see Amelia again. When June changed her telephone number, she lost contact with him. Although she initially commented that "it was just that sort of series of circumstances that cut it off," she later observed that she herself had engineered some of the conditions that led to their loss of contact.

Although Ivan had been physically absent from June's life for several months, she was still hearing his voice in her mind. While she hadn't heard the sound of his real voice, in her head she heard his two-hour rampages in which he tore her to shreds:

> I could hear every word of them goin' over and over and why couldn't I get away from that? What was this doing to me? . . . It's supposed to be over but it's not over. Why not? This is more

than just not having him right beside me. There's more to it than this, and I started thinking, how do you ever get away? . . . And how did I get into this? And why did this happen to me? I'm a smart woman—how did I end up with this asshole for six years? And why did I put up with this? And why did I blame myself? This wasn't my fault . . . so how come I lived with this for six years? The questions started coming up, all the questions that had been there for years.

June was dealing with the effects of Ivan's abuse, but something more was happening than reliving the rampages. The contradiction and conflict in her own consciousness had become visible to her. How had she come to believe in things that constructed her as powerless and undeserving? Why had she "just accepted them without question" and clung to them for so long? Why did she respond to Ivan's exertions of power the way she did and assume that she was the cause of his anger? Why had she perceived herself as "completely powerless" in the relationship? Why had she made herself "invisible," denied her own needs, done everything in her power to please him, and "kept silent about what was happening"? If she had believed in things that were not in her best interest, how could she trust herself in the future?

This process was painful because it involved not only self-questioning but casting a critical eye over significant others who had been part of her formation: everyone from her parents and teachers to her grandfather and brother.

Part of giving that up [what I had believed in] was questioning the people who gave it to me in the first place. . . . Why did they teach me that and such nonsense? In order to give up those ideas I had to look at myself and why I kept them for so long—why I just accepted them without question. . . . It's horrendous to look at every person in your life and see them for what they are. . . . It's really hard to see how shitty women are treated in the world. It's very painful to see that. . . . I don't think anybody says. . . . now that I see this I'm enlightened! That's not fun! It's not fun to have to look at your mother and how she treated you when you were a kid, and look at her mother and see how she treated you and your mother, and to look at . . . your friends [from childhood]. . . . All of a sudden I realized that kid had a lot of accidents when he was a kid. A lot of things are not what I thought, not what they seemed . . . It's like admitting to myself that, yes, my grandfather abused me when all through my life my grandfather was the only person I ever thought loved me. Well, he sure as hell did, that's hard to give it up, but . . . it's all part of the same work.

To admit that others had not acted in her best interest but rather had taught her some of the very things that contributed to her oppression engendered feelings of loss and betrayal. June also confronted the reality that her grandfather had masqueraded his sexual abuse of her as love. Acknowledging that significant others had helped her to see herself as a lesser person also brought home the painful reality of the social worth accorded to women: now she recognized to a greater degree not only her own pain but the pain of other women.

June's self-questioning evoked feelings of loss and letting go. She described this nexus as one in which, despite her desire to know some truth about her life, a part of her did not want to know. She strove to reinvest in exactly what her new knowledge had begun to dislodge.

I fought it, I mean I fought it. I tried so hard to stay with everything that I'd learned all my life, but I couldn't. It just got to a point where you just can't . . . not start to put these pieces of the puzzle together, so it all started to fall into place. . . . It's like walking into the front lines of a war. . . . There are lives that are destroyed. Nobody wants to see that, you know. . . . I found it's hard because you never can let it go. . . . Once you open your eyes you can't ever say, oh, I don't want to see that 'cause it's just right there in your face all the time . . . It's scary but you can't walk away from it. I can't walk away from it.

Paradoxically, as hard as she tried not to know, she could not stop herself from putting the pieces together. The different factors that had converged to heighten and accentuate her dissatisfaction with "the way it was" had also generated a desire for something more.

As June became conscious of each little parcel of her history and more attentive to her desires and needs, she "dragged down that early stuff" one bit at a time, saying, "No, that doesn't fit for me. Do away with that one." As her gaze moved from seeing some intrinsic flaw inside herself to examining the ways in which she had been shaped by her social world, including significant others, she began to construct a different sense of herself. When she rejected pieces of what the world had told her and recognized how she had invested in them, she needed to put something else in their place. In her meaning-making process, the coming together of certain pieces depended upon other pieces being in place. One such piece was self-acceptance.

> Somewhere along the line you realize that it's okay to be a square peg. . . . That's a huge leap. It really is a complete about-face because then you have to look at . . . everybody. If you're blaming yourself for being a square peg, then you're only blaming one person, but when you stop seeing that it's you that's wrong for being a square peg and it's them that's wrong for trying to fit you into a wrong hole, then you have to look at all of them. I mean that's the whole question of where I fit. Why do I see all of them being wrong and not just me?

June recalled that at this point in her journey, her difference, her misfit status, what had been "wrong" with her, became a strength, something formative in rebuilding her sense of self, rather than a weakness or flaw.

Another piece of sorting out her relation to the world involved answering the question: Why are women subjected to such violence? The "cycle of violence" theory presented at Turning Point did not give any real reasons for the systemic nature of violence against women. In second-stage housing June was introduced to what has become known as the power and control wheel (Pence and Paymar, 1993). This wheel depicts the different tactics that men use to exercise their power and control over women, for example, by using male privilege, coercion, and threats. With this information June put words to what she had already intuited: gender relations based on unequal power pervade every realm of society.

Instead of just one person, I started seeing it as a bigger picture. I started thinking about the politics of it, how scary it was for me to go to court . . . How come I was being abused and I had to go to a shelter? I was the one that was being hurt here. . . . How come it happens that way? . . . [The power and control wheel] finally gave some reasons that I could see. It was one of those eye-opening things you look at and say, yeah, this applies! This is it! This is the way it works! And it wasn't a great leap of intellect to take that from a personal point to the bigger picture. . . . Realizing it was about power and control on an individual level showed me how it was about power and control in the bigger picture as well. . . . Power as not just being physical power but about being social power. . . . Once I looked at it in terms of power then the whole thing, employment and everything, fell into place because it was all about male power, and it was very easy to relate the big picture to the personal picture and the personal picture to the big picture. It all fell into place with that.

The social structures, institutions, and practices that give rise to women's subordinate social status were now exposed, laying bare all that had maintained Ivan's advantage and organized June's disadvantage. Recognizing woman abuse as a "huge thing," a systemic issue addressed by only a handful of predominantly women's groups and organizations, June felt a growing urgency to take action. Why wasn't the rest of the world as furious as she was at such injustice?

I was absolutely furious! Somebody's gotta do something about this and at that point I really felt that I was gonna make a difference. . . . All it was gonna take was for me to start telling people what was happening and . . . once people started talking about it, then society as a whole was gonna be outraged and . . . that was that. Ha! As I learned that people really didn't care that this was happening and, yes, that everybody knew it was going on . . . was the same time that I was making the connections with the whole social structure. . . . So I was saying, well, of course, if this is what's happening then of course they don't give a shit because they're part of it. . . . So those two pieces kind of happened hand in hand and one explained the other, so it didn't fuel the anger. I don't think I've ever not been angry since that time. That anger that built there then is still there and it's always gonna be.

June first reasoned that people's inaction was due to ignorance alone. When everyone found out what was happening, surely they would be compelled to act. However, when she realized that social misogyny permeated every realm of patriarchal culture (Grosz, 1990), including people's psyches, she saw that this would not happen. Rather than giving rise to despair, this realization affirmed the urgent need for change.

Before her year of residency in second-stage housing was up, June began to look for decent, affordable housing. She became cognizant of the lower status accorded to her as a "single mother" on welfare and the lack of good housing for women and children.

How hard it was to find housing that we could afford and that was decent for your kids. . . . They put us in shelters and they put us in second-stage housing and then what? We had to go out and live in a slum with our kids because we couldn't afford to do anything else. . . . How come we couldn't get enough money to pay for day care and how come we had to put our kids in second-class day cares and we were treated differently? I was treated differently at the day care center . . . than the people who paid full fees. You know, my daughter wasn't as important as those other kids and why was that happening?

She rallied others to "make noise" about the lack of housing. Shortly afterward, June moved into cooperative housing. Still wanting to do something about woman abuse, she went to hear a lecture given by the profeminist director of Turning Point. If woman abuse was to end, June reasoned that men would have to change, and if they wanted to change, then they could do so. Volunteering with this program, she contacted female partners in order to monitor men's progress in the program. In her role, she observed that many men did not want to undertake the difficult project of change. She felt compelled to move on in search of more answers.

In telling her story, June found it ironic that she chose to work with Turning Point, a program that had been such a source of anger for her, at the very juncture that she uncovered the systemic nature of violence against women. In retrospect, she concluded that her observation about men's resistance to change had produced a subversive rage that propelled her to let go of men's professed intentions to change.

> To put a visualization on it, it was like I had a hand behind me pushing me along. I think at a certain point I dug my heels in and said, okay, this is it [I won't go any farther], but it just seemed to happen without my volition. There really was some goddess's hand or something behind me saying no, go farther, you have to go farther.

Feeling a sense of hope, June yearned to better understand her own life, other women's lives, and the ways in which they sought to improve them. She decided to work with women in second-stage housing in order to "do it better for women."

During her residency in cooperative housing, she became friends with some of her neighbors. Her friendship with a lesbian woman gave her permission to accept feelings that she had previously felt for women. To actually know a woman who was out there living what June had experienced and been told was "sick and twisted" challenged the institution of heterosexuality and encouraged self-acceptance. While in cooperative housing she did not identify herself as a lesbian, but she reflected upon everything that she had learned about what gay and lesbian people were supposed to be. For example, in her family, the worst insult was to call someone a "damn queer."

Pursuing her desire for more knowledge, June took courses on violence against women and on women's sexuality, which were taught by feminists. In one course, the professor asked students to talk about what feminism meant to them. June had known a staff person, Linda, at second-stage housing who talked a "feminist line" but did not live it. Because of her experience with Linda, she refused to "take the label" feminist.

> We went around the class . . . and I said, "I'm not callin' myself a damn feminist." I said, "I believe in women and I believe in the strength of women and I believe that the world

really needs to change and make lives better for women, but I'm not one of those feminists who goes around preaching all this fancy word stuff and then not practicing it. I live what I preach." . . . Linda . . . had all these words, right, . . . and I thought, it's not that, that's not what it's about. It's not about having all the right answers—it's about what you do every day. It's about living your life and making changes in your life, not about preaching one thing and doing another thing. You know, you have to live it to be it.

June recalled that her experience working collectively with other women at second-stage housing had been positive and constructive. She had experienced women's strength and power to make change. Shortly after this classroom discussion, June happened upon a cartoon in *Ms.* magazine depicting the contradiction between women's desire for equality and their rejection of feminism as a means to achieve this. This cartoon, seemingly created just for her, provoked her to reevaluate her refusal to identify herself as a feminist.

The cartoon was this little woman and she's going, "Well, I think that women should get equal pay for equal work but I'm not one of those feminists." And in the next panel she's a little bit smaller. "Well, why is it that nobody wants to do anything about violence against women? But I wouldn't want to join up with that feminist organization." And it's about [five] panels like this, and in each one she gets a little bit smaller, and she ends each one with "but I'm not one of those radical feminists." And in the last one she's saying, "I'm not one of those feminists" and there's this big male hand patting her on the head going "Thata girl," and I thought, holy shit! Is that me or what!

This cartoon was powerful because it so clearly mirrored the contradiction between her belief in the goals of the feminist movement and her refusal to identify as a feminist. It became clear that her denial of feminism signified preservation of the status quo.

So the old wheel started working again and I thought, gee, you know, if I'm not going to call myself a feminist, what am I doing to the women who are out there? Not all women who call themselves feminists are Linda, so what am I gonna do? I'm going to either refuse to identify myself with women who are out there doing the work, and that puts me on my own and them on their own, or I'm gonna be one of them but I'm gonna challenge everybody.

If her failure to identify as a feminist buttressed existing power relations, then solidarity required that she identify as one. June saw her immersion in a feminist learning environment as significant in this process of self-identification. Once she took this step, she could not turn back.

Things just came into my life that made me make choices, that I just couldn't anymore. . . . I think once you see it then you have to take on a responsibility. . . . It's an awful responsibility just to yourself, never mind to the other women in the world . . . a responsibility to yourself to say no, I'm not going to be part of this. I'm not going to collude in this or I'm not going to take part in or participate in this anymore, and then the responsibility goes further to say, I'm going to pass this information on.

At this juncture June assumed the responsibility to pass on her knowledge to other women. Thus she committed herself to monitoring whether she was practicing feminism or contributing to the diminishment of others. Her experience with Linda had demonstrated how a formally educated, middle-class woman employed language to intimidate less privileged women such as June. Feminism had to be much deeper than what can be quoted from books. It is a political theory and practice about how to live, cognizant of how one's actions affect others. June's self-identification as a feminist had a profound effect on how she proceeded in her everyday life, in her work with others, and in her understanding of power and privilege. It was important for her to learn about the different ways in which systems of domination affect diverse groups of women. At the same time that June felt freer to progress in her journey, her path became more demanding in a different way. As she stated, she felt it was "harder but freer to be at the same time."

June's self-definition as a feminist occurred a few years ago. Reflecting on her journey from the time of her court appearance to her self-definition as a feminist, she emphasized that she struggled every step of the way to survive with her daughter with scarce resources, make sense of her life, and follow her obsession with piecing together the puzzle. Her politicization affected every aspect of her being: her way of seeing, her sense of herself, her relations with others, and her material world.

As June differentiated her way of seeing and being in the world from that of others, she faced real consequences in terms of loss of relationships. Almost every support she had had before she articulated her political perspective changed significantly or was lost to her. This distance and feeling of aloneness initially caused her much distress.

> You have to feel that you have some kind of support out there to do it [to reject a piece of what the world has told you] because you give up everything. The price is really, really high. . . . You give up family support. When you start questioning in your place of employment why men are making more than women, you give up your peer support there. When you start questioning why all these women are sitting around putting down other women, you give up that support network . . . so it's a high, high cost. . . . I don't know if I had realized that when I started on this path [if] I would have carried on, because it's not a real popular place to be. It can be quite a lonely place because you really are in opposition to most of the men and women.

June's friendships with women mitigated some of these losses, but her declaration—that if she could have foreseen the cost she might not have pursued this path—suggests that such a journey is full of difficulties, challenges, and risks. Despite the cost, however, she asserted that she would not change it.

What kept June moving forward? More than anything else, she felt that it was unanswered questions, questions that she could not ignore. Constantly thinking and reflecting, she would develop an analysis of something and then find that some piece did not quite fit. "Why doesn't this fit with this?" she would ask. "Why doesn't this feel right anymore?"

Paradoxically, the questions she did not want to ask and the contradictions she did not want to see led her to develop a different set of principles for living. Her refusal to collude with the status quo has become an integral part of her identity. Even though she is aware that she still makes mistakes and will only be able to recognize them in hindsight, she is unwilling to punish herself for only being able to get one piece of the puzzle at a time. She is trying to figure out what feminism and political action mean to her and how to work in ways that do not reproduce oppressive discourses and practices. Thinking of "the master's tools" (Lorde, 1984, p. 110) and examining how her ways of making sense of the world and acting in it might perpetuate the status quo, June says:

> I've been thinking a lot about Audre Lorde and [how] the master's tools will never dismantle the master's house, so when I evaluate my life. . . . I have to evaluate my life based on whether I have used the master's tools in attempting to dismantle the master's house. . . . whether I have taken feminism beyond what I read in books . . . and actually lived it. . . . Have I used my knowledge and my exposure to knowledge about oppression and patriarchy . . . to further it? . . . Am I using that knowledge and that position of privilege that that knowledge gives me to . . . put myself up here and women who don't have that knowledge down here? So I have to evaluate my life differently in order to get rid of the master's tools because the master's tools are in here [inside]. The master's tools are how I've been raised to treat other people in my life, the racism, the ageism, all the isms. . . . It's not just out there.

In ending her story, June said, "I am a born-again woman . . . but me then is not me now."

Chapter 4

Rewriting a Survivor's Life:
Revisiting the Past to Form the Future

June's desire for knowledge that would illuminate her lived experience and her strength and resilience in rebuilding her life stand out as formidable accomplishments. What is also impressive and exceptionally instructive for us is not the fact that she lived contradiction and conflict, as I believe we all do, but the processes through which she became conscious of and confronted contradiction and conflict, thus shifting her consciousness about herself and her relation to the world.

What, then, is the significance of contradiction and conflict? According to Sandra Bartky (1990), contradictions are lived subjectively as internal conflicts, anguished consciousness, inner uncertainty, and confusion. "A 'contradiction' connotes dynamic tension between two opposing forces. . . . contradictions are never fully resolved; instead, they are continually being transformed into new situations of tension. Unlike problems, which may be 'solved,' contradictions require continual struggle" (Sable, 1978, pp. 335-336). Contradictions arise from disjunctures between dominant modes of consciousness and experience.

Making meaning out of contradiction and conflict in our everyday lives can produce new ways of seeing that call into question dominant social meanings and open the way for change (Weedon, 1987). In her discussion of feminist pedagogy in the classroom, Linda Briskin (1990) states that

> Naming the contradictions is a powerful motor for change. The recognition of "opposing forces" suggests choices; challenges the obvious, the accepted, the "natural," and forces

> students to seek understanding in order to take a position. The
> struggle with contradictions shifts consciousness. The recog-
> nition of alternatives highlights the possibility of change, if not
> the possibility of resolution. (p. 21)

When conflict between the meanings of experience becomes intense, women may challenge what they had accepted as given and
arrive at a different understanding.

June lived many contradictions in the course of her life. She had
rebelled against doing what girls and women "were supposed to do"
but had gone along with what was expected of her; she had been
told not to ask for anything, let alone contentment in her relationship, yet she believed that she could obtain it if she could just "do it
right"; she thought that all relationships were just like hers and that
other women were even worse off than she was, yet she was
shocked to discover that so many women were being beaten and
that shelter staff knew the details of her private life; and she had
been attracted to women but had repressed her feelings, telling
herself that she was sick and twisted. If it was important for June to
become conscious of and confront contradiction and conflict, then
how did she do so and what was the significance of such an
achievement?

The notion of common sense knowledge is important in understanding the role of contradiction and conflict in survivors' stories
for two reasons. First, at the starting point of June's process of
politicization, her understanding of the violence and abuse Ivan
inflicted upon her was embedded in a set of gender norms and
practices that formed the ground of her common sense knowledge.
Himani Bannerji (1995), drawing on Antonio Gramsci's work
(1971), describes this knowledge as "the submerged part of the
iceberg which is visible to us as ideology," what Fredric Jameson
calls the political unconscious (p. 44). She specifically discusses
how common sense racism operates in an imperialist, capitalist
society such as Canada. Notions of beauty, good mothering, good
housekeeping, and family forms are rooted in an epistemology of
common sense racism. Bannerji explains how common sense
knowledge consists of "diffused normalized sets of assumptions,

knowledge, and so-called cultural practices" that are pervasive and therefore powerful (p. 45). Common sense knowledge, then, is

> accretional, and being unthought out it leaves plenty of room for contradictions, myths, guesses and rumours. It is therefore by no means a unified body of knowledge, and as a form of our everyday being it is deeply practical in nature. The general direction of its movement as such comes from common socio-economic and cultural practices which, in turn, common sense helps to organize. (pp. 44-45)

Common sense knowledge is powerful because it constructs reality as "society's givens" (Patai, 1988, p. 143).

Many dominant everyday definitions and representations of women's place, whiteness, "race," the family, and heterosexuality, as well as the stereotypes and myths that work to hold these in place, "are so much a daily currency, they have been around for so long in different incarnations, that they are not mostly . . . objects of investigation for they are not even visible" (Bannerji, 1995, p. 45). Racism, sexism, and other systems of oppression that are inscribed within the social relations of everyday life become an invisible "everyday life and 'normal' way of seeing" (Bannerji, 1995, p. 45). June's understanding of Ivan's violence as "normal" worked to naturalize and reify heterosexual relations and notions of "woman" as well as account for and justify social relations of inequality. Her normalized way of seeing had the effect of editing out whole por-tions of reality outside the range of "normalcy," indeed, a whole world that she did not know even existed.

June had perceived the social norms and practices producing women's subordination as self-evident truths. Marilyn Frye (1983) suggests that this is precisely what secures the efficient subordina-tion of one group by another: "what's wanted is that the structure not appear to be a cultural artifact kept in place by human decision or custom, but that it appear *natural*—that it appear to be a quite direct consequence of facts about the beast which are beyond the scope of human manipulation or revision" (p. 34). This naturalism, socially constructed to explain women's place, creates the sense that the social world is a solid and immutable formation to which we must adapt, feeding personal and political immobilization (Briskin, 1990). Even though June sometimes sensed that "something didn't quite fit," she relied on the naturalism of "the way it was," "accepting things without question" or challenge.

The normalized lessons we learn about ourselves and our social world are produced through ideological and social processes that are largely unconscious (Bannerji, 1995; Elliot, 1995; Haug et al., 1987; Lather, 1991; Weiler, 1988). Mimi Orner (1992) encourages us to think of ourselves and our realities as the products of "meaning-making activities which are both culturally specific and generally unconscious" (p. 79). Therefore, one of the tasks that June had to undertake was to become aware of the political unconscious, those ways in which she understood the world that were not immediately accessible to her through conscious awareness but rather lived as "unreflexive, unexamined ways of thinking" (Brittan and Maynard, 1984, p. 185). These spoken but unrecognized and unnamed common sense patterns of thought, absorbed uncritically, do not merely reflect the world but, since they are used to live in the world, work to reproduce it.

The notion of common sense knowledge is important for a second reason. As Arthur Brittan and Mary Maynard (1984) point out, common sense knowledge about social relations, patterns of interaction, and habits of being constitutes the basis on which people make sense of and react to a range of everyday social experiences. These "normal" ways of seeing and making everyday sense and judgments about the world also form an integral part of a person's unconscious sense of self and are locked into structures of identity (Brittan and Maynard, 1984). Frigga Haug and her colleagues (1987) examine the concept of subjectification, "the process by which individuals work themselves into social structures they themselves do not consciously determine, but to which they subordinate themselves" (p. 59). These authors maintain that the active participation of individuals in their formation as social beings "gives social structures their solidity; they are more solid than prison walls" (p. 59). Thus, identifying how "individuals have constructed themselves into existing structures and are thereby themselves formed; the way in which they reconstruct social structures; the points at which change is possible, the points where our chains

chafe the most, the points where accommodations have been made"
becomes a challenge in conscientization (Haug et al., 1987, p. 41).

If it is true that our subjectivities are formed largely through
unconscious processes, then a goal of liberation within these hegemonic patterns of thought must be

> to make conscious the ways in which we have hitherto uncon-
> sciously interpreted the world, and to develop resistances
> against this "normality." Only then will it become possible for
> us to identify the points at which our morality hinders the
> development of our thinking, the points at which images from
> the past reassert their hold on us in the present; the feelings we
> live as productions of our own. (Haug et al., 1987, p. 60)

Making conscious the ways in which we understand social norms
and practices and the structuration of our identities as normal and
natural could challenge the powerlessness associated with "ideologies of naturalism" and lead to possibilities for change (Briskin,
1990, p. 18). How did June become conscious of the ways in which
she had interpreted the world and what did she discover about
herself when she became conscious of them? A particular configuration of conditions and psychic processes was required for this to
occur.

In telling her story, June clearly emphasized her adolescent rebellion against social directives to fit into the mold. What had happened to her early desire to depart from a gendered social script?
Had it been repressed or completely subjugated? Why and how did
it reemerge at this particular time in her life, and was this early
resistance related to the path upon which she had now embarked?
My image of June's process of conscientization is one of a balance
or scale, weighted on one side by her implicit acceptance of the
status quo and her justification of unequal gender relations. On the
other, less weighted side, existed scattered fragments of her adolescent rebellion, jagged edges that chafed her consciousness, things
that did not fit, and desires and needs that were repressed or subjugated. For June to see and challenge "the way it was," she had to
engage in a process that would fortify the less weighted side of the
scale.

June did question why she was treated differently from men, and on some level she was aware of other contradictions in her life. For example, early in her relationship with Ivan, the reality of her life with him conflicted with her fantasy of finding contentment and happiness. Rather than looking directly at this contradiction to see what her experience might tell her, June, like some participants, told herself that something must be wrong with her. In effect, she was discounting her own knowledge that things were not acceptable. While Ivan's violence toward her blatantly refuted her dream of a happy marriage, at that time she could not give herself permission to validate her own knowledge. Repeated invalidations evoked a strong feeling of being wrong, of offending the self by not seeing what the world did not give her permission to see. June's journey was thus about acquiring the knowledge and opportunities which would bolster her insights that contradicted dominant interpretations of reality and help her to dismantle her inability to look at what was happening to her.

June's shock during Sheila's court hearing was a pivotal point in her journey because it produced a small fissure in her belief in a phallocentric discourse that justified Ivan's actions. It also brought into sharper relief the contradiction between her daily reality and the promise of contentment and happiness as a reward for doing "her womanly duty." According to Maria Mies (1983), such a crisis could provoke "a rupture with normalcy" in which "women are confronted with the real social relationships in which they had unconsciously been submerged as objects without being able to distance themselves from them" (p. 125). While this rupture was insufficient to crack open once and for all the mystification of patriarchal relations, it was instrumental for June in beginning the process of exposing her own common sense knowledge about gender relations and disempowering self-understandings.

My examination of June's process of transformation is not intended to undermine her agency or status as an actor in her life but rather to show that this process was contradictory and complex, involving both conscious and unconscious dynamics. A particular set of discursive and material conditions was also indispensable to the unfolding of her journey. If, at this juncture, June was unable to look directly at the contradiction between the contentment for which she hoped and her experience, the possibility existed for this to happen given an adequate eliciting context.

In the meantime, questioning her understanding of abuse was an excellent way for June to proceed. Two and a half years after the incident with Sheila, she went to a shelter for the first time. She did not talk much about what was going on during that period, except to say that she held her knowledge about Sheila at bay. Given that she had realized that Ivan's violence toward her "wasn't okay anymore," I suspected that she might have been ashamed to reveal that she had kept on doing everything to make her relationship work. In fact, the frightening actuality that she was routinely assaulted and verbally degraded probably worked against her ability to affirm that Ivan's actions were wrong. However, when he threatened her daughter, June took action, a pattern common to women who are abused (Bowker, Arbitell, and McFaren, 1988; Hooper, 1995). Ivan's violence against both her and her daughter heightened the disjuncture between that elusive contentment and the anguish of her day-to-day existence.

In the shelter, however, even though June already knew that battered women existed, she was unprepared for the shock of finding out that her individual, private experience was both known and familiar to shelter staff. Magda Lewis (1993) suggests that dominant social meanings about women's everyday lives mask our subordination: "Our subordinations are lived precisely in the context of the details of our individual experiences which, to the extent that they can be made to seem to be private, cannot then offer the ground for a collective political practice" (p. 10). Yet if June had thought that what went on in her relationship was "just the way it was for everybody," then why was this knowledge such a shock to her and why did she resist it?

At this juncture, June glimpsed the implications of questioning her relationship for her notion of who she was in the world. To confront the fact that many women were being beaten "for no reason" questioned the foundations of an identity that she had had for many years of her life. Ronnie Janoff-Bulman and Christine Timko (1987), in their discussion of the role of denial in coping with traumatic life events, suggest that one holds a relatively coherent set of assumptions about oneself and one's world.[1] These assumptions, which organize understanding and experience and guide behavior, often operate outside of conscious awareness. However, crises may bring these assumptions to the forefront of consciousness, leading to their objectification and examination. When assumptive worlds are threatened, intense emotions are aroused, and the task of incorporating new knowledge is salient. Rebuilding an assumptive world that is different from the previously accepted one without allowing one's conceptual system or worldview to "crash" in the interim is a difficult task, but one which most victims of trauma successfully complete (Janoff-Bulman and Timko, 1987, p. 142). Its completion is facilitated by the adaptive function and process of denial.

According to Janoff-Bulman and Timko (1987), denial as a defense mechanism functions to protect the individual, operating outside of awareness in the preconscious or unconscious. Denial can serve an adaptive role in maintaining internal stability and coherence to prevent a collapse of one's worldview and cognitive/emotional functioning. Denial allows for "a proper pacing in the revision and rebuilding of one's basic theories and assumptions," enabling a person to process new information and insights, deal with emotional responses, and reduce confusion and anxiety, particularly when one's resources are insufficient to act in alternative, more growth-producing ways (p. 145).

June's denial of the gendered dimensions of her private experience served a protective function while she was frightened, overwhelmed, and struggling to survive. However, it also functioned to ward off knowledge and insight that threatened to unsettle her relatively stable notion of identity. Her resistance to questioning the belief that she was to blame for everything in her life was tied to her self-image and sense of herself. Her resistance was a force that kept her from knowing something that she suspected but wanted to repress and not know (Alcorn, 1994). At the same time, however, this reprieve afforded her the opportunity to further explore the ground of her subordination.

One of the most valuable insights to be gleaned from June's story concerns the potential significance that questioning dominant beliefs and disempowering self-understandings has for unsettling our notions of identity, evoking pain, and transforming our sense of who we are. Kathleen Rockhill (1987b) captures how frightening this can be: "We don't let ourselves know in part because we are terrified to see, and then to name and live by what we see" (p. 15). June's story clearly demonstrates that critically examining one's life can be a difficult undertaking precisely because of the tenacity of dominant modes of consciousness, the ways in which these are tied to identity formation, and the emotions and psychic dynamics that are evoked in questioning one's interpretation of reality.

Several factors were critical to the advances that June made during her recurring shelter stays. First, she was increasingly able to identify the social and material barriers that she faced as a woman trying to deal with an abusive partner. Second, shelter staff encouraged her to critically reflect on her life and to believe in her own self-worth. She also learned a great deal from shelter residents about the social and structural forces outside their immediate comprehension that shaped their lives. Third, she had access to a feminist discourse about violence against women, which she drew upon to understand Ivan's violence toward her and develop an alternative interpretation of his behavior. Questioning dominant interpretations of her situation, she refuted self-blame and constructed new meaning about her experience of abuse and aspects of her past. These factors facilitated her movement beyond self-blame to interrogate notions of "woman" and the ways in which she defined herself. This method of interrogation coaxed into conscious awareness contradictions, fragments of things that did not fit, and repressed longings for something better.

Just before June left Ivan, she became more cognizant of how her life had been curtailed by him, by the social lessons she had been taught, and by material constraints. For many years she had acted according to notions of what she should or should not be doing. Drawing on feminist discourse about the oppression of women, June was able to disrupt dominant meaning systems that made certain modes of understanding and being seem worthwhile, desirable, or unalterable. hooks (1988) affirms that oppressive social arrangements "attempt to destroy our capacity to know the self, to know who we are" (p. 31). Disengaging from what she thought society gave her permission to be and do, she increasingly validated thoughts and insights of her own and acted on desires that were previously subjugated, cultivating that part of her that wanted to know. In a misogynistic world that often supports women's development along gendered, scripted lines, June's desire for growth manifested before she was able to consciously recognize and admit her desire. In this respect, her process of conscientization encompassed more than conscious understanding and self-reflexive knowledge. This manner of proceeding also shielded her from fully grasping the psychic and social losses that her progress would inevitably entail, permitting her to strengthen her capacity for facing these losses when they would occur.

A feminist analysis of violence against women was also critical in cultivating June's anger and outrage. The emergence of her anger at Turning Point depended to some extent upon the groundwork laid by her growing analysis of woman abuse and the politics of her subordination. In her essay on women's anger, Marilyn Frye (1983) declares that women become angry when they see an obstruction or hindrance as unfair. To be angry is to have some sense of the rightness or propriety of one's position and interest in whatever has been harmed: anger is "the logical mate of respect" (p. 86). While anger can be a spontaneous response to obstruction, June's anger at injustice arose when she began to discern the social organization of her experience and its harmful effects on her well-being.

Living in second-stage housing, June continued to take Amelia to visit Ivan at considerable risk to herself. June talked about the custody issues she dealt with during this period, but for the most part she left unspoken her struggle to stay away from Ivan. What she did say about changing her self-representation and the desires upon which her identity was based was that she felt like a fish on Ivan's hook. Despite this feeling, she had achieved a greater space in which to ask critical, pressing questions of herself by gaining some physical and psychic distance from him. Her struggle in second-stage housing was a much deeper and more profound quest than simply leaving Ivan. June was immersed in changing her consciousness about herself. A critical piece of this process involved uncovering the ways in which her self-understandings formed part of her disempowerment.

The fact that June unearthed her internalized oppression does not imply that Ivan would not have abused her if she had reacted differently or been a different person. Women who refuse to believe that abuse is their fault are also subjected to a partner's violence. Rather, June's discovery points to "the relations of subjectivity to subjection and of objectification to internalized self-image, the conflict of representation with self-representation, the contradictions between consciousness and ideological (unconscious) complicity" (de Lauretis, 1990, p. 123). June had become conscious of how dominant representations of "woman," as an internalized product in her own consciousness, formed part of her identity and were linked to her subjugation in unequal gender relations. She had uncovered both her investment in her identity and her complicity with abuse.

The process of uncovering internalized oppression and shifting structures of identity is a difficult and gradual task because it involves dislodging deeply entrenched desires and assessing the implications of change within a particular set of concrete social conditions and practices. June was able to consciously confront and articulate the contradictions in her life because she had gone through a process of developing an understanding of her experience and social world, connecting her ways of thinking and being to her subjugation, dismantling her resistance to knowing, and building on those aspects of her self that contradicted the messages of what she ought to be and do. Once aware of how she had hitherto unconsciously interpreted her world, she could develop "resistances against this 'normality'" (Haug et al., 1987, p. 60).

In June's journey, a configuration of different conditions and psychic dynamics tipped the balance of the scale toward conscientization. Magda Lewis (1990) defines transformation as "the development of a critical perspective through which individuals can begin to see how social practices are organized to support certain interests, and the process whereby this understanding is then used as the basis for the active political intervention directed toward social change with the intent to disempower relations of inequality" (p. 469). Although June's politicization did not resolve the poverty in which she lived, it was significant in redefining her sense of self and making a personal commitment to resisting oppression.

In summary, June's story poignantly illustrates that giving up old ways of seeing and being is a tenuous, painful, and growth-producing process. The lessons that we can learn from June's journey to collective action concern the multifaceted, contradictory, and complex nature of processes of conscientization, the length of time required to become conscious of contradiction and conflict, the importance of liberatory discourses in sense-making activities, and the anguish entailed in changing notions of self and identity. A number of factors converged to assist June in questioning society's givens, breaking through her resistance to knowledge, and dealing with the emotions and dynamics threatening her well-being. Changes in the ways that she experienced and defined herself were undertaken over time as she incorporated new knowledge and insights into her life and encountered losses and gains. While the discursive and material conditions critical to her growth and movement from individual survival to collective action could not guarantee her conscientization, at the very least these conditions made it a possibility.

Chapter 5

"Rediscovering
What These Bones Are About,
What This Flesh Is About"

SHIFTING THE GROUNDS OF CONSCIOUSNESS:
NAMING AND CHALLENGING HEGEMONIC
CONSTRUCTIONS OF VIOLENCE AGAINST WOMEN

The first theme captures the complexities involved in naming experiences of violation as abuse or violence. Nine of the eleven participants named their partners' actions as abuse while they were living with them. These women, either by accident or design, had talked with someone (a close friend, co-worker, family doctor, housing worker, women's service staff member) who suggested that they were being abused and might benefit from speaking with shelter staff, a women's service, a support group, or a therapist. In addition to mistreatment by male partners, nine of the eleven participants had experienced physical, psychological, emotional, and/or sexual abuse as children (abuse by foster parents, mothers and fathers, male neighbors, and other relatives). As adolescents and adults, some participants had also been sexually assaulted by men they were dating and had been sexually harassed in high school, the workplace, and the university.

Participants' stories of how they became involved in collective action cannot be considered in isolation from a constellation of everyday conditions and social inequalities as well as experiences of abuse that shaped their lives. Poverty, loss of family and community, spoken and unspoken messages about being female, living under a dictatorship, racism, and low-paying jobs replete with sexual harassment may contribute to participants' future actions. Jackie spoke about growing up poor and her lifelong struggle to overcome deep feelings of inadequacy:

> The first feeling to come up for me would be inadequacy because that's what society has made me feel: inadequate. You're poor, you're female, you're uneducated, so that's a feeling I deal with a lot. . . . I grew up and went to a Catholic school. Most kids going to a Catholic school were middle class. We were the ones that were made fun of; we were the ones that were put down. . . . Among the peers in the social network you were still oppressed—you were oppressed within your home and you were oppressed out in society too. I feel like it's been a struggle to get out of that situation and I'm still fighting and I still will continue to fight. Being brought up or having been given that message, my biggest fear is that when it's all over and it's all done with, it's going to be no, you're not good enough . . . you came from those people [living in] poverty. Your family was cursed.

Ruth's removal from her community at an early age by child welfare authorities and her subsequent placement in a series of foster homes greatly affected her self-image.

> I remember back as far as age three. Back in the 1950s and 1960s is when the government came in with the child welfare authorities and took us out by the hundreds. . . . They took us out and we went into various foster homes and we were victims of a lot of racism because I grew up to hate who I was as a[n] aboriginal woman and the same with my sister. We would be embarrassed to walk on the street together, for someone to recognize us as so-called Indian persons, and at a point for me, if I saw a Native person walking up the street, I'd turn around and go the other way all right. I'd cross the street. And I would avoid the sun so my skin would be white instead of dark. So I had a lot of self-hatred for myself, who I was, and hatred for the Native people, and I didn't want anything to do with them for what they stood for as a result of all the racism.

Sources of inspiration, such as a mother's political activism or a father's spirituality, as well as poverty and racism were also central to the stories women told and the meanings they made of their experiences of abuse. Paola spoke passionately about what it was like growing up in a politically active family under a repressive regime, particularly with a mother who was "a natural-born feminist." Her mother's activism in popular neighborhood organizations significantly influenced her formation. Paola's sense-making activities about her suffering were intertwined with her culture and country, her awareness of herself as a woman of color in a dominant white society, and her analysis of class differences in a culture of consumerism and individualism.[1]

> My family has always been very political. My mother has had a very strong influence in the political work that I've done. She's somebody who's been very, very active and a very empowered woman, not only back in Chile since we were really really young, and also even here not knowing the language . . . so she is somebody who takes a lot of things into her own hands. . . . In countries like Chile if you don't solve it for yourself nobody's gonna come and give you a hand, so you better get together with other people in your neighborhood. . . . Those kind of actions were what my mom was always involved in, a lot of it through the Catholic church. We were also living under a dictatorship, so there was a lot of political oppression that influenced us greatly. . . . My mom doesn't have more than grade one [education] . . . so she always had the concept of you have to get as much education as you can afford so you don't have to suffer as much of the oppression . . . so you're never going to have a man that's going to treat you badly . . . so you're never gonna be stepped on as a woman or as much as other women are going to be in the same social class that you come from.

Victoria viewed her adoption and female status as influential factors shaping her identity because they gave her a unique perspective on the world. Her father's spirituality was especially significant, weaving its way into her meaning making about her spiritual being and how her husband's violence toward her damaged her spirit.

> From the day I was born there was a big minus sign put next to the F in my name, F for female. . . . I can go back to my birth because I didn't have parents. I was left at the hospital, a girl child left at a hospital, and then for a year I was put in foster care, which everyone knows in our society, as a foster parent you're not supposed to—you can handle a child, you can feed it, you can change a child—but you must not show that child love and affection. So I think that probably helped a lot, whatever was part of that complex situation . . . to make me who I am. . . . So from the time I was born I guess I had a crystal in my pocket and that crystal was always there for me and it gave me a unique way of looking at the world. Because even though I couldn't perhaps grow up with my direct bloodline, I was able to grow up in an environment where I had many opportunities to look at the world through very interesting eyes. And I was really fortunate to have a stepfather [adoptive father] who was very, very spiritually advanced for a man who lived in a farming community and who grew up in a very abusive home. . . . I think my understanding comes from those experiences in my life and knowing that all my life I was in pain and that I was suffering.

According to Deborah Brock (1993), analyses of the dimensions and effects of any one form of abuse cannot be considered separately from other abuses of power or from everyday conditions such as poverty, racism, or neglect. The effects of social and material conditions on participants' lives, such as poverty, converged with the effects of different kinds of abuse, shaping their experiences of abuse and the stories they told about them.

In telling their stories, most participants found it difficult to articulate precisely how they had understood their experiences of violation before they had the language through which they presently make sense of them. Some women described them as part of the fabric of everyday life or "just the way it was," what Paulo Freire (1994) calls immersion in oppression. This did not mean that women explicitly accepted abuse, nor did it diminish their pain.

Others recalled sensing that "something was wrong," "something didn't quite fit right," or "it was not okay." Two participants who were abused as children by a parent (mother and father, respectively) clearly identified that their partners were abusing them when they found themselves experiencing the same fear and apprehension that had been beaten into them at an early age. They struggled against accepting the inevitability of abuse and enduring it for the sake of their marriage. In talking about how they coped with, survived, and resisted abuse, women recalled feelings of confusion, numbness, uncertainty, humiliation, and betrayal of self as well as conflicting emotions and fears of losing contact with reality.

June, who was sexually abused by her grandfather, related that she did not have the sense that something was wrong, believing that her grandfather was the only person who loved her. Deborah Brock (1993), in her discussion of popular discourse on sexual abuse, affirms the importance of depicting the range and complexity of women's and girls' experiences of violence and abuse as well as their everyday character. A wider range of stories might better convey how "normalized (and therefore all the more insidious) sexual abuse can be in the lives of women and girls" (p. 110). Much of the discourse on sexual abuse is supported by horrifying stories of coercion and trauma inflicted upon the survivor/victim. Although this is the reality for some girls and women, she argues that women also experience sexual abuse in noncoercive contexts and in many different ways.

How did women come to identify and name what was happening or had happened to them as abuse? I refer to naming as the process through which women connected their experience with abuse or violence. Barbara DuBois (1983) suggests that

> the power of naming is at least two-fold: naming defines the quality and value of that which is named—and it also denies reality and value to that which is never named, never uttered. That which has no name, that for which we have no words or concepts, is rendered mute and invisible: powerless to inform or transform our consciousness of our experience, our understanding, our vision: powerless to claim its own existence. (p. 108)

In order to name what was happening and/or had happened to them as abuse, the majority of participants required ample concrete opportunities in safe places to make connections between the concept of abuse and their experiences of violation, feelings, and sense of unease, that "inexplicit consciousness of something wrong" (Cain, 1993, p. 83). Maureen Cain (1993) explains that it is not clear if such ways of being/experiences cannot be spoken because there is no language for them, or because the language in which women speak and express their existence is politically subjugated, that is, rendered illegitimate by dominant discourses.[2]

Women explicitly recognized and named their experiences of violation as abuse in different ways, under a range of circumstances, and at different moments in their lives. Recognizing and naming abuse was not an instantaneous or definitive event but rather a process that involved facing, working through, and coming to understand their experiences of violation in a different way. Although each woman's naming process was rooted in the specific details of her life, all women had sustained engagement with feminist/antioppressive discourses within social spaces such as women's support and self-help groups, educational programs and groups in shelters and second-stage housing, feminist organizations, and communities of women active in the antiviolence movement.

Several factors mediated women's process of naming abuse: (1) concrete opportunities to name experiences of violation as abuse and make sense of them; (2) conditions such as homelessness, financial dependency, and systemic discrimination that impeded their naming efforts; (3) the disjuncture between what women learned was abuse and the ways in which they had previously understood their experiences of violation; (4) the ways in which women digested and applied new knowledge about abuse to their lives and sorted out its implications; and (5) the degree to which alternative interpretations of their experiences threatened to dislodge repressed pain and unsettle relatively stable notions of self and identity, evoking fear, denial, and resistance to knowledge. In the following discussion, I will give examples of each of these.

A year after immigrating to Canada, Paola had the opportunity to name her experiences of violation in the context of learning about gender and feminism. She identified as sexual harassment what had happened to her when she stepped into the male-dominated field of economics in a university in Chile. She did not then have a name for her experience but clearly recalled her apprehension and strategies for negotiating the situation:

> We were five women among 250 men in the first year and it was terrible because it didn't matter what you wore . . . jeans or . . . pants or . . . a shirt or skirt. You could try to pretend that you were a man and it was like, no way, constant sexual harassment, like constant, constant. . . . It was the whole thing of sitting next to the door in case something happened so we can get out . . . things like that, it was really, really a constant fear and I lived through it for three years. . . . It was scary, this struggle for three years of university, thinking, what should I wear today? What is going to make me feel safer? And it was a point in which my way of dealing is that I wear the tightest things that I have . . . so I'll defy, I'll be defiant. . . . I felt very uncomfortable but I never—I knew that it was not okay but at the same time it comes also from the same point of view. It's like all women go through this, so what's the big deal? Or also even sometimes blaming myself. Oh well, I got myself into this, so I knew that this was something I would have to put up with. It's that kind of thing.

At the time of these frightening encounters, Paola believed that, like any other woman, she would just have to contend with this reality the best she could, and that perhaps this treatment was a consequence of stepping outside the boundaries for women of her social class.

Removed from her mother and aboriginal community at age three, racism had distorted Ruth's ability to name the abuse she had suffered as a child and adolescent. She had perceived "sexist/hetero-sexist racism" (Bannerji, 1995, p. 37) as something that had happened to her because of an intrinsic flaw.

> One Native person in an all-white school—you were blamed for everything that went wrong even though it had nothing to do with you. . . . Indian people were the bad people and so then after class people would say things—'cause you're Indian and

all these remarks. And then the family that adopted me, they were non-Native so they had no idea on how to deal with stuff 'cause I was getting into fights with people and I'd be blamed, you know, it was my temper and I'd just say well, he calls me all these different names. . . . But nothing was ever done. There was something wrong with me, everybody's fine but me. . . . When I was thirteen I was raped by . . . my friend's father . . . and I told my mom all the various people before that since I was little and she dumped that all on me, saying that it was all my fault. Even her own son was doing that to me between nine and eleven, so I was blamed. . . . Something went wrong, it was me.

Ruth's efforts to resist racism were constructed as her own deficiency and a reason to feel ashamed. Singled out as wrong, she carried the displaced emotions and hatred of others. "A child that grows up hating or being ashamed of her own looks, body, language and people can be traumatized and self-destructive. . . . This is what racism or sexist/heterosexist racism can theoretically produce" (Bannerji, 1995, p. 37). As Elsa Barkley Brown (1992) points out, white women's experiences of violence are also shaped by "race," but because of the dominant position of whiteness in the hierarchy of ethnicity and "race," white women are generally not conscious either of their whiteness or of how their experiences of violence are shaped by their skin color.

After years of silence, Ruth found opportunities, first in a feminist shelter and later in a college program on violence against women, to speak about and make sense of her experiences of abuse.

It was there at the shelter that I learned about abuse and they had women come in to do feminist counseling groups. . . . That's where I started to really look at my life and see other women, knowing that other women, too, didn't know anything about the shelters and learning about what they went through. And also being a Native woman too, it's not easy to seek help sometimes with non-Native. . . . It was just sitting with a group of women and the counselor, just openly asking questions . . . and knowing you're not all alone, too, which you think you are . . . and looking at the situation differently. . . . Normally, I was always silent, I wouldn't say anything because that's, like, years of programming. Either I tell you what to do or my opinions didn't matter. Again racism falls into that too. Well, you're just an Indian, how would you know?

In dealing with her partner's mistreatment of her, Ruth had also been searching for the meaning of past violations. Upon leaving the shelter, she continued her lifelong search for "some kind of outlook out there" that would help her understand herself and her past. For other participants in this study, recognizing a partner's actions as abuse also provoked a redefinition and reevaluation of childhood and/or other experiences of violation.

The disjuncture between Donna's belief in commonly held myths about abuse and her understanding of the treatment she received impeded her naming process. She did not see what was happening to her as abuse or violence. While she knew that "something was wrong," she had always believed that she had failed to "cope properly" with what everyone threw at her. For her to name what happened to her as abuse meant deconstructing the notion that the source of her life situation was something inside herself (Freire, 1994).

I couldn't see that I was being abused, and especially with the sexual assault [date rape], because most sexual assault that you hear about is violent . . . plus there's all the stereotyping that women deserve it. . . . There was still this kind of a socialization that date rape isn't as bad as regular rape and baloney! . . . like, the rape and everything else [sexual assault by a male neighbor at age ten and forced sex with partner] I internalized because I felt like, okay, I deserved it. And what happened to me as a child [sexual abuse by grandfather], I really didn't see as sexual abuse because it wasn't actual intercourse. . . . Everything was kind of implied that I deserved it. It was always "you get what you deserve" sort of attitude and it was always "good people aren't treated badly" and so I always thought I was doing everything wrong because people were treating me badly. . . . I guess I saw abuse in everybody else but I couldn't see that I was being abused.

For Heather, the fissure between the concept of abuse and her way of seeing her early experiences made it difficult to identify that she was abused. She described growing up in an environment where chaos and yelling formed part of everyday familial interactions. With her second partner, she recounted that she focused her energy on surviving, fighting back when she could, and trying to figure out how to avoid "ticking him off":

> I don't think there was much really running through my mind [when my husband was abusing me] because I thought it was normal. My whole childhood was abusive . . . my mom was married three times. . . . The third husband is where I really started to notice abuse, alcoholism, because my mom never drank—she started drinking. . . . For myself, growing up, I didn't know that a lot of things that were happening to me were unpleasant because they were just everyday, common. Oh well, there's some screaming going on, just kinda avoid it. Up to your room and drop your books off and change your school clothes and okay, we'll do our best and grit our teeth and go out the back door. And hopefully we've done everything that we needed to do so that anger doesn't get shifted toward us. But that was our lives and I think you're . . . used to that. . . . It's not like that's really normal but it's something that you become accustomed to so when I was being abused . . . I don't really recall what I was thinking. You kinda think, Why me? What did I do? Who did what? So you can go and change for that person. There was a lot of trying to figure out what was going to tick him off and fixing it before it was going to do that.

In second-stage housing Heather was amazed to discover the more subtle operations of power: her husband's comments with double entendres, a compliment containing an insult, a look from her husband when she was on the phone, a threatening undertone in an interaction, the pretense that something was not directed at her when in reality it was.

> When growing up, there was physical abuse, and in my relationship with my two husbands, there was physical abuse . . . I

didn't know the subtle stuff. . . . That's how I became more aware, sitting in a room of women and to hear a woman say that she was never physically abused. But she was abused! I just kinda went, huh? So then you need to understand that more and I went, wow! That happened to me. I was being abused and, yeah, the strength that persuasive power has . . . the manipulation tactics, and you start understanding how subtle an abuser can be . . . to take control of your life. . . . Those started really coming out and scaring the shit right out of me, going, wow! That was abuse, the emotional stuff. . . . You really get into the whole thing. It's scary, the whole process of how they can manipulate you for years and you not even know anything. . . . Once you come through here it's a bigger, wider thing.

As she learned about woman abuse, she named her partner's exercise of power in badgering her and making innuendos and insinuations as harmful rather than part of "normal" heterosexual relations. Other participants also named sexual putdowns, name-calling, mind games, and threats, once perceived as commonplace or "trivial" in comparison with physical beatings, as abusive behavior that was denigrating and hurtful.

When Jackie went to a shelter for the first time, she found it difficult to digest and apply her new knowledge to her life because she was struggling with a complex, difficult situation. She had contacted Family and Children's Services (FCS) when her daughters told her that their father was touching them sexually, and was trying to protect her children from him by going to the shelter. Gradually, she began to break through her perception that what was happening to her was "just the way life was."

I have a vivid memory of walking into the women's shelter . . . and saying to the counselor, "Well, I really don't think I should be here 'cause actually I was only hit five times" and then she said to me, "Well, once is too much." In the shelter I learned what abuse was. There was so much abuse that was happening there that I didn't know was abuse. It was just the way life was . . . that's the way it was going to be. I come from a home where there was violence, so what? I mean, it was normal to me. Someone calling someone a stupid fat bitch is just something that happened. I mean, it hurt but, you know, it's just the way it was. It was the way a man talked to a woman. . . . What the heck is emotional abuse anyway? Is it all that stuff that happened when you were a child, and it was supposed to happen, and it's just the way it is? . . . You look at the surface stuff and then you start looking at the other stuff underneath and it's like, oh my God, it's bigger than I thought. . . . I felt relieved. There was a name put to what was happening to me, and at the same time I was overwhelmed at the fact that this is really what's happening to me. You can't—at that point in time, when you're in the shelter, you can't take everything in because it's too overwhelming, the knowledge and the fear.

Although Jackie initially did not define much of her husband's abusive behavior toward her as abuse, she clearly identified what her husband was doing to her daughters as wrong.

You're there for the children. I can stick this out. What am I going to do, leave here and go on welfare and have this bloody stigma attached to me that I'm a welfare bum? Let's just kinda stick it out. I can survive it for the kids. I can survive it. I mean I can put up with being called stupid and the other things, but when you find out that your children are being abused, you can't look the other way. . . . I was a sexual abuse survivor myself. I just know it was wrong. I mean, you know it's wrong. That is one boundary that you don't cross at all; that's really not acceptable.

Upon her daughters' disclosure, FCS placed Jackie in a group for incest survivors as a way to encourage her to protect her children. Her process of naming abuse and dealing with her relationship was compounded by the complexity of her situation and by the treatment she received from FCS. Although Jackie made incredible efforts to protect her children, she received messages from FCS that she had failed as a mother. These messages implicitly communicated that, as a mother, she was the sole person responsible for the care of her children. FCS neither recognized her caring for or about her children, nor her own needs at that particular point in her life. For Jackie, her participation brought up the sexual abuse that she had experienced as a child, overwhelming her and exacerbating her fear and confusion. Given this situation, it was difficult for her to name and deal with the abuse she suffered from her husband.

In her thirties, Barbara began to remember that she was sexually abused by her father and stepgrandfather (her mother's stepfather). When her partner began to mistreat her, more memories began to surface for her, threatening to dislodge years of repressed pain.

> I kept remembering this one incident. . . . I had actually remembered one incident but I hadn't . . . [put together] that this was sexual abuse, and you didn't hear as much about it at that time. And then when I heard more, read more, then I realized, whoa! And then I started to have more memories. . . . Sometimes I'd have body memories but I wouldn't remember—I wouldn't know at that time that that's what it was . . . I was frightened of having a bath . . . because he used to abuse me in the bathtub when I was very little. . . . Because of David's and my relationship and his abuse I started to recognize more that some of the things that happened to me were abuse. I didn't look at that in the first place so I didn't see it.

For Victoria, her naming process evoked both a fear of going mad and the pain of childhood memories of always feeling wrong, that she did not fit anywhere. She began keeping a journal to document the incidents and verbal barrages in which her partner claimed that she was wrong, even though she did not comprehend his claims.

> It was too difficult to pinpoint situations on any given day and to be able to psychologically analyze for my own self whether this was [abuse]. . . . I knew this was happening to me and I knew that the way I was being treated was not at all the way my parents had interacted. Sure, they had their disagreements, but it wasn't an ongoing daily sense of oppression and psychological warfare. . . . It wasn't that I wasn't sure it was happening. I was very sure it was happening but I wanted to confirm—I wanted to be able to open up something and see exactly when it was happening and how often. . . . Because when it happens so often and it's disjointed and you're disconnected and you're being kept off balance, it's very hard to be

able to say, well, in the month of January out of twenty-eight days, there were twenty days where I know I was being abused. I wanted to know, am I crazy? Am I just fantasizing this? Or is this really happening to me? . . . I had to be able to put it down in front of my face and go, oh my God, oh my God, it's worse than I thought. . . . I was my own advocate. I was advocating on behalf of my soul. Soul, this is what's happening to you—you're being chipped away on a daily basis. No, yesterday you had a good day, oh wow, you're lucky! . . . Let's see, the other side of my consciousness is saying, no, I think the odds are against you. You better get out, your idea was right in the first place, go for it!

For participants in my study, the act of naming experiences of violation as abuse was the beginning of a process of situating and reinterpreting their experiences in the context of unequal social relations of power. Himani Bannerji (1995) identifies this process as "conscious attempts at recovery, exploration and naming, or re-naming in politically actionable terms" (p. 21). Such renaming "extends beyond the individual to a historical and a collective one" (p. 21). For participants, naming experiences of abuse initiated a process of grasping the historically and politically constructed nature of their experience and social world, and deconstructing some of their fundamental self-understandings.

In summary, naming abuse provoked a series of dilemmas and contradictions specific to each woman's life, demonstrating why it involved a much more circuitous, difficult, and tenuous process than simply finding the name "abuse" and connecting it with experience. Popular discourse about woman abuse often assumes that women should unequivocally be able to identify what is happening to them as abuse. If they do not, they are perceived as deficient for failing to see what so obviously constitutes abuse. This position, however, obviates the power of hegemonic discourse about woman abuse, the complexities involved in naming experiences of violation as abuse, the concrete realities of women's lives, and the conditions and factors that facilitate the process of naming abuse.

THE PROCESS OF MAKING SENSE: RECOGNIZING CONTRADICTION AND CONFLICT AND MAKING CONSCIOUS THE INVISIBLE AND THE UNCONSCIOUS

The second theme that I identified in participants' accounts was their struggle with contradiction and conflict. This was key in shifting women's consciousness about woman abuse, taken-for-granted views, and the ways in which they defined themselves and their relation to the world. Women's confrontation with contradiction and conflict had the effect of bringing into conscious awareness common sense knowledge, thus unsettling disempowering self-understandings. The processes through which women became aware of contradiction and conflict in their everyday lives and exposed the political unconscious, however, were complex. A convergence of several factors was required, often involving a parallel task of breaking through resistance to potentially liberating knowledge.

Naming abuse and learning more about it produced a ripple effect, stimulating participants to critically question many aspects of their lives, habits of thinking and being, and notions of self and identity. They questioned the values, norms, and practices that had defined their experiences of abuse as insignificant and constructed them as persons unworthy of dignity and respect. Renaming their experiences in politically actionable terms, women confronted contradictions between their ideas and beliefs and the realities of their situations; the fantasy marriage and ideology of man as protector and the actuality of abuse; and the social messages about what they were supposed to be and enjoy, and their experience. This growing questioning of the ways they had been treated by significant others, the social lessons they had learned as children and adolescents, the justifications made by family and friends (and sometimes themselves), as a way of accounting for what was happening to them, unsettled women's assumptions about themselves and where they fit in the world.

The ways in which participants became aware of and confronted contradiction and conflict differed. As with June, women's lived experience of violence and abuse sometimes opened up disjunctures between dominant patterns of thought and the reality of abuse, but this was insufficient for them to become conscious of and confront contradiction and conflict. For some participants, contradictions emerged for them as they dealt with abuse, including going to shelters, attending support groups, and encountering the "systems." For the women I interviewed, the "systems" referred to the criminal justice, child protection, social assistance, legal, and mental health systems, for example, Family Court, the police, mediation services, psychiatry, and mental health. Women did not include women's shelters, support groups, or second-stage housing in their definition of the systems. Encounters with systemic oppression quickly brought into focus contradictions between the purported equality of women and their lack of access to resources that would protect them and their children, and the presentation of mothering as a valued role and the simultaneous devaluation of mothering. Other participants had lived contradiction and conflict but hadn't acknowledged them or "brought them into the light" for examination. For some women, contradictions had existed latently in the subconscious but had been suppressed or glimpsed only fleetingly.

Donna recounted: "Maybe I didn't realize the contradictions were conscious," suggesting that they were unconscious and that her pain was repressed. At the cost of great anguish, she had tried to keep contradiction and conflict from coming into consciousness, but several factors converged to make this an impossibility: she was being sexually harassed at a low-paying job, she was living in poverty with her daughter, and flashbacks of painful memories kept prodding her consciousness. She could no longer repress her pain or protect herself from conflict that threatened to destabilize her sense of self. Before Donna's breakdown, her mind had contained a "jumble of thoughts" such as, "don't wear that skirt, it's too inviting; what did I go out with him for? I asked for it. I didn't deserve what I got." Her contradictory understandings about her experience of being raped by a date finally "popped out" at this particular point in her life. Following her collapse, the contradiction and conflict that had previously been inaccessible to her became conscious and she began to clearly articulate them in therapy and a support group for sexual abuse survivors.

During a course in Native studies, Ruth came face-to-face with a central contradiction in her life: she was an Ojibwa woman, yet she loathed herself as an aboriginal person.

> I didn't really have my true identity yet either about myself, too, because I have a foot in both worlds, the non-Native and the Native. You're Native physically but you're not in the culture either. . . . It [the college program] uproots you because all your own stereotyping or your own ideals are all looked at from various ways whereas it's either myth or fact. If you're gonna deal with racism and any kind of hatred in any form, you really have to take a good look at that . . . to really take a good look at your own gender or your own race. So that hit a clinger with me because I had to look at Native people, and then they're talking about racism. Well, if you hated your own race, I was beginning to accept them but I still didn't accept them, for who we were or what I was.

For Paola, learning about feminism ignited a contradiction that had been smoldering since her political activism in Chile. Her image and experience of herself as a fighter contrasted sharply with her reactions to her partner's violence against her. She questioned how she could have had a revolutionary class consciousness but yet have been "so blind" to her partner's abuse. Enrolled in a social work program, she began to unravel this contradiction with feminist colleagues, becoming aware of her previous acceptance of her role as subordinate.

> We did not have a gender analysis—that came for me when I came here to Canada. . . . We were all fighting for liberation and revolution . . . but most of the time it meant liberation and revolution for the men. We were going to continue being married to them and suffering their oppression! There was not the concept of us as women . . . there was a lot of our sharing of our common pain but not as a common cause in terms of male-dominating society. . . . Because I have always thought, how did I get myself into such a bad relationship, me knowing so much about the world? I think a big part of it was my understanding that, well, it doesn't matter how much I

struggle, my role in society is always going to be determined by my gender and there is nothing I can do about it. . . . If I had had more of a gender analysis it would have been easier for me to see why this was happening to me. . . . Even with all the political consciousness I had . . . I could not see myself being abused by somebody . . . from my own class . . . I can look at it now and I could see at that time in my mind how something didn't fit right, but I didn't have the elements to sort of challenge it and say, well, something doesn't feel right here. I'm talking about liberation but at the same time I'm being oppressed in my own home.

Jackie lived a contradiction between her implicit acceptance of "the way it was" and her spiritual desire for a better life. The image of her grandmother in her subconscious produced feelings of powerlessness against destiny while her subjugated knowledge affirmed her personhood. Through therapy, residency in shelters, and facing the unfair treatment that she received from FCS, she was able to articulate and challenge the social messages she had received throughout her life.

I didn't have the education then that I have now. I didn't realize that what was happening was happening. I was doing exactly what women are supposed to do. . . . I can remember thinking, this isn't right and it shouldn't be happening. . . . That was the spiritual side . . . the inner self that goes right deep into the core of who you are. That's the part, the survival . . . . But the other part of me, the feeling part saying, Jackie, this is normal. It happened to your grandma, remember Grandma? This is who you are, this is where you're supposed to be and . . . you're destined for it. This is what life has dealt you out and you can't change it. That was the feeling part or subconscious . . . but when you get educated . . . or the more knowledge you feed into yourself, the more you can shut that down and make the changes on the inside.

Her contact with FCS provoked another, related conflict about her competence as a mother. She had stayed in the relationship for the sake of her children, yet "sticking it out" for the children conflicted with her husband's sexual abuse of her daughters. For Jackie, coming to some resolution about her survival strategies, her competence as a mother, and the judgments of FCS was central to her sense-making activities.

> I always felt like I was being judged. . . . It [the sexual abuse of her children] never got to the courts. The whole onus was put on me. It was, "you're the mother, you're supposed to protect your children." . . . They put me in an incest survivors' group thinking that would shock me into being able to protect my daughters, when in fact all it did was bring back some incest [memories] from my childhood. So there I was, I had three things to deal with. I had to deal with my incest from my childhood, my victimization by my husband, and the fact that my children were sexually abused by my partner. . . . It's so confusing because in the back of your mind you're thinking, I gotta protect my kids, I have to protect my kids. At the same time I have to survive, so how do I do that? . . . I felt like the only way I was going to get out of this relationship was that I was going to get killed and then there wouldn't be anybody there to protect my kids, so I just had to survive. If my husband wanted sex then I just had to lay there and perform because. . . . I was made to feel by Family and Children's Services that, they ask questions like "How's your sex life?" And it makes you feel like if maybe if I was giving something more he wouldn't be going to the children. Questions like "Is your daughter provocative?" My daughter was three years old. . . . Instead of protecting, instead of doing the things that the law needed to do to protect my children, they put it back onto me. You go to . . . the experts, you get a little pat on the head. It's like, yeah, well, it may have happened but there's not much that we can do—your children are too young. And at the same time you're being pressured to protect them and you're being judged.

Jackie's strategies for coping with her complex situation were complicated by the fact that she was emotionally shut down, overwhelmed, and dealing with an agency that failed to take into account both her needs and her efforts to protect her children. FCS maintained her inequality by failing to recognize her economic dependence on her husband and placing sole responsibility on her to protect her children from their father's sexual abuse. Marilyn Frye (1983) aptly calls these situations in which women frequently find themselves the "double bind." "One of the most characteristic and ubiquitous features of the world as experienced by oppressed people is the double bind—situations in which options are reduced to a very few and all of them expose one to penalty, censure or deprivation. . . . One can only choose to risk one's preferred form and rate of annihilation" (pp. 2-3). If Jackie had been outraged, then she would have been perceived as a vindictive, manipulative woman trying to get custody of her children. Despite being a deep source of anguish, her encounter with FCS served to politicize Jackie. Her experience of abuse and the service she received from FCS served as the ground on which to develop an analysis of the social norms and practices that position women as mothers, devalue them, and place them in a perpetual double bind.

Like Jackie, other participants faced multiple barriers and a host of other factors and life changes in working through experiences of abuse and sorting out their lives, for example, a partner's alcoholism, homelessness, custody and access proceedings, loss of income, racism, grief at the loss of their country, immigration difficulties, social assistance appeals, oppressive encounters with the systems, and other destabilizing events. Heather's devastating contacts with Family Court, the criminal justice system, and Family Benefits highlighted the contradiction between the value accorded to her as a woman and a mother by social institutions and her own self-valuation and needs.

> This whole legal system and a lot of the processes, it's always focused on the abuser no matter if he was a wife abuser or sexual abuser. You're left out. . . . They're telling you that you are involved when you're not. It's your lawyers and the legal system—they just take it right away and you're left there as a physical empty shell. . . . I lost a lot, and they can never replace what they've taken from me, not just the physical stuff but the emotional stuff that they've taken away and what they've done to my youngest child. . . . For them to sit there and tell you that

that was for the benefit of my child—go and blow your horn somewhere else, because I know they're saying it's for the benefit of your child so you'll buy into it, and they're feeding you something else. . . . The hell with the good of the kids, give us what we need as women to function and maintain our homes. Our children would be just fine, healthy, happy. They'll have what they want. . . . Even the court process . . . a woman . . . thinks that Crown attorney is working for her. Well, he's just working for the town, he's not really actually her lawyer. . . . I went through it all by trial and error. It's a very intimidating process, and not being told that abuse is gonna be right there in your face and no support systems. I had my abuser's lawyer say to me, we haven't got the regular judge that's supposed to be here today. We've got some real aggressive blah blah. If you're not going to agree to these terms, well, your abuser's going way down the road. If I woulda had proper support at that point in time, I'da probably said let him go way down the road. . . . Why did the Crown attorney allow his lawyer to come in and intimidate me like that? So it was like, let's get on the stand. He's gonna go get counseling. Okay, fine. Like, let's just leave. I wanna go home. Meanwhile, no, he shoulda had the damn book thrown right at him. He got off his year probation and he phoned me right up. "Now whatta ya gonna do?" Started running me off the road. The whole system sucks big time.

Through an educational group in second-stage housing and individual therapy, Heather also confronted the painful reality that her relationships had not measured up to her hopes. For both Jackie and Heather, understanding the social organization of motherhood and how their mothering had been shaped by circumstances outside their immediate comprehension was key in their sense-making activities.

Participants' struggles with contradiction and conflict called into question dominant social meanings, shifting consciousness about their world. Conceptualizing how shifts in consciousness produce changes in subjectivity, Abdul Janmohamed (1994) suggests that one develops a relationship of nonidentity with a part of oneself.

Yet, in order to develop such a relationship, one would in effect have to adopt another subject position from which to critique and distance oneself from one's "own" subject position. A relationship of nonidentity with one's position amounts to the development of an antagonism with oneself, which can only be accomplished when one has already begun to identify, tacitly or deliberately, with another position, whether that position is fully formed or nascent. (p. 246)

Thus, this process simultaneously requires a disidentification and an identification, a shift away from disempowering parts of identity and toward an engagement and identification with something different (Janmohamed, 1994).

To struggle with contradictions signifies that "a process of change and transformation" is underway (Childers and Hooks, 1990, p. 70). As Chris Weedon (1987) points out, "recognizing contradictions and the power relations which inhere in specific definitions of women's nature and social role is only the first stage in the process of change both for individual women and in the struggle to transform social institutions" (p. 5). This process also requires alternative senses of ourselves as women as well as visions and strategies for changing institutions and practices (Weedon, 1987). However, participants' changes in self-understanding did not happen through erasing or replacing prior consciousness; rather, it was accomplished by working through contradictions in subjectivity that resulted from the coexistence of the old and the new (Hollway, 1984). In the space created between the old and the new, between society's givens and alternative visions of what might be, there exists a lacuna in which a new subjectivity can begin to articulate itself.

In summary, for the majority of participants, the process of becoming conscious of and confronting contradiction and conflict in their lives, thus exposing and challenging "society's givens" (Patai, 1988, p. 143), took place over substantial periods of time through naming and dealing with abuse, encountering the systems, and connecting with people and discourses that questioned dominant social meanings about violence against women and about women's place. Although access to liberatory discourses and spaces does not ensure that women will work through contradiction and conflict since these are not always easily or readily accessible, it may provide significant opportunities for recognizing and confronting them.

TENSIONS, TRANSGRESSIONS, AND THREATS: PAIN AND PROMISE

Participants' processes of naming abuse, becoming conscious of contradiction and conflict, and making sense of them were constrained not only by material conditions but by psychic processes that worked to suppress contradiction and conflict, repress pain, and resist potentially liberating knowledge that threatened to unsettle notions of self and identity. As different writers have suggested (Elliot, 1995; hooks, 1994; Lather, 1991; Lewis, 1993; Tatum, 1992), learning about oppression and engaging with contradiction and conflict is not undertaken without some degree of pain and loss. While this process was sometimes arduous and threatening, it also contained the possibility of insight and growth.

Participants recounted that they struggled with many emotions and dynamics in their processes of transformation. They described "big holes" gaping in front of them; experienced fear, "engulfing rage," "immobilizing emotions," confusion, and uncertainty; wavered back and forth between wanting and not wanting to see and "blocking out" and "not accepting" certain knowledge and insights; and described "living in a state of denial and reality at the same time." This complex array of dynamics, both conscious and unconscious, were often known to participants only in retrospect.

Maryanne recounted that she lived in a fairy-tale land for years, convincing herself that everything was going to be just fine. At the time that she was surviving in her relationship, she was unable to see this dynamic.

> Strange games, isn't it? It's scary when you think back. Like, I think, God, I coulda been a psycho killer and told myself I wasn't. . . . How could I have thought that everything was going to be fine? It wasn't. . . . Like, I lived in a fairy-tale land for so long where I played so many mind games on my own just to keep myself sane, that if I'm not honest and tell you

exactly how I feel then I'm afraid I'm gonna slip back into trying to make everybody happy again. . . . Survival was number one. . . . I think that was just it, you just kept everything nice and calm and cool and everybody was happy. Life is much easier when everybody else is happy! Ernie'd never be happy . . . and that's what's so amazing, isn't it? That you can fix things, you can fix anybody if I just love 'em enough. . . . That's the hardest thing [to question yourself]. How could you live for that long that way and then start to think it's not right? 'Cause you're actually telling yourself you were wrong. You can't look at that. . . . When I was eighteen, nineteen, twenty, I was hell on wheels . . . and then to be molded into this house-wifey mouse at home and sit back and go, my God, how did I ever get there? . . . That is a failure if you're trying to look back and go, yes, you're supposed to be strong. . . . What's happened and you don't want to see that. I turned into a wife, one of those things I vowed I'd never do. . . . I'm being my mother all over again.

Rosario lived a profound ambivalence for several years about facing the hurt that her husband's behavior caused her. She clung to the belief that she was not being abused.

The hardest thing was to accept that I was being abused. I think the biggest step—at the time it isn't that you don't realize it but you don't want to accept it. You see, it's something out there, you don't want to know. It's something that you consider normal because of the traditional way that we have been educated. . . . When I looked at my situation to see what solutions there were for me, the more they told me that he was abusive, the more I didn't want to accept that he was, that that was violence. I used to say, "but he doesn't hit me so, no, it isn't violence," but deep down I knew that, yes, it was, and that, yes, I felt terrible.

For participants, the act of naming partners' actions as abuse evoked anxiety and fear about the loss of the relationship, and a redefinition of childhood experiences of violation. For example, for Jackie to name what her husband was doing to her as abuse was a double-edged sword. While it provided some relief, it also generated anxiety and distress, carrying with it an internal momentum and a foreboding of loss and grief.

> If I recognized what my husband was doing to me as abuse, then I would need to recognize that what my parents did to me was abuse too, and there it was, give up the fantasy childhood, give up the fantasy marriage. Again, it's recognizing the other things in life and giving up.

Recognizing that her partner was abusing her meant revisiting the pain of past sexual abuse and shattering the image of her fantasy childhood and marriage. Engendering feelings of betrayal and abandonment, this was a demanding task given her priority of protecting herself and her children from her husband and trying not to do anything that would "rile him up."

For participants, coming face to face with contradiction and conflict required that they cast an ever-widening net over the past, particularly the ways in which they had been treated as girls and adolescents. Making sense of abuse included making sense of many patterns, events, and pieces of their past, including patterns of surviving and coping that had been formed early in their lives. For example, in her adolescence Barbara was coerced by her parents to give up her child for adoption. Working through her past experiences, she learned more about her pattern of giving up her self to "just be a good girl." Integral to women's sense of self, these gendered patterns of coping and surviving were often tied to unpredictable, unsafe environments, where fragmentation and denial were necessary for survival. Participants required time and space to examine the origins of these patterns and power dynamics in order to reveal the links between patterned ways of coping, fear, survival, and disavowal of the self. Feminist/antioppressive discourses and social spaces helped women identify and understand these patterns and begin to change them.

For some participants who had repressed memories of childhood sexual abuse for many years, looking at the past produced trepidation, because to fully feel emotions created a sense of being overwhelmed, engulfed, and annihilated by them. For Barbara, learning to feel emotions again was a momentous step forward.

> You can't go back to that naive person that you were. You've got to keep going. And I remember going through it and thinking, what do I have to do next? . . . I remember one of my counselors did tell me, made me aware of my feelings, 'cause I was sitting there and she was asking something and I was responding. And I was starting to get really emotional and then, like I always had done, I would push that down so I wouldn't let out that emotion. She said, "Stop! What are you doing?" And I said, "What do you mean?" And she said, "This is what you just did," And I said, "Yeah, I was pushing that down." And she said, "You have to let that come out." And she said, "Just sit there. It'll be okay, you'll be okay." And I started to do that and I used to always hear people say you have to feel your feelings, but nobody ever explained to me how do you feel your feelings. . . . Through the help of the group and the counseling, it helped me through that and through readings. It's hard to describe.

Both Donna's and Barbara's participation in therapy and support groups for incest survivors provided a safe environment in which they could express their emotions, name what they were feeling, and experience and contain their feelings.

For years, Donna had repressed painful memories of her family's treatment and her grandfather's sexual molestation of her. She had suppressed all her feelings, the good and the bad, and tried to blank out painful memories.

> I had to admit: okay, I did have these emotions. Okay, this did happen. I reacted this way. I had to know who I was and why I was. . . . I knew it happened but at the same time . . . it was like, oh, that's just a bad dream. I just denied, suppressed more. . . . I would concentrate on the good events. . . . Things just gradually built up. . . . I ended up going into a major depression and so they asked me to go to [a psychiatric hospital]. . . . For the first time in my life I was told, well, how do you feel? And it was like, whoa! I don't think right, I don't feel

right, and I'm not supposed to talk cause that's being [selfish] . . . . I started off by trying to understand where my brothers were coming from. . . . That's how I always tried to deal with things. See, well, that person's doing that and then I could understand a bit about myself. . . . As soon as they said, well, how did that make you feel? I felt like I was doing a huge betrayal and doing something really sinful because. . . . I had no right to even think about myself. . . . I didn't know anything else. I just tried to be a better person and I couldn't see that I was a good person.

For Donna to be able to say "I feel, I need" transgressed psychic boundaries that formed an integral part of who she was, boundaries that were related to admonishments about pleasing others and unselfishness. Having wandered around like a "zombie" with everyone "pushing" at her all her life, this transgression of psychic and social boundaries was the renewal of a process of self-definition. Frightening in itself, this process required substantial support and interpretation of her feelings in the context of gendered expectations of girls and women and sexual abuse as an abuse of power. To refuse to transgress these gendered psychic boundaries would have signaled perpetual incapacitation for her. Donna credits the support group she attended during this time with saving her life when she was feeling suicidal.

As with June, resistance to knowing served a protective survival purpose, but it sometimes also worked to avert knowledge that would bring up painful memories, threaten to undermine notions of self and identity, and expose internalized oppression. Denial, as an unconscious defense mechanism, worked "to ward off full conscious awareness and verbalization of warded off thoughts and feelings" (Blum, 1985, p. 12). Harold Blum (1985) clarifies that denial can include "not noting or perceiving, withdrawing attention and signification, disavowing what has been perceived, distorting and misperceiving, and isolating a percept from affective or contextual meaning, as in minimizing danger or anticipated adversity" (p. 8). In her essay on the dynamics of students' resistance to a feminist curriculum, Patricia Elliot (1995) explains that denial "is a defence against unacceptable or unpleasurable affects such as shame, guilt, depression and, ultimately, against anxiety" (p. 6). Participants did not automatically embrace new knowledge and fleeting insights, experiencing them as both hope and fear, as both "threat and desire" (Rockhill, 1987a, p. 320).

Ruth lived in a state of ambivalence for some time, wanting to explore aboriginal culture and forms of oppression, yet avoiding them. During field trips to museum displays about aboriginal peoples she would distance herself from the exhibits, yet she found herself deeply offended by certain remarks and actions by students during these visits. In her discussion of Freud's concept of ambivalence, Jane Flax (1990) states that

> ambivalence refers to affective states in which intrinsically contradictory or mutually exclusive desires or ideas are each invested with intense emotional energy. Although one cannot have both simultaneously, one cannot abandon either of them . . . . It is often a strength to resist collapsing complex and contradictory material into an orderly whole. (p. 50)

Ruth's ambivalence was bound up with the effects of racism and sexism: her self-hatred and the repeated abuse that she had suffered as a child and adolescent. Gradually she broke through her ambivalence with the help of a teacher in her college program. She began her journey to heal herself and become aware of her hurts and their social origins.

> I struggled with that [looking at racism and sexism] . . . because they would bring up scenarios—they would trigger some memories with me. It was hard for me to look at that pain. . . . And then again, the one teacher helped me through a lot of things. . . . It's a risk. You're vulnerable to it. When you deal with it you're vulnerable and . . . you have to deal with whatever has been suppressed and to look at this new information, 'cause information is knowledge, right? Knowledge is power, so it was having to confront whatever it is that you've suppressed for years and taking the risk to sort of rehash over that or go through it, that your healing journey goes through.

Ruth's resistance to knowledge about her culture suggests that she was warding off or defending against some unacceptable ideas or effects. Since the desire not to know is unconscious, the goal of naming what is left unsaid is "not about forcing people to 'face reality,' but about undoing the mechanism of denial (or other defence mechanisms) that distorts our perceptions and our ability to think and to feel" (Elliot, 1995, p. 7). The hope engaged by resistance is located "in the possibility that the insight it defends against might become conscious" (p. 10). For Ruth, this meant integrating her insight and reclaiming her identity as an Ojibwa woman. Breaking down the desire not to know, the knowledge that she claimed and integrated into the self produced changes in consciousness and subjectivity. Knowledge about the effects of racism and the pain of her childhood years promised the hope of an outlook and self-understanding based on self-respect rather than self-hatred. Formative in breaking through her resistance to knowing was her lifelong search for an outlook that would illuminate her past.

Undoing mechanisms of denial and integrating new knowledge and insights were also difficult for participants because their own and their children's daily survival was jeopardized by violence, degradation, loss of family support, and financial hardship. According to Magda Lewis (1993), defensive behaviors may be necessary for survival, requiring attention "to the ways in which women have been required historically to invest in particular and often contradictory practices in order to secure their own survival" (p. 179). As participants made changes in their lives, they faced emotional and economic survival issues such as how they were going to pay the rent and feed their families if they failed to "keep everyone happy." Some participants lost connections with or became isolated from family and friends, while for others, relationships with their families of origin changed substantially. This isolation and feeling of aloneness were discouraging for some participants.

For Donna, the acts of knowing and speaking transgressed the boundaries of the social order. One consequence of speaking out was the collapse of her relationship with her mother. After she told her parents about her grandfather's actions, their small flutter of support was followed by her mother's claim that she had made it all up. Once Donna was hospitalized, her mother pretended that she did not exist and tried to get the psychiatrist to declare her permanently mentally disabled. Furthermore, her mother convinced Donna's daughter that Donna was crazy and persuaded the daughter to live with her rather than Donna. While her mother's actions were perhaps a reaction to her own sexual abuse by her father (Donna's grandfather), this did not lessen Donna's sense of betrayal, nor the consequences of naming the unnamable and speaking the unspeakable.

Donna also talked about another consequence of speaking out against violence toward women, particularly in a small rural community:

> You end up being victimized all over again. You lose everything. You're totally revictimized over and over and over again. So, like, every newspaper article you do, every time, or even admitting that I'm a volunteer for the women's shelter and second-stage housing, people raise their eyebrows and it's like, whoa! She's one of those man-hater, feminist, argh, bra burning, and—stay away from her! It's like you have the plague.

Ruth felt that she had to say good-bye to friends of twenty years. They objected to her enrollment in a course of studies that had feminist and lesbian participants, and also objected to her interest in Native spirituality, calling her a traitor to her Christian faith.

> Listening to other Native women, they've gone through the same things as I have, too, but they hadn't given up their faith either. . . . They [friends] were looking at it very bias[ed], judgmental, and discriminatory. . . . Like what was that going to do to them? Is that going to destroy them? . . . I guess through everything that I've gone through I looked at the church as a kind of a refuge kind of thing. People were there to be able to pray with me or counsel me, but when it came time to recognize what all these different oppressions and "isms" were in my life, then it was like I was going a little step beyond them. Because they didn't recognize it either and then it became a threat to them, and then they dumped it on me.

Eleanor, however, framed the cost of losing friends in a different way.

> The way I look at it is not so much am I giving something up as I'm moving toward something that I can be more comfortable

with. That's what I see, a seed that you plant in the ground. . . .
It's not so much what I've left behind as where I'm going that is
important. . . . Look where I am and where I'm going.

For Heather, who sees herself as a fighter, speaking out also had a
price. Although her treatment by the systems served as a source of
politicization for her, it exacted a high price. She lost her share of
joint property in her divorce settlement, almost lost custody of her
infant son to her ex-husband, and was cut off from Family Benefits
when she called her worker to clarify that her husband had been
harassing her and hanging around her home. She also challenged
her role in her family of origin:

> I had gone through this [Family Court] process for almost
> three years, and I just said, ach, every time I walk in there I
> lose more. . . . I lost everything. . . . The grounds for his
> visitation was that he's supposed to be paying [child support]
> since November and he has only made one payment. So now if
> I take him to court, what am I going to lose? It's like I have to
> sit here and go, what am I ready to give up? Before you even
> challenge anything, a woman has to sit there and say, what am
> I gonna give up? . . . I was the oldest in the family and . . . I
> was brought up to be the problem-solver, the mother, the nur-
> turer. . . . I found out that I really had become so strong
> because emotionally my mother had abandoned me. . . . I
> needed to do that [stand up to my mother]—otherwise I was
> not going to know my own personal identity because of having
> been tied into the family and solving everyone's little issues
> . . . . I don't know who Heather is. I'm just finding that out
> now. I don't think they [family] have a very clear focus or
> understanding of abuse and power . . . They don't want to see
> it, and I think when somebody chooses not to see something
> that's because if they did recognize something they would
> have to deal with the issues in their lives. . . . I made a deci-
> sion, a choice to do that, and I feel like right now my family is
> not my family sometimes. . . . We feel two worlds apart.

For many participants, significant social costs were associated
with challenging the status quo, speaking out about injustice, and

taking action. In her discussion of feminist pedagogy in the class-room, Lewis (1993) asserts:

> Thus, we cannot expect that students will readily appropriate a political stance that is truly counter-hegemonic, unless we also acknowledge the ways in which our feminist practice/politics *creates*, rather than ameliorates, a feeling of threat: the threat of abandonment; the threat of having to struggle within unequal power relations; the threat of psychological/social/sexual as well as economic and political marginality; the threat of retributive violence—each a threat lived in concrete embodied ways. (p. 178)

Critical education must acknowledge and help women prepare for the risks that they face in making change and the negotiations involved in maintaining their connections to family and community.

In summary, participants' responses to violence and oppression as well as their identification, recognition, and resolution of their experiences of abuse were both shaped and hindered by dominant society's culture of silence and denial. "Repression, dissociation, and denial are phenomena of social as well as individual consciousness" (Herman, 1992, p. 9). Society's wish is often to banish knowledge of violence against women from consciousness. The tasks that participants undertook are not supported in our everyday lives, at least in dominant white culture. Clearly, disrupting "the tyranny of the familiar" (Gunew and Yeatman, 1993, p. xiii), what one has learned is normal, requires sustenance and connections with others that can attend to both the political and psychic aspects of questioning the self and the social.

LIBERATORY DISCOURSES AND SPACES: SELF-RECOVERY, SOCIAL ANALYSIS, AND COLLECTIVE ACTION

Through making sense of contradiction and conflict, participants cultivated a critical social analysis of their experience. By critical social analysis I mean a process of politicization in which participants made connections between their personal experiences and the social and material conditions engendering these experiences, what bell hooks (1988) calls a "critical understanding of the concrete material reality that lays the groundwork for that personal experience" (p. 108). She points out that understanding "that groundwork and what must be done to transform it is quite different from the effort to raise one's consciousness about personal experience even as they are linked" (p. 108). Drawing on feminist/antioppressive discourses and building on what they already knew, women began to more clearly articulate and discern the patterned ways in which the social world constructed their disadvantage, encouraging them to "see through rose-colored glasses." One effect of this process was the interrogation of dominant meanings of "woman," "mother," and "Native." This was key to their construction of an alternative sense of self.

In putting together pieces of the puzzle, women engaged in theory making, ways of explaining what had happened to them. Emphasizing the political importance of theory, Gloria Anzaldúa (1990) states:

> Theory produces effects that change people and the way they perceive the world. Thus we need *theorías* that will enable us to interpret what happens in the world, that will explain how and why we relate to certain people in specific ways, that will reflect what goes on between inner, outer and peripheral "I"s within a person and between the personal "I"s and the collective "we" of our ethnic communities. . . . We need theories that examine the implications of situations and look at what's behind them. And we need to find practical applications for those theories. (pp. xxv-xxvi)

bell hooks (1988) links theorizing to the political processes of self-recovery and collective liberation, to education for critical consciousness, and to "the overall effort of the oppressed, the dominated, to develop awareness of those forces which exploit and oppress" (p. 30).[3] Feminist and antioppressive spaces and ways of interpreting the world helped participants in several ways: to elucidate and reinterpret their experiences; to comprehend power relations and oppressive social structures and institutions; to reconstruct and recover parts of themselves that had been lost, repressed, and subjugated; to use their knowledge and redefine their relation to the world; and to discover ways and avenues to work for change.

Describing growing up without a sense of home, hooks (1994) speaks about finding "a place of sanctuary in 'theorizing,' in making sense out of what was happening" (p. 61). When theorizing is directed toward liberation and healing, it can be a place "to recover ourselves and our experiences in language" (p. 175). Paola found a language that illuminated her experiences of political oppression, woman abuse, and incest and their relation to her social position as a woman from a particular class.

> It was a very rich time for me when I finally started putting things into words. . . . It was like naming things for what they were when in reality I had already understood the theory. . . . When I finally got to read a lot more stuff here. . . . it was finally the point in which I put two and two together and said, oh my God, this is what's going on! . . . That's the process in which I became a lot more knowledgeable about saying this is the route that I'm going to take, a lot more in control of what I will do with my life experience and in terms of understanding why . . . violence happened to me. You know, I have survived incest as a very young child, which caused a very, very, very strong pain in my family, and I have survived political violence and oppression, and I have survived the violence of my relationship, so putting them all together and not only looking at them as very specific and individual experiences but trying to analyze them in context made me realize that my experience as a woman and as a woman of color, as a woman of the social class that I come from, made it all sort of click together. . . . That was . . . a very important turning point when I was able to say, oh yeah, all of them are connected and it has to do with my experience as a woman. . . . To also realize that the whole concept of gender was missing for me, and that as a woman . . . no social or political change was going to bring a real solution to me [if it did not] address the issue of gender and race and class.

For Paola, theory making furnished the conceptual elements with which to resist structures of domination. Although gender had not been a salient category of analysis in her political activism in Chile (Sternbach et al., 1992), she realized that feminist theories about women of color and social change must take into account her multi-dimensionality.[4]

Theory making also accorded Paola a greater sense of what she would do with her knowledge and a greater degree of consciousness about her life.

> I think when you've gone through abuse, you go through a time [when] you don't know where you're going. . . . It's not even living at the moment because it's like just dealing with things as they come in the best way you can, or—with . . . no real idea of what you're really doing. . . . And it's important for me through raising political consciousness to say, okay, I have all the elements. This is what's going on. I can understand what's going on in my life. This is what I can do about it. . . . I think abuse puts us so much out of control, it takes so much control away from our life . . . that we somehow feel that we have no control of anything. . . . We need to recover, women need to regain the control . . . to do things consciously.

Linking theory with self-recovery and acting in the world, Paola identified the personal changes that she needed to make as well as social changes that would improve women's lives. Using her knowledge in organizing work with women constituted a form of "effective and meaningful resistance" for her (hooks, 1988, p. 30).

Jackie had already been working for change in her community when she joined the work of second-stage housing. Elaborating a critical analysis of her experience there gave her a structure for understanding the immobilizing emotions that she had felt during her relationship and following her separation from her partner. A feminist understanding of woman abuse and child welfare policies and practices gave her permission to feel sadness, grieve, and come to a place of self-acceptance. For Jackie, theorizing about her experience encouraged critical self-awareness and political consciousness and effected a containment of emotions, facilitating her movement beyond immobilizing feelings and her tendency to be verbally abusive with her children.

My involvement [at second-stage housing] helped me to take it from that personal scene that was just happening to me to society and wow! A lot of my growing has happened here because I've been able to look at myself and to see exactly what happened, to grow given the opportunity to grow. . . . You need to be given the opportunity to go ahead, to get the education and to learn that it's not just you, it's women. . . . There needs to be a time when you . . . look back to examine things, to say why I feel that way, but do you really need it all? . . . You have to get to a point where you let go of your past. You try to normalize things. At the same time you take your rose-colored glasses off and put them on the table and you go on. . . . But I think, you know, it's not woe is me, look what happened to me, I'm going to [work to end violence against women]. But it's like this shouldn't be happening to women, this shouldn't be happening to children. So I could sit on a therapist's couch for ten years . . . and it's not going to change. For me it had to be moving ahead and doing the work to change it.

Critical to Jackie's learning was the space in which to grow without anyone attributing her thoughts or actions to the fact that she had been abused. Jackie, like some other participants in this study, sought to refute the assumption often made by professionals and workers within the systems that everything a formerly abused woman does or says derives from her ascribed status as a "battered woman."

Theorizing about the social and material conditions engendering her subordination helped Rosario comprehend why she felt that she had failed as a partner and establish some goals for herself. She attended an educational support group for women of Latin American origin.

I think it's really difficult to challenge and let go of your customary ways of being because, for example, in Latin American countries we are raised with the idea that the highest honor for a woman is to find a good husband and make a good home. It is a woman's duty to make a good home and if your husband leaves you, then it was because you didn't attend to him well. You didn't do your part. You didn't understand him, but they never tell you that it has to do with both partners. No, you have to attend to him, understand him, treat him special, be flexible. My mother used to say to me, it isn't the same when you are with me. I'm your mother and I understand you and you're my daughter, with me it's different, but he's your husband and you have to adjust to his needs.

hooks (1988) points to the dehumanizing effects of oppressive social forces: "We oppose this violation, this dehumanization when we seek self-recovery, when we work to reunite fragments of being, to recover our history" (p. 31). For Rosario, situating her life in a social context illuminated her own struggle to let go of self-blame.

As Magda Lewis (1993) affirms, "we are able to uncover the politics of our subordination as we interrogate our experiences for how they delimit what is possible for us" (p. 12). Reflecting on her past, Donna made connections between her belief that she must please her partner, her partner's "mind control" over her, and her earlier experiences of violation. She gained insight into the gender norms structuring heterosexual relationships, engaging her to rethink her investment in what "society" expected her to do.

He forced me into some experimental sex that wasn't the nicest. . . . I knew it was wrong 'cause I didn't feel right, yet it's like, okay. . . . You basically become their property to do with, like it's your job to please them and you have no rights to say no. I can't say that he really raped me but he did. It's a fine line. I guess I feel he didn't really rape me, but it was like a mind control sort of, which maybe it does go under rape . . . I didn't want to do it all but I never said anything to him because he probably wouldn't listen anyway and "keep your mouth shut or it could be worse." And I guess because of my own experience with sex, it was sort of, well, maybe he isn't wrong. Maybe I was the one that was at fault because I'm feeling this way. Like I'm supposed to be enjoying this and it was, like, get me out of here! Like he would say, is that hurting you? And it was kind of like ha, ha, ha, don't you dare say you're not [liking it].

Donna uncovered her own self-representation as an object and began to dismantle its power. This shift in consciousness resulted in a monumental change from seeing herself as a piece of property to seeing herself as someone who could define what was good for her. This process was a source of power and pleasure. Renaming her experience in politically actionable terms generated self-acceptance and a refusal to carry the burden of shame.

For Donna, like other participants, putting together pieces of the puzzle about experiences of abuse extended to theorizing about a host of other life experiences, for example, her ostracization as an "unwed mother" in her small community and the discrimination against her practiced by employers on that basis.

> It was always that kind of attitude—women were supposed to be barefoot and pregnant, and you can get an education and a job, but when you get married, you stay home, take care of the kids. That's always been instilled in me, and looking around I always knew women had the low-paying jobs. I knew all that before but then when I had my breakdown then I guess [I could] apply it to myself and I could see that okay, they had no right to hold it against me even though I knew before it was still an issue [her status as an "unwed mother"] that I hadn't dealt with emotionally. . . . I could say, okay, this isn't just me, this is a huge problem because I was internalizing that . . . I was too stupid and dumb and I wasn't the right personality for decent places to have on staff.

As Linda Briskin (1990) affirms, naming the personal as political "challenges the ideology of individualism which suggests that we are each able to shape our lives through individual will and determination, and that any failure is due to personal failure or laziness" (p. 22). This analysis granted participants more freedom for rewriting the self.

Participants in this study identified the kinds of liberatory environments and knowledge that helped them in their sense-making activities and provided avenues for affirming the self and creating community. They emphasized the importance of connecting with other women who believed in them, being treated with respect, having their voices heard, and belonging to community. They underscored the key role of significant people in helping them grow, not by providing nonchallenging support but by inviting them to struggle and confront facets and issues that they sometimes wished to avoid. Access to liberatory discourses and spaces provided them with avenues for learning about themselves, creating community, and for affirming the self.

Heather described the significance of second-stage housing in her meaning-making journey:

> Second stage has been very strong, very strong support for me . . . . I've had very strong influential women that supported me . . . . For myself it was the stronger the support system, the stronger I was because if you don't have a support system out there, you can be barricaded down just as fast as anything. . . . The more I was supported and confirmed, then I just continued fighting and challenging the systems. . . . I think that's why I got so much out of second-stage [housing] because of that confirmation. I don't think when I was a child there was much of that, if any at all. It was always do, do, do, you gotta do, do, do. . . . When people start really saying this is valid what you're feeling and this is what you need and this is what you deserve and this is what you should have, then you start saying whoa! I'm really a human being and whoa! Look at these feelings that are starting to come back, and you don't shut yourself down so much, you don't try to avoid things so much. . . . I'm just allowed to be who I always was . . . to have those feelings. What we believe in gets validated instead of being shut down or covered up or stepped on or swept away or ignored.

For Maryanne, second-stage housing provided an environment in which she could act, question, and make changes without fearing the consequences.

> I think it was just that calming effect when you're used to pins and needles. They [staff at second-stage housing] were helping you but yet you still had to do it. They wouldn't completely smother you and look after you but they would give you the knowledge to go out and do it. . . . I guess, too, challenging

rules. . . . They said, well, if there's something in there that you don't think is right, bring it up at the residents' meeting. So that's what we started doing and that's where I started. That's where I learned that I could question no matter where it's written. . . . The safety here, you knew the counselors weren't gonna put you down for it. If the other residents did, well, it was all right because nothing else was going to happen. You would just talk about it and sometimes it did get changed. Things changed, that was the big thing.

The respect for their personal process and decision making shown by staff in various women's organizations and by other program participants enabled them to learn new skills and build on their strengths. The social networks that they developed were critical in maintaining connectedness and meaningful relationships within their communities. They gained confidence, learned about reciprocity, accountability, and respect in these relationships, and often supported one another during difficult times. For some participants who had been relatively isolated before contacting a shelter, second-stage housing, or support group, forming friendships with other women was a new and sometimes uncertain experience, requiring the breakdown of myths about women and friendship. Women's social networks helped them counter the isolation that women leaving abusive relationships often face. In her study of women's experiences after leaving a shelter, Susan Gadbois (1999) found that the majority of the twelve participants experienced severe isolation both pre- and postshelter. They did not have a broad, stable social support network, thus affecting their reestablishment in the community.

In summary, as participants unravelled contradiction and conflict, they drew on feminist/antioppressive discourses to elaborate a critical social analysis. This was a critical element in constructing an alternative sense of self, underlining "the relationship between experience and meaning-making as the basis of subject formation" (Lewis, 1993, p. 12). Particularly significant was the role of theorizing in facilitating women's understanding of their feelings and responses to the violence and oppression they experienced. As Sasha Roseneil (1995) affirms, liberatory spaces provide opportunities for women to actively rethink and reconstruct ways of understanding themselves and their world. Feminist/antioppressive discourses and spaces resonated with women, validating their realities and experiences, and providing friendship and community. They expedited women's articulation of previous ways of seeing the world, gave meaning to their experiences, and constituted an explanatory framework through which they could understand their past and present.

CHANGES IN SUBJECTIVITY: SELF-ACCEPTANCE AND SHIFTING STRUCTURES OF IDENTITY

For participants in my study, an alternative sense of self emerged from their struggle with contradiction and conflict; their understanding of how social norms, messages, and practices had shaped them; and how they themselves had taken up and lived dominant representations of "woman," "mother," and "Native." Changes in subjectivity occurred primarily in two areas. First, women came to self-acceptance through making connections among self-blame, woman blaming, and the social devaluation of women. Second, although it was difficult and painful for women to uncover, transforming subjectivity entailed exposing internalized oppression, the ways in which their own self-understandings formed part of their disempowerment.

One effect of developing a critical analysis of lived experience on women's subjectivity cannot go unmentioned. A powerful factor in the transformation of women's sense of themselves was what Freire (1994) identified as "becoming a person," recognizing one's reality as oppressive. Some participants expressed this as "realizing I was a human being," "seeing that I was okay," and "realizing I deserved respect." For others, it was shedding a sense of being "wrong," a "misfit," and "not good enough." For some women, what they had perceived and defined as their weakness or "misfit status" became their strength. Participants came to realize that they alone were not responsible for everything that had happened to them, including the violations that they had suffered. Refusing the notion of some intrinsic flaw in the self appeared to be a necessary condition for establishing the grounds on which to set personal boundaries and demand respect, to find out what worked for them, to refuse to absorb the projections and emotions of others, to cultivate strengths and new facets of themselves, and to develop new principles for living.

Jackie explained how she came to a place of self-acceptance:

> Part of that process [of growing] was establishing personal boundaries and . . . how did I build the skill that I needed? I guess a lot of it was going back and it was self-acceptance. There's nothing wrong with me. Because I don't have a confrontational personality, because I'm not aggressive, it doesn't make me any less of a person. . . . I don't have any sign on my back that says "kick me" or I'm not passive because you're made to feel that something's wrong with you again. . . . It was the blame. "Jackie, if you would have spoken up, if you would have yelled at him the first time he went out, if you would have done this and if you would have done that, if you wouldn't have been quite so passive, he would never have abused you" . . . all the messages, the whole messages that society comes with, "if you wouldn't have been quite so pretty as a little girl they wouldn't have abused you," just all those messages. Part of the process is going back and examining those things and reasoning out why they happened and the wrongs there. Like, that's bullshit, because a child is pretty doesn't mean that they need to be abused or because a woman is a quiet woman doesn't mean that she doesn't speak up or stick up for herself. Some of those messages, too, came from my partner. You're such a wimp—why don't you ever speak up for yourself? Okay, I will. And then swat. Okay, okay, excuse me!

Donna spoke about a transformative moment in which she experienced herself differently. It occurred after she began attending a support group for sexual abuse survivors:

> How can I explain it? I felt like I was the ugliest, terriblest thing and I justified my existence on this earth as being—like I was here on this earth to prove to people what not to be. . . . Once I started dealing with things, that was gone, not totally . . .

but it's like I realize I do do some things right. . . . It happened in a split second. . . . I call it being born for the first time in my life. It was just a feeling. It's just so different, like I'd never felt that way, like it's so light inside. . . . It's like I'm still light. It's like, whoa, I can deal with this and get on sort of thing. . . . It made me feel a lot and I still wasn't in good shape then. . . . I don't feel so weighted down. . . . There was six tons taken off my heart and insides. . . . I don't know if you just stop taking the world on . . . saying oh, I'm not responsible for all this. . . . I even noticed, like, colors, not that they turned tremendously different in shades, but they seemed just that shade or two brighter and everything just looked [different] and I just felt so different inside. Maybe I realized I was a person, I don't know. And I made up my mind then nobody was taking that away from me.

Although Donna still struggles with self-punishing patterns of thought, she feels better able to interrupt them, realizing that change is not automatically achieved through the effort of will alone.

In recognizing how she had been encouraged to give her power over to others, Maryanne developed an inner strength that helped her resist losing herself in an effort to keep everyone happy.

It's back to that inner strength again, not being pushed to do anything that I don't want to do. Like, I'll still compromise, but nobody's gonna tell me what to do. And I think if I hadn't been through that, it wouldn't mean so much to me. It wouldn't be so important to have that right and to know that I have to have that right. . . . I value my opinions more, as a person. . . . I know what's there instead of always second-guessing myself. . . . I have an independence that I didn't even know could exist because I went right from home to marriage. The independence circles everything, like having to make choices. There's still times when I want to run away and tell somebody else to do it, like, tell me what I should do! . . . Take some time . . . see what qualities you really have instead of having to be with somebody. That'll make all the difference in the world, instead of that desperation—yeah, what am I gonna do?

Participants' feelings of inadequacy, not fitting, being wrong, and being not good enough, which were constitutive of self to varying degrees, were not solely the effects of abuse. This complex of feelings arose in several ways for women: from feeling that they had not measured up to social imperatives as well as from the outcomes of gendering processes, defined by Jane Flax (1993) as the social processes that constitute a gendered subjectivity (expectations to "absorb things," "always respond to somebody else's needs," "keep everyone happy," and be "the fixer and problem-solver"); from a perception of having failed in their responsibility to shape their lives according to certain standards; from transgressing or rebelling against social expectations (having or expressing desires when told to "not ask for anything," for wanting a better life after being "somebody else's scapegoat or punching bag or maid"); and from shutting down and crushing their experience, their desire to resist, or their acts of resistance in order to survive ("crushing your rebellion"; "not giving yourself permission to see things differently").

These everyday experiences reinforced women's knowledge of the ordering of the world and the social and cultural boundaries and limits beyond which they ought not to go (Haug et al., 1987). As a young girl, Donna faced shaming and consequences when she crossed the lines of the social order and resisted her grandfather's infringements on her body:

> I was dodging his hands when I was about three and—well, he got his actual hands on me when I was about nine. . . . I can even remember actually hitting my grandfather and yelling at him, "keep your paws off." And you shoulda seen the looks I got. Like, there was a kitchen full of us in my mother's house and he had gone to the washroom and, on his way, he had felt every one of us on the way there, okay? He deliberately went around and felt every one of us in the kitchen and then went to the washroom, came back, and started doing the same thing. And I, well, I have this automatic response sometimes, like jah! Doesn't always work. I love it when it does, though, and I come back with my elbow and I yelled at him, "Don't you ever do that!" And everybody give me the dirty looks. They all just

glared at me and my mother says, "You don't do that." And he just stood there and he was shocked, but I'm the one that was in trouble.

The effect of this practice was that Donna learned to feel shame for her transgressions of the social order. Inger Agger (1994) identifies shame as the emotion that acts as a powerful mechanism to enforce women's adjustment to their cultural environment. Shame, the voice of society within the individual, is legitimated by a system of domination and reinforced by power strategies. Agger suggests that these power strategies, which include the use of shame, are "elements in an almost unconscious *structural violence* embedded in the cultural and social structure itself, which simultaneously contributes to maintaining this structure and the existing distribution of power" (p. 40). The everyday relations and language that construct the cultural, social, and psychic boundaries of the permissible are enforced through concrete sanctions, violence, and abuse. Girls learn to feel responsible and wrong for transgressing social, cultural, and psychic boundaries and for resisting and rebelling against the order of things, an order of things guarded by sanctions that threaten transgressors.

Of course the experience of violation can give rise to shame and doubt. In her clinical work and research with victims of sexual and domestic violence, Judith Herman (1992) states, "shame is a response to helplessness, the violation of bodily integrity, and the indignity suffered in the eyes of another person" (p. 53). My reading of women's stories suggests that although shame results from experiences of violation, it is, as Sandra Bartky (1990) suggests, a broader emotion closely intertwined with women's status in society. In her examination of the relation between shame and gender, Bartky sets out the structure of shame as an affective attunement to the social environment, a sense of personal inadequacy that as an emotion is profoundly disempowering. As an emotion of self-assessment, it plays a strong role in women's oppression, "both in the constitution of subjectivity and in the perpetuation of subjection" (Bartky, 1990, p. 98). Bartky clarifies that shame involves "distressed apprehension of oneself as a lesser creature" (p. 87). What is insightful about her discussion of shame is that, unlike emotions/affective states founded on cognitions, the feelings and sensings that make up women's shame often do not "reach a state of clarity we can dignify as belief" (p. 95). The sense of being a lesser creature is apprehended unconsciously as self-doubt and ambiguity. For this reason, shame, suffered at the level of feelings that have no name, is all the more corrosive and undermining, lending legitimacy to the power that occasions it.

The social regulation of women is achieved, then, not only through oppressive social formations that legitimate violence, abuse, and the use of force, but through feelings and deficits that women come to recognize as their own. Therefore, the social norms and practices that oppress women are isolated and removed from social relations of power and established as aspects of the psyche. Valerie Walkerdine (1985) states that "powerlessness can hardly be recognized as an effect of regulation in those practices in which power itself is denied" (p. 218). For participants in this study, uncovering the politics of their subordination significantly diminished their feelings of inadequacy and shame. Established as aspects of the psyche, these feelings were transformed when women recognized that it was a combination of social conditions and practices that constructed them as wrong and inadequate. Letting go of this weight signified a different relation to the world, one that affected self-definition, habits of being, and relationships with others.

The second area of transformation in subjectivity concerned becoming aware of internalized oppression and unconscious investment in oppressive relations. bell hooks (1990) affirms that self-recovery, becoming aware of oppressive and exploitive forces and their effects, entails throwing off "the colonizer mentality" (p. 218). Through unraveling contradictions and theory making, women exposed "the image of the occupier lodged somewhere" in their minds and bodies (Fanon, 1967, p. 52). As participants became conscious of having internalized dominant representations of "mother," "woman," and "Native," they examined the ways in which they had taken up and believed in them. This was expressed by participants in different ways.

Ruth uncovered her loathing of herself as an aboriginal woman, transforming those feelings that kept her ashamed of who she was.

I didn't have a full knowledge of what all those words [racism, sexism] meant, but it was when they got into a more inner depth thing, looking at society as a whole or over the generations, that I really opened my eyes to them. . . . I never knew which label or which "ism" went with what, really, and why it's there, or why society or how society put it in place. And people believing in that kind of thing subconsciously or consciously, and just recognizing the different levels of systematic oppression or racism, never really looked at that either. And even, like, to begin my own healing too, recognizing that it's okay to be a Native woman. You can't change that. . . . We'll never forget. You can go along through your healing—you'll never forget what's happened to you. But you're not going to be held in that state of oppression or those internalized feelings you've had, like you go through that where it's not holding you down or caging you as an individual to keep you from accomplishing whatever you have to in your life.

For Ruth, like June, internalized oppression formed part of the very knowledge and pain that generated threats to identity, part of the knowledge that women resisted. However, their stories attest to the rewards of attending to ambivalence and uncertainty in processes of conscientization. Because shifts in structures of identity occur through both conscious and unconscious dynamics, critical education must acknowledge both the threat and the promise that it poses and embrace ambivalence and uncertainty.

As a poor woman with little education, Jackie felt that she had been set up and was doing exactly what she was supposed to be doing as a wife and mother. As she described, "When you get educated then, or the more knowledge you feed into yourself, the more you can shut that down and make the changes on the inside." Part of this process involved looking into oneself, recognizing where the changes needed to be, and if there were resistances to change, asking, "Why are they there?" Part of Jackie's process involved coming to terms with her self-valuation as a mother and the messages from FCS and society in general that somehow she had been responsible for allowing the abuse she experienced from her partner, the sexual abuse of her children, or even the sexual abuse she suffered as a child. Although Jackie didn't directly talk about her implicit acceptance of "the way it was," I suspect that it was painful for her to look at her previous investment in her fantasy marriage and childhood. She also had to come to terms with her tendency to be verbally abusive with her children, another difficult undertaking.

As Chris Weedon (1987) points out, we are all emotionally and psychically invested in our identities, consciously and unconsciously, and challenges to the ways in which we understand ourselves and our world threaten our sense of who we are. Women's resistance to seeing and knowing is intimately bound up with uncovering "the organization of knowledge and the production of ignorance" (Lather, 1991, p. 144). Patti Lather states that critical examination of experience and the politics of subordination can help us comprehend our own collusion: "To begin to understand how we are caught up in power situations of which we are, ourselves, the bearers is to foreground the limits of our lives and what we can do within those boundaries" (p. 144). This task of exposing and working through internalized oppression and realizing how they, too, were the bearers of power relations was more difficult for some participants than for others.

Some participants appeared to have worked through multiple facets of internalized oppression, arriving at self-understanding and acceptance. Like Jackie, other women found it difficult or impossible to speak directly about how their personal beliefs and actions had disempowered them. Others were beginning to examine their investment in "the way it was" and ask themselves how their beliefs and actions contributed to their own or others' oppression.

In her journey, Heather had discerned how social institutions upheld men's interests over those of women and children. She was also beginning to examine how she, too, was the bearer of power relations, discovering that she had been living according to everyone else's rules: her husband's, her mother's, and her family's.

> I was expecting the white little picket fence, the three or four kids, and the nice little house. . . . They pump that in your head when you're a little girl, that Cinderella process. . . . They don't actually let you know that that's not what life's about. . . . Part

of the process in getting involved in social change is finding out who you really are because somebody's kept you locked up for a long time. Well, like, the whole thirty-five years of my life I haven't been me or never was allowed to be me. You're always somebody else's scapegoat or punching bag or maid. . . . I think that's a lot of it, to actually find out what it is that I really like or want to do. . . . That's the scary part after the abusive relationship. . . . You're sitting there and what do you do? Which way are you going to be? . . . I don't even know who I am or what I even like or dislike because someone's always controlled all those thoughts or what you're even good at, because you've always been told you were good for nothing.

Deepening her understanding of the oppressive social and material practices organizing our lives, she began to see that she, too, was part of this formation.

Other participants described that they had been "brainwashed" or "molded" into being and acting in certain ways, with less acknowledgment of conscious or unconscious investment in identity. For example, Victoria found in radical feminism an explanation for why she had always felt pressured to conform to society's expectations of her as a woman. Although she came to some resolution that she will never fit into what she called a "normal" lifestyle, she may need to revisit the conflict she experienced between her own investment in and desire for what society pushes upon her (a "normal" heterosexual relationship) and her resistance to society's "molding" of her.

We live in a society where daily we betray ourselves because we allow ourselves through our socialization to continually, minute by minute, be betrayed by what is going around us. It's very complex. . . . I was really fortunate to have been able to take the eight months in my life . . . to start making some sense out of a lot of stuff that had gone on. . . . Just one by one take out the bricks, rearrange the foundations. . . . There was just no way, after what I'd been through, that I really felt there was a different way to be programmed. Well, I knew that there was a different way to be programmed, but I didn't think it was part of the way I was. . . . I've had to fight all my life from the time

I was born and then fight through everything I learned, only to realize that I had to unlearn everything that I was taught because, for me, it was wrong. . . . I was always taught that I was wrong, and I always felt that there was something wrong, and I could never understand why whatever it was that I did or I said was wrong, because nothing was wrong with me. But society and everyone . . . was trying to mold me into what they wanted me to be so that I would fit in where they wanted me to fit. And for me it was the wrong way because there never was anything wrong with me, other than the fact that I fought tooth and nail every step of the way.

To move beyond the victim perspective, Victoria would need to recognize her insight regarding self-betrayal and examine her investment in her identity and her failure to be accountable to herself and other women. The more we can "examine and question self-consciously the conditions of our own meaning-making and to use it as the place from which to begin to work toward change" (Lewis, 1990, p. 470), the more constructive will be our ability to create alternative senses of ourselves, communicate with others about what kinds of changes can be growth-producing, and plan effective strategies for change at the personal and collective levels.

However, for us to adopt this position, we need to address the silence and shame attached to internalized oppression and domination, and provide safe environments that enable us to reach a psychological place where we can work through our inability, not unwillingness, to examine the difficult issue of complicity with the status quo. A great deal of silence and shame surrounds this issue, particularly for women who have been abused. Our complicity with the status quo is further complicated when women who are abused also abuse their children, or live with a partner who abuses them. Feminist theory and practice must begin to openly address these areas within feminist discourses on woman abuse and child abuse, with women who are being abused, and within professional journals and circles.

Participants in this study made many changes in their lives. They refused to shoulder the blame, demanded dignity and respect, stood up and spoke out, became angry and found their voices, called injustice by its name, learned that trust is earned, changed the ways they raise their children, refused to continue to put other women down, and made a commitment not to partake of the master's tools. They were no longer willing to tolerate sexist remarks and degrading putdowns about women, nor to put on the rose-colored glasses that enable them to accept certain attitudes and behaviors that are harmful to themselves and others. Some participants realized the importance of making connections between systems of power and oppression based on "race," sexuality, class, ability, and other categories and figuring out how they reproduced everyday oppression.

For Barbara, working through her own experiences of violation helped her connect and empathize with others who are marginalized in our society.

> It's amazing how people treat other people poorly. We have someone coming in [who] has a disability. This woman's in a wheelchair and she has cerebral palsy. . . . Here's this highly intelligent woman and she's happy because we're going to allow her to work for us for nothing! For nothing! I mean she is going to be paid because of the program that she's [in], but I thought, this is ridiculous, this is disgusting, because it has nothing to do with her intelligence. . . . And seeing how people treat racial minorities, it's all just progressed, and it started with me dealing with what I had to deal with. I don't like anybody to have anything like that happen, you know. I will now speak up and say, "hey, that isn't right" or "stop that" because it happened to me and I know how bad I felt and how awful I felt, and nobody deserves to be treated like that.

Changes in subjectivity meant becoming more emotionally interdependent, developing inner strength and a sense of deserving dignity and respect. Participants' connections with women's organizations, communities, and support groups helped them maintain their sense of worth, enabling them to break away from unhealthy relationships. Jackie, like Maryanne and Heather, questioned the norms and practices that encouraged her to give her power over to men and understood her feelings of emotional dependence on men that created desperation and panic. She rejected modes of heterosexual relations that position her solely as "giver," sacrificer of self:

> I came to the realization that because of the experience in my childhood, I had love and control mixed up. That sense of him having power over me—I thought that I was in love but I wasn't. No, that's not what it [was]. And then having the desperation when you're in the process of leaving, that person's no longer there . . . feeling the panic . . . my body's shaking, what am I going to do? . . . He's getting the power, which takes the power away from me. . . . It's like one little piece at a time till the day comes something's missing. Something inside me's been taken and what is it? . . . When you get into another relationship and you start seeing the signs, don't think, oh my gosh, this is stuff from my past coming up. Damn it, it's not! It's right from today and you're seeing exactly what you should be seeing. . . . I wouldn't change it . . . I wouldn't change it at all. It's worth the price that I pay and—it's worth the price that I pay every day, hopefully. . . . There's not going to be someone that's going to come and they're going to take and they're going to take and then I won't be anymore.

For some participants, naming, feeling, and expressing anger was important in their journey, but its meaning differed among women. For Victoria, it was important not only to be able to name it but to articulate the source of her anger in the social devaluation of women:

> I didn't know what anger was because I had been taught to always swallow that emotion. I was denied that expression. In this relationship it was hard for me to identify anger, and yet I could see so much of it coming from my partner because he was very angry all the time. . . . I couldn't respond to it because I had never been allowed to express it or respond to it. . . . The biggest transformation in my life was finding my voice and being able to stand up and use it, to know why I'm angry, to name that. Far too often we recognize anger but we don't recognize the cause, we're that far removed from ourselves. . . .

I've spent all my life swallowing; I'm not swallowing anymore. I don't like [it]. It tastes horrible and that's it. No! No! No!

Jackie had to transform her anger into a constructive force because she experienced it as unmanageable and potentially destructive.

That kind of anger [unfocused, destructive anger] is something that holds you back, that immobilizes you. If you're using it in a negative way, if it's affecting the quality of your life today, then it's not to your benefit. . . . I could go through life being really pissed off at the people from my childhood and . . . my husband, focus all my energy into really being angry at these people, or I could take that energy and channel it into making change for the future. I know that I can't change what happened to me. I can't change my past, but I can change the world for my children, so if I make one change that's one change they don't have to make. . . . I was immobilized by my feelings and I knew that's not the way that I could be doing the work that I wanted to do, so if you take those feelings and direct them, you take your anger and make the changes.

The kinds of subjective changes that women achieved differed among participants. In constructing an alternative sense of self, Paola challenged the concept of "woman," rejecting the social role of woman as primary caregiver and redefining caregiving as appropriate and necessary for both men and women in various family and social forms. She also challenged a definition of professionals as all-knowing experts on women's lives, thus reproducing women's roles as fixers and caretakers. For Jackie, subjective change meant redefining herself as a woman and a mother, and a recognition of the need for a world that truly values women and children. In such a world, the illusion of choice for women would not mean a "choice" to survive and stick it out for the sake of the children. Like Jackie, the majority of participants emphasized that if they had access to the resources they needed to sustain their families, the rhetoric about society's concern about their children's well-being would not ring hollow. Jackie pointed to the importance of recognizing how a social world based on a gender hierarchy denigrates women's strength and spirit:

> When they talk about women and women's safety . . . you need to be, too, thinking about their spirit, the importance of the spiritual part of a woman, the inner strength. And society has just pushed it all down. [If] you go out to work, you're not being a good mom because you're not there when your kids come home from school—you're not there to nurture them. If you stay home you're a welfare bum and you can eat bologna and tuna sandwiches. Oh God! Women that you see that are shut down, those are the ones that have been spiritually wounded and how [do] you get them back from there and get the twinkle back into their eyes and the vitality?

Participants reclaimed and reconstructed the self in different ways. Although it is difficult to define the exact nature of the relationship between changes in consciousness and identity, the deconstruction of old forms of consciousness and the (re)construction of identity are inextricably linked. Teresa de Lauretis (1990) conceptualizes these processes as "a series of successive displacements" (p. 136).[5] "Each configuration of identity is examined in its contradiction and deconstructed but not simply discarded: instead, it is consciously assumed in a transformative 'rewriting of herself in relation to shifting interpersonal and political contexts'" (p. 136). The work of self-deconstruction and reconstruction does not simply involve discarding pieces of the self that were conflictual and disempowering but appropriating them into the self with new understanding.

In summary, the nature and depth of resolution to contradiction, conflict, and internalized oppression that each woman achieved differed according to the ways in which she made sense of it, the degree of pain elicited, and the particular stage of her own development. To reclaim and reconstruct the self, women had to claim and integrate into the self the very knowledge that had caused them pain in unsettling their notions of identity. Becoming aware of their own, "often unwitting, collusion in clinging, even against [their] will, to old invisible paradigms" (Schuster and Van Dyne, 1985, p. 170), the insights gained through analysis of the production of experience exacted a greater commitment to critical self-questioning and resisting oppression.

The degree of changes in subjectivity that participants were able to make depended on a number of factors that came together to forge an environment conducive to confronting contradiction and conflict, recognizing the social organization of their lives, letting go of old paradigms that constrained their forward movement, and undertaking risk, pain, and change. Participants required environments that supported them in giving up old ways of being, growing into new ways, and confronting the consequences of stepping outside the status quo.

WOMEN'S COLLECTIVE ACTION: KNOWLEDGE, CONSCIOUSNESS, AND TRANSFORMATIONS OF IDENTITY

The sixth theme concerns the relation between changes in women's consciousness and subjectivity and their participation in different forms of collective action for social change. Each participant constructed her story around a central thread of meaning that was rooted in her specific history and shaped by a tapestry of discursive and material conditions, events, moments, and significant others. This central thread of meaning making about her experiences of abuse was connected to her desire to participate in collective action.

Although I did not find clear, linear stages of politicization or one homogeneous entry point into collective action for the women I interviewed, I did identify a nexus where changes in women's subjectivity intersected with opportunities for collective struggle. The impetus for women's action arose from the convergence of several factors: (1) their desire to make sense of their experience and work through the contradiction and conflict they faced; (2) the meaning that they made of their personal experience of abuse and violence by drawing on the feminist/antioppressive discourses available to them, including an analysis of the politics of their subordination; (3) their desire to grow and develop various new, subjugated, and repressed aspects of themselves and their access to opportunities and spaces where they could do this; (4) their desire to speak out and resist oppressive relations and structures; and (5) their connection with feminist and women's organizations and groups and their access to different avenues of collective action. In the following discussion, I will give an example of each of these.

June had always wondered about contradictions she experienced in her life, for example, why her life as a girl differed from her brother's life. After residency in shelters and second-stage housing, she became aware of a series of unanswered questions. This time she was ready to look at them.

> The questions started coming up, all the questions that had been there for years. How come I got turned down for that job because I might go and get pregnant someday? Then I started really, really asking the questions and asking them openly of myself and saying, What's happening? Why did this happen to me? . . . to her? Why can't I do this . . . and that? . . . I guess all the questions were there, and I started looking at the history of my life and how I'd always been asking these questions but always thinking there was never gonna be an answer for them, that that was just the way it was. I started thinking, why is that just the way it is? I don't think I like that and what can I do about that?

When Ruth was driving to college to begin her program, she had a vision of herself in a circle looking outward at her experiences of abuse (sexual abuse by her foster father, rape by neighbors, and abuse by her partner), and knew that one day she would speak out against injustice. Drawing on antiracist and feminist discourses, she made meaning of her personal experiences of racism, abuse, and violence:

> I think it's not a matter of unforgiveness, it's the justice and what they've even done to my own cousins. And who's accountable for my cousin who hung herself because of the abuse? And then I think of my sister before she died, how she would say to me, "you're a woman warrior" and she was very proud that I could do something about it, whereas she had fear [of people who would hurt her if she spoke out]. I think about all that, too, and women that have come through these things have to stand up for that. . . . To me, I've been silent so many

years, so many deaf years, so now that I've come a long way in my healing journey, you know people need to hear that, too. Because it's like going back to the first shelter I was in—it was by sitting there listening to others [talk] about their past, about their abuse, that brought me out of my shell too and made me look inwardly.

Ruth honored and fortified the early resistance that she had expressed as a young girl when she told classmates to stop calling her names. In reclaiming her identity as an Ojibwa woman, she refused to accept the burden of a society that can only know itself by constructing an Other (Hall, 1991). Ruth's commitment to telling her story and acting on her knowledge is echoed in the message of Andrea Benton Rushing (1993). Hearing other women's stories of struggle and survival gave Ruth, like Rushing, the courage to tell her own, adding it to the "frayed pieces of the patchwork quilt" (p. 139). Ruth hopes that other women will benefit from her witness.

Heather's engagement in collective action not only provided opportunities to challenge the systems but also to develop new and subjugated aspects of herself. During her residency in second-stage housing, staff there reinforced her growing sense that she was a human being, supporting her desire to know herself better, stay away from partners who were not good for her, and make a better life for herself and her children.

I got real angry. . . . I just kinda thought . . . take this anger and refocus it and really challenge the way these systems are working because they're not working for women. I don't know who the hell they're working for, but they're sure not working for us women. . . . When I left [second-stage housing] I really felt like I was abandoning something. Part of me wanted to stay. I think that's why I started getting involved, and I started doing all the work that I do . . . It's because I didn't feel like I wanted to abandon something that I felt was so vital and valuable. It gave me something so vital and valuable. . . . Another part of that is that I don't want my own children to grow up in the life that I had. I want my children to know that they have rights and choices, whether they're male [or] female. . . . Doing the work, it's stimulating, it gives me a lot of energy. It gives me a lot of hope. . . . It means change, it means support for myself and others, it means strength. . . . I just really see myself being one hell of a fighter. I'm not giving up being in a lot of people's faces and making them answer to and for a lot of women. . . . This is what we've lived through every day. This is what we experience every day. This is my life.

Jackie became involved in collective action because she wanted to speak out about the injustices that had happened to her, especially about the power that FCS and other professionals had exercised over her life. Her work for change was a way to resist her oppression.

That's where my passion is . . . I want to be right there in their faces. . . . I'm a survivor and I don't have a "kick me" sign on my back, and for them to realize that society set me up for those things to happen to me. I was a female, I was poor, society set me up, so society owes me the opportunity to be able to get myself back up to where I should be. Well, you'll never be the person that you're supposed to be, but you know what I mean, to be the best that I can be. . . . There's still a lot of work to be done . . . the faces change but the stories don't change. When is this going to end? When are people finally going to get the answer, that no, it's not about pointing the finger at what is wrong with her? . . . When is society going to see exactly what's wrong with society, quit victim blaming and asking those questions that do the same thing?

It is difficult to differentiate the changes in subjectivity that occurred as women engaged in communities of struggle. Jackie's confidence and determination grew as she learned more about working for change. Part of this change involved confronting fears of being labeled or misjudged by others.

The first time I took part in political action and I picketed, I was really scared. I thought, oh my God, they're going to come . . . arrest me and . . . put me in jail . . . I think, now here I am with my picket sign and two months from now I am going to be looking for a job, and these people in the community are going to remember my face. I'm that troublemaker from in front of [the MP's] office. But do you know what? I don't give a shit. . . . I'm not going to let them take that away from me. What is happening is wrong and I'm making a stand.

Politicizing the personal and participating in collective action provided her with opportunities to develop different aspects of subjectivity, part of which was a sense of identity rooted in resistance. This resistance, consciously articulated, became part of who she was.

While attending a support group, Donna learned about her neighbors' complicity with her grandfather's abuse. Donna's anger, "grounded in a personal and collective sense of self-worth" (Culley, 1985, p. 216), was a critical source of energy (Lorde, 1984; Culley, 1985). When she was ready to use her anger at complicity as an energy source, she could readily identify an avenue for action in the group's wishes to form a sexual assault self-help action group to educate high school students about abuse.

I guess it was my anger, like once I found out that my neighbors knew what my grandfather was like. . . . Half the town knew what he was like. . . . Then you could see through the whole system, like the blindness. . . . It made me so angry. . . . It was my way of fighting back, and I'm still fighting. . . . All this was going on. It's been known for so long and people admit it. Yes, it [sexual abuse] destroys lives, and yet it's like, so what! . . . It's fighting the ignorance. . . . It was the fact that it doesn't have to happen. . . . It made me so angry 'cause I don't want anyone feeling and going through this. . . . I don't feel I should have gone through this. It's just not right. . . . Everyone is allowing it to happen and I hold everyone responsible. I guess that's why I'm being so vocal about it. I had always wanted to act but in a group I could act and do something.

Rather than perceiving her anger as something "dangerous to the social order" (Briskin, 1990, p. 19), Donna could see it as a healthy response to injustice. She became an activist and advocate with the local shelter and second-stage housing through the connections she made as a member of the action group.

In her research with survivors of sexual violence, Liz Kelly (1988) found evidence of a process of personal politicization (women's questioning of men's power and their commitment to personal independence) as well as evidence of a wider political perspective (women suggested that men's violence could be prevented through changing society, gender relations, and the organization of the family, and educating women and children, thus enhancing their individual survival). However, the majority of women in her study did not become involved in collective action. They did not perceive feminism as a framework for analysis, support, and action, and most had no contact with or knowledge of feminism, feminist services, or feminists.

For the women I interviewed, feminist/antioppressive discourses and social spaces were critical to their process of becoming involved in collective action. Integral to participants' engagement in collective action was the fact that they were already connected, in various ways, to women's communities and social spaces when they decided to take action. Women knew about and belonged to networks and communities and therefore identified with feminist/antioppressive frameworks for analysis, support, and collective action directed at ending violence against women. For example, June lived in second-stage housing where she participated in a feminist educational group, and then moved to cooperative housing where she met other socially conscious people. There she joined others to demand decent, affordable housing for abused women and children. It had been over four years from the time she had recognized that she was being abused to the time of her involvement in the antiviolence movement.

For the majority of participants, this route was typical of their involvement in collective action. In general, as women felt comfortable in community and learned about themselves, they were also learning about the social organization of their lives. When they felt moved to work for change, they could identify where this was possible, and they already had some background and preparation for it. Their desire to act on their knowledge arose out of these circumstances. Therefore, women's previous involvement in these communities was critical to both their process of politicization and becoming involved in collective struggle.

Two participants deviated from this pattern. Barbara had attended a number of educational support groups for victims of incest. Upon invitation of the staff, she became involved in the work of a feminist organization, providing support for other women in their healing process. After gaining confidence in her abilities, she engaged in many of the organization's community efforts to better women's lives. Jackie's situation also differed. After leaving the shelter in the town where she relocated, she experienced a spiritual moment and immediately knew that she would be "one of those persons that will make the changes." She went to therapy for a year and then began to speak publicly about the barriers she faced in seeking help and rebuilding her life. When she joined the work of second-stage housing some time later, Jackie developed an explicit political perspective, making connections between her life and the lives of other women, particularly poor women.

For participants such as Jackie, her commitment to social justice formed an integral part of who she was. She has been active in the struggle against violence against women for ten years. For participants beginning their involvement, their learning and action may translate into a long-term personal and/or social commitment to change. Most likely, continued involvement will depend on many factors, for example, their paid and unpaid work lives, financial circumstances, poverty and discrimination, the availability of child care, the political dangers and risks of participation, risks of loss of family and community, the inclusiveness of women's organizations, opportunities for growth, and organizational structures that make survivors' repetoires of knowledge an integral part of their functioning and programming. The forms and intensity of personal and social commitments may change over time, ebbing and flowing over personal and historic time.

Susan Gadbois's (1999) study of women's experiences after leaving a shelter is important to consider here. She found that women leaving a shelter identified feelings of abandonment, and the support they received there diminished or ended upon leaving it. Participants in this study especially valued and benefited from the relationships and social networks they were able to maintain after their residency in second-stage housing or participation in educational programs and support groups. These relationships helped them affirm their self-worth and connections to their larger worlds. A community development and capacity-building approach that encourages connections and solidarity among women may be especially beneficial in helping women reestablish themselves in their communities.

Participants' previous involvement in therapy, support groups, self-help groups, and feminist educational programs requires discussion here. Ten of the eleven participants had belonged to some kind of feminist educational program or support group (for woman abuse or childhood sexual abuse). Paola, the only participant who had not participated in such a program or group, had been a member of a feminist group in her social work program. Some participants had taken courses on woman abuse and initiated self-study on women's issues. Six women attended educational programs and support groups while residents of second-stage housing, and two participated in short-term groups in shelters. Five participants undertook individual therapy. Of these, two began therapy after learning about systemic oppression and violence, and three had been in therapy while they were elaborating a political understanding of their situation.

Only one participant attended therapy that was nonfeminist. Liz Kelly (1988) emphasized that women must have access to a name with which to describe their experiences. But access to a name does not necessarily mean that women's experiences will be located in a social and political context. In retrospect, Donna concluded that while her therapy helped her immensely, she was disappointed that the therapist attributed all her difficulties to the abuse she suffered rather than to a combination of oppressive elements in her life as a poor woman. He had also reinforced the idea that she could not cope adequately with reality (Hutchinson and McDaniel, 1986).

> I know when I started into therapy I was dealing with it, that I was a rare case. . . . It bothers me that the therapeutic process says, "This is normal everyday life." Well, if this is normal everyday life and if every female is going through this, I think it's time, 'cause this isn't right! . . . Therapists say, "This is

normal, you just don't cope with it" . . . like you have to learn to cope with the world—it's not these jerks out there that are creating real issues for you . . . I still get that. It's like, well, gee!

Later, she also realized that staff at the shelter and second-stage housing affirmed her anger at the gendered dimensions of woman abuse, while her therapist encouraged her to discharge her anger in private within the four walls of his office or her home.

In her analysis of the depoliticization of feminist discourse on incest, Louise Armstrong (1994) points out that to "shift the focus to women's self-rehabilitation can only lead to a victim-blaming theology that says that those who (allow themselves to) suffer violences need only learn to love themselves" (p. 211). This is a critical point in any discussion of how women come to understand their situation differently. In telling their stories, two participants sometimes emphasized women's psychosocial construction, or what is often called their vulnerability to abuse, to the exclusion of social and material conditions, as if women's psychosocial construction constituted the source of their oppression. While we must examine how our personal beliefs contribute to our own disempowerment, we also need to clearly emphasize the social, political, and economic realities of our lives and how these realities structure and condone violence against women. This piece of critical understanding was what feminist/antioppressive ways of seeing offered to participants.

For participants, making sense of their lives and belonging to women's communities were simultaneous, mutually illuminating processes. Women learned about themselves, grew, and made changes in their lives through their engagement in collective action. Through working for change, women can grow and deepen their critical analysis, what Paulo Freire (1994) calls praxis—action and reflection. These experiences can themselves produce changes in women's consciousness and subjectivity. As Sasha Roseneil (1995) states, "the challenging and reconstruction of consciousness and identity are both the medium and the outcome of feminist politics" (p. 136). Engaging with others in ways that build collaborative, respectful relationships and communities can contribute to women's process of personal growth and conscientization, and continue to illuminate what is required for social justice.

Rosario recognized that both her silence and her action were connected to the well-being of other women. She took up what Sandra Butler (1995) calls the "the burden of witness," recognizing one's own oppression and the pain of others' oppression.

> What I've learned more than anything is not to keep quiet. To the extent that we talk about our issues and I learn more about myself, I can help others. . . . To keep quiet is a comfortable way of saying, "I've resolved my problems and I'm not inter-ested in those of others." . . . At this point I feel that I have to speak out because it makes me very angry, and when it hap-pens to other women, I feel as if it is happening to me. I feel her pain too. I feel that we have an obligation to help each other because if we don't do anything, if each of us resolves our problem and we stay inside our homes, then it's something that's never going to stop. I might have a daughter and it might happen to her. I have a son and I feel that my conscientization has helped me to raise him differently, because the ideas that I had before were very different than the ones I have now.

I found that what participants in this study claimed most was knowledge. What engaged them was the act of learning and articu-lating how the world was fundamentally organized in unjust ways: constructs of masculinity and femininity that were bound up with violence against women; racism that shaped both white and aborigi-nal identities; institutions that sanctioned their subordination; and systems that denied them resources. As Chandra Mohanty (1994) states, "knowledge, the very act of knowing, is related to the power of self-definition" (p. 147). Women's knowledge gave them a sense of power with which to speak out and act. For example, for Paola, combining her knowledge about community organizing in Chile with her analysis of systemic violence gave her the power to act.

> Yeah, the bird that burns down and then comes up [the phoe-nix]. . . . My life has been in pieces and in such destruction and from it I've been able to build another life. . . . There are pieces of my life that have died and I mourn, I really grieve them, but

at the same time I had to get rid of those dead parts in order to grow new ones, and so it has meant a lot of work and changing and I think also it has been very determining in terms of my work here with women. The whole experience that I brought from working in Chile with the organizations, I think, gave me an understanding of women's issues. . . . It was so much easier since I had some basic understanding already of social issues in general, to just understand, to put them together, to put the two of them together. . . . It's been also important to honor my own way of survival of many kinds of violence.

In her organizing work with women, Paola has been able "to rescue pieces" of her past life, reconstructing from them a part of herself linking the past and present. Her power to act is part of her larger struggle for "humanity," mindful that when she needed help, it was a friend of hers, a male co-worker, who helped her when female friends were unable to do so.

My reading of women's stories suggests that politicizing the personal helped participants understand themselves and their lives in ways that bridge the dichotomy between feelings and action for social transformation, between the realm of the personal and the sphere of the political, and between healing and social change. Participants' stories are testimonies to the possibilities of transformative learning for survivors of abuse. "The language of healing and the language of political change and solidarity need not be mutually exclusive. Healing can and does take place within the language of solidarity, collective resistance, and social change" (Profitt, 1996, p. 35).

June's words illuminate a possible relation between women's singular histories and their collective work, and between self-recovery and social transformation:

I think when we think of healing . . . we think about the spirit that's been wounded by the belief that you're less than human . . . that you don't deserve anything different than what's been handed to you, and I think those wounds are very deep . . . wounds to the soul and spirit from violence. . . . Political action can be part of a healing process. . . . But it's not just about healing, that's not why you should do it. That [healing] can be sort of a subconsequence [of political action], but I don't think that's why we do it. . . . Being a political activist can also be a very painful thing to do. . . . It's swimming upstream. . . . When you become political as a woman . . . the people who supported you when you were doing all your womanly duties aren't going to like you as a politician . . . and being politically active is going to make you change a lot. . . . It's solidarity among women that heals those kinds of soul wounds, realizing that there are many others with you, and not that I believe every woman is my sister . . . but I think there are women out there that we can be sisters with and it's that that heals the wounds to the soul, making connections with other women . . . healing as effecting change.

In summary, my study demonstrates that the processes through which women move from individual survival to collective action are much more complex and tenuous than the feminist social work and related interdisciplinary literature suggests. My findings suggest that we need to take into account a number of points: (1) the process of becoming conscious of and making sense of contradictions and conflict takes place over substantial amounts of time; (2) women require sustained engagement with feminist/antioppressive discourses and liberatory social spaces in order to politicize their personal experience, work through resistance to knowledge, and develop a political analysis of women's oppression; (3) consciousness-raising has significant implications for changes in women's values, identities, and habits of being, and can be a threatening as well as liberatory process; and (4) women experience significant gains as well as risks in their processes of transformation, pointing to the need for communities that support women's personal growth and deepening political analysis.

Chapter 6

Finding the Self in Other: Reflections on a Researcher's Life

REFLEXIVITY IN FEMINIST RESEARCH

Feminist theorists and researchers have emphasized how a researcher's own politics and experiences, rather than constituting a hindrance to inquiry, can, if engaged reflexively, contribute in significant ways to the production of knowledge (Klein, 1983; Fonow and Cook, 1991; Mies, 1983; Olesen, 1994; Stanley, 1990). Both reflexivity (Fonow and Cook, 1991; Stanley, 1990) and transparency (Klein, 1983) are hallmarks of feminist research. Reflexivity means that we include ourselves in what is being studied. Transparency means revealing who we are and how our location shapes the research process (Klein, 1983). Through ongoing reflection about all aspects of the research process, we strive for self-consciousness about how our values permeate our research, and the nature of the nonexploitive relations we develop with research participants (Fonow and Cook, 1991; Reinharz, 1992; Stanley, 1990). Janice Ristock and Joan Pennell (1996) suggest that reflexivity in feminist research includes reflecting on the assumptions underlying our perceptions and bases for decisions, the aims and impact of our research and the ways in which it is and is not empowering for participants, and how we adjust research methods and practices to reflect learning from our community and our own observations. Reflexivity, then, involves the researcher's engagement with herself as an active producer of the research (Stanley and Wise, 1993).

Early in the feminist research literature, Maria Mies (1983) argued that since feminist women researchers experience a double consciousness as both oppressed and privileged, they "must deliberately and courageously integrate their repressed, unconscious female subjectivity, i.e., their own experience of oppression and discrimination into the research process" (p. 121). Sandra Harding (1987) points to the difficulties involved in examining how our locations and identities as researchers inform and shape the research process, but she ultimately affirms that our "fragmented identities" can be a "rich source of feminist insight" if we try to understand how they inform the research process (p. 8). Thus, consciousness about our own locations, subjectivities, and the narratives we construct about the research we do is a key component in feminist and empowerment research (Ristock and Pennell, 1996).

Renate Rosaldo (1993) aptly observes that "All interpretations are provisional; they are made by positioned subjects who are prepared to know certain things and not others" (p. 8). If feminist research is concerned with " 'the discourse of possibility' implicit within the constructed nature of social experience" (Kincheloe and McLaren, 1994, p. 139), by definition the researcher must examine how she opens and closes off possibilities of understanding based on her own politics, experience, and exercise of power. In this study I monitored this by attending to and critically interrogating the psychic dynamics and emotions that I experienced during the research process. Extensive journal writing on my personal journey constituted part of my "intellectual autobiography," that is, documentation of the processes by which understanding and conclusions are reached (Stanley and Wise, 1993, p. 189).

In this chapter I examine a small piece of the personal journey I undertook while seeking to understand the processes through which survivors of woman abuse made sense of their experiences of violence, abuse, poverty, and racism, and became engaged in collective action for social change. I will describe how my own process of politicization unfolded in relation to the repressed issue of complicity with the status quo in women's stories, and analyze the meaning of the psychic dynamics and emotions that occurred in my life as a researcher. I will argue that my interpretation of the interview texts was ultimately tied up with what I was willing and able to hear, and that only by recognizing and working through issues of silence, shame, and responsibility in my own life was I able to constructively consider these issues in the lives of the women I interviewed, and ultimately, in my public writing about them. Feminist researchers need to carefully attend to their own personal narratives as they conduct their research, ever alert to the possibility of unearthing repressed issues in need of a voice.

I am aware that my desire to share my personal journey as a researcher transgresses the boundaries of the speakable more or less set out by academia and by my profession. As Kathleen Rockhill (1987b) points out, "the body, the emotional, the private and the personal are systematically and sometimes tragically eliminated from the world of legitimate academic performance" (p. 14). Certainly, academic forums and forms of expression, at least in dominant culture, reinforce the fear of speaking the truth and challenging authority, and this fear is especially intense when speaking about experiences of violence. My understanding of the dichotomies that have been constructed between the academic and personal worlds, the speakable and the unspeakable, does not render the vulnerability that I feel in discussing the personal realm any less potent.

MY JOURNEY THROUGH
THE RESEARCH PROCESS

I experienced a variety of emotions and reactions during the data collection and interpretation phases of my research. Listening to women tell their stories, I was deeply moved by their pain, determination, and fighting spirit. Early on, I became aware of one of the effects of conducting qualitative interviews with survivors of woman abuse. I began to experience some of the very processes that participants described in their sense-making journey. For example, some women recounted that when they first named their experiences of violation as abuse, they were inundated with memories of childhood abuse. For me, the faces of women who had sought refuge at places where I had worked passed incessantly before me. Remembering was painful: the woman whose military husband had sewn parts of her genitals together with a needle and thread; a woman of eighty who felt that the pervasive sense of worthlessness she had experienced all her life condemned her to endure beatings from her son; the woman whose husband had beaten her so badly that she could not get up from the cot where he had thrown her, and since he claimed that she was no better than a dog, he threw her out on the front lawn and left her there in the rain until a neighbor arrived and carried her inside.

In telling their stories, participants also told how, upon critically remembering the details of their lives, they had attempted to turn away from revisiting the past. I, too, actively tried to forget experiences in my own life, how when I was a child, my great-uncle, a minister and a well-respected member of the community, would accost us under the pretense of tickling. Even then I knew that if I did not get out of his grasp without exposing what he was doing, I would be dismissed by others with an admonishment to stop being "so foolish." At that young age, I sensed with a heavy, dull feeling that if we were to say anything, we would be the problem, the unfit, the shamed. The privilege of hearing participants' stories evoked these reactions and, while they furnished additional insight into women's change processes, I was unprepared for the intensity of the effect I experienced.

Of course, one might anticipate that listening to women's experiences of oppression and resistance would evoke powerful and painful feelings, and that one might need to give voice to them. My wish here, however, is to recount and analyze another process, the process of dismantling a psychic defense which, as it was much more complex, affected what I was willing and able to see and hear in the interview texts. Defense mechanisms are "constructs that denote a way of functioning of the mind" while "defenses . . . are the specific behaviors, affects, or ideas, that serve defensive purposes" (Wallerstein, 1985, p. 222). Although defense mechanisms, as theoretical abstractions, cannot be conscious, "defense behaviors—that is, behaviors that serve defensive purposes—may be conscious or unconscious" (Cramer, 1991, p. 4).

Early in the interpretation phase, I experienced a disturbing sense of disconnection with the texts and a reluctance to interpret them. Part of this reluctance was justifiably rooted in my fear of reinscribing power relations between myself as a white, privileged woman from a working-class background and the "Other," that is, participants less privileged than I was. As a witness to and participant in acts of "othering" in my shelter work, the haste with which we workers set ourselves apart from "battered women," I feared reproducing classist and racist stereotypes of women who had been abused. In my journal, I had also noted something else, perhaps related to this reluctance: my desire for women's stories to constitute perfect examples of an enviable critical consciousness and impassioned commitment to social justice. Surprised, I asked why this was so.

Although I did move forward in interpreting women's stories, my angst continued as I sought to disentangle and make sense of a complex set of issues in the texts. My journal writing at that time reveals a nagging feeling that I was still analyzing them uncritically. For example, participants had described how, in developing a feminist understanding of their experiences of abuse, they had arrived at a place of self-acceptance, self-valuation, and self-empathy. This was expressed as "realizing that I was a human being" or "realizing that I deserved respect," what Paulo Freire (1994) identified as "becoming a person." Participants had come to realize that they were not responsible for everything that had happened to them, including the violations that they had suffered. At the same time, however, some participants, in coming to terms with their past, declared that "there never was anything wrong with me" or "I was doing exactly what women are supposed to do." Although these women's realization that they were human beings was a powerful factor in transforming subjectivity, I suspected that claims such as "there was nothing wrong with me" signified something different than their insight into oppressive realities. Something here did not quite fit, but I was unable to grasp it.

My journal writing at that time clearly reflects my intuition that a deeper issue was present, both in women's claims that "it was just the way it was" and in my personal story. What was telling at this point was that as I tried to distinguish among internalized oppression, complicity, and unconscious investment in the status quo, issues present in women's stories, I experienced my mind going numb and a "blanking out" whenever I undertook this task. How, I asked, was women's profound sense of "being wrong," which was transformed by their realization that they were human beings, related to internalized oppression, complicity with relations of domination, and shifting structures of identity? In my journal, I had posed these questions: Have I overidentified with women's struggles? Where am I in all of this? What has happened to me?

I began to suspect that my inability to clearly name and sort out these issues had more to do with psychological resistance than with obtuseness on my part. How was my personal story affecting my ambivalence about examining women's internalized oppression and investment in oppressive social norms, whether conscious or unconscious? Ultimately, a colleague commented directly on what she saw as my unwillingness to critically examine women's stories. Her observation effectively broke through my immobilization and resistance to knowing. My resistance to directly facing the issue of complicity, responsibility, and accountability in women's stories had at least partial roots in my personal story. It had taken just over ten months to break through my defenses. For me, interpreting women's texts and dismantling my resistance to knowledge about my own life were parallel, intertwined, and equally critical processes.

CONFRONTATION WITH THE UNNAMED AND REFLECTIONS ON THE SELF

The repressed and unnamed issue that I identified in women's stories was their failure to examine their own investment in the status quo. To confront this issue in their stories would mean that I would need to face my own painful feelings, memories, and realities if I was to work through this impasse. As Robert Wallerstein (1985) clarifies, "resistance is a defense against insight" (p. 147). In naming the repressed and unnamed issue, I was speaking the unspeakable, an act that elicited feelings of guilt and betrayal. I felt as if I was betraying not only the participants in my study but also a significant other, my mother. As it does to many victims of violence, that feeling of being wrong, the terror of being exposed as wrong and/or bad, contributed to my unwillingness to see and speak, compounding the silence of what I could not name.

After the resistance was broken, however, I faced the painful task of examining the silence that surrounded different facets of my mother's life. As Kathryn Church (1995) suggests, silences are often significant in speaking and writing because they point to places in "thought/feeling which require transformation or are in the process of being transformed" (p. 100). The defended content, then, reveals a clear relationship between the degree of repressed pain and resistance to insight. To critically examine the discourses through which participants made sense of their unconscious complicity with the status quo was to look directly at my mother's investment in it and its effects on her, on me, on all of her children. Her adherence to oppressive gender norms and practices profoundly shaped us as girls, particularly in our adolescent years. This act of knowing, laden with visceral emotion, made explicit the knowledge that she had failed me, a rebellious daughter. If the act of speaking about these issues threatens to overwhelm us with grief, hurt, and rage, how can we come to speak the words "mother," "daughter," "complicity," and "oppression" in a way that, while still provoking a resonance that is highly emotive, allows us compassion for and insight into our lives as mothers and daughters?

Connected to my analysis of my mother's investment in the status quo was my own confrontation with my complicity with the status quo. I recalled how I had been invested in discourses of "helping" third world women, arrogantly thinking that our role as community workers from a "developed" country was to empower them. I also recalled how dominant representations of "woman" had formed part of my identity and way of being in intimate relations. As I remembered the feelings and sensations that had burned through me when I became aware of internalized oppression and domination, I relived it, this time consciously facing and articulating the nature of this shame. Because shame is often experienced as feelings that have no name (Bartky, 1990), I began to comprehend its power as corrosive and undermining, demanding concealment and producing isolation. For this reason, shame as an emotion rooted in pain must be contextualized in order to understand it, work with it, and transform its power as a profoundly disempowering emotion.

CRITICAL ANALYSIS OF THE PROCESS OF UNCOVERING THE REPRESSED

The unnamed, women's failure to examine their own investment in oppressive relations, is shrouded in silence and shame. My own silence concerning my mother's life mirrored the silence and apprehensiveness in feminist discourse about women's complicity with the status quo. As feminists we must begin to address this issue in discourse about woman abuse and about child neglect and abuse by mothers. Why are we reluctant to address this issue? "Why is shame, not about abuse, but about one's complicity with a patriarchal and misogynist worldview that blames women for male violence, the unnameable here? Why is complicity with abuse and the resulting shame the repressed issue?" (Elliot, 1998).

There are several reasons for this. In my situation, I found it troubling to look at my mother's complicity with the status quo because it evoked strong emotions and painful memories of growing up as a girl child. Thinking of her as brainwashed and molded by oppressive forces was more comforting to me than acknowledging her complicity, a much more emotionally exacting endeavor. How was it possible or even thinkable to speak about responsibility and accountability when I knew that my mother had been hurt by her oppression as a woman? For me, this question is the most difficult one to grapple with in sorting out issues of responsibility and accountability in conditions not of our own making.

Patricia Elliot (1998) suggests three reasons why complicity with abuse and the resulting shame is the repressed issue. The first reason is that "we often do not trust our gut feelings, particularly when and if they indicate something unethical" (Elliot, 1998). Some part of us, at some level, may know that we were complicit and we feel ashamed because ultimately we know that we are accountable to ourselves and to other women for this complicity (Elliot, 1998). We do not want to admit our complicity to others, partly because of our shame, and this is particularly so when there is no safe context or place to do so.

The second reason is that we often confuse responsibility with blame (Elliot, 1998). Responsibility can mean a sense of obligation and duty, being accountable for the care of another, personal accountability, considering ourselves answerable for our behavior, and being capable of making moral decisions on our own, and therefore accountable to others. Responsibility has to do with the way we respond to events in our lives (Elliot, 1998). Depending on the circumstances, we may or may not associate blame with our responses to particular situations, in the sense that we see ourselves at fault or as the source or cause of something. Being condemned or blamed by others for something can reinforce the association of our responses with blame. Particularly now, given the current anti-feminist climate, we may be hesitant to raise issues that could be construed as woman-blaming. This may hinder us from naming issues of responsibility and accountability in oppression and victimization.

The third reason why complicity with abuse and the resulting shame is the repressed issue has to do with "the lure of positive thinking, or the desire to vindicate the oppressed [which] leads us to minimize (if not repress) the negative or complicit or inadequate responses of the oppressed" (Elliot, 1998). For me, this desire to vindicate the oppressed, my mother in my case, was intense. I believe that this desire has silently, but firmly, shaped over a long-term period, my reluctance to directly examine this issue in feminist theorizing. If this reluctance is experienced by other feminist social workers, which I suspect it may be, this suggests the need for a compassionate feminist approach to exploring these issues. Such an approach may enable us to speak more openly about the personal/political investments we all make in our identities and the meanings we ascribe to our experiences (Lewis, 1990).

Our minimization or repression of the inadequate responses of the oppressed sometimes correlates with the adoption of the perspective of the victim. In her discussion of perspectives on responsibility and choice in situations of oppression and victimization, Susan Wendell (1993) states that the perspective of the victim acknowledges the oppressor's responsibility in situations of oppression and assigns blame to the oppressor. However, this perspective recognizes "little or no responsibility of the victim for her/his victimization" (p. 28). Although it is important to recognize the reality of women's victimization and that perspectives on choice and responsibility are fluid and multiple, this perspective sometimes hides the choices and power, albeit limited, that we do have in our lives. Such a perspective may position women as "unwitting, unaccountable, and therefore dehumanized, objects of other's [sic] actions. . . . As long as feminist discourses of woman abuse continue to adopt the perspective of the victim . . . we will not be able to examine our investment in our identities, our complicity with abuse, and our failure to be accountable to ourselves and to other women" (Elliot, 1998). I believe that we would benefit from a more holistic perspective that both recognizes our victimization and the power and choices, however limited in any particular situation, that we had, and do have, to respond to oppressive forces in our lives. Responsible action (Wendell, 1993) that forges radical, progressive change requires that we acknowledge our own investments in our identities, choices, and responsibilities as well as our accountability to ourselves and others.

DIRECTIONS FOR FEMINIST
SOCIAL WORK RESEARCH

"What we are able to learn from our research is surely tied into what we are willing and able to hear" (Elliot, 1998). Indeed, "the process of social enquiry is not complete while silence exists around the places where it has rubbed the research raw" (Church, 1995, p. 128). Our willingness and ability to see and hear important issues will, to a great extent, determine what shall and shall not be spoken about in public accounts of our research. In my experience, the interrogation of my emotions and psychic dynamics and the interpretation of interview texts were mutually illuminating and constitutive processes, fraught with ambivalence, hope, and fear. Ambivalence characterizes resistance because resistance involves a struggle between insight and the blocking of insight (Rangell, 1985). Contained in this struggle lies the hope that insight will become conscious, contributing to self-knowledge and the possibility of knowledge about others. My efforts to understand, explain, and reexplain my experiences as a researcher, sustained over a period of time, intersected with other factors in my life to ultimately dismantle my resistance to knowing and coax insight into consciousness.

Kathleen Rockhill (1987b) suggests using the power of our subjectivity to determine what is and is not significant in our research. She describes how, in reanalyzing a prior research project with women, she drew upon her own experiences of violence and came to see the power dynamics that had framed her original project and previous analysis. In this analysis she had not addressed the devastating effects of men's violence on women's education for literacy. Rockhill advocates that "we must learn how to use our subjective formation more effectively, politically, educationally and in our research" (p. 13).

For me, this does not mean narcissistically or egocentrically focusing on our individual subjectivity. Rather, it means recognizing that although pain is often experienced as purely personal, it can have significant political meaning (Findlay, n.d.). As Linda Carty (1991) clarifies, the recounting of experiences, while seemingly personal, has political relevance, providing insight into the way that structures and relations of power are reproduced. I believe that we need a framework as well as an arena in which to talk about reflexivity and explore more fully how the complexity of struggles with our subjectivities shapes and affects our research.

As a researcher, I believe that part of the challenge is to use my subjectivity as a point of departure for understanding how I open and close off possibilities of understanding the complexity and depth of issues in women's lives as well as in my own. Michele Fine (1994) suggests "working the hyphen" of self-Other that "both separates and merges personal identities with our inventions of Others," and rethinking how researchers "have spoken 'of' and 'for' Others while occluding ourselves and our own investments" (p. 70). My personal journey of working through silence, shame, and responsibility had definite implications for my professional and personal practices. I could have maintained the status quo by failing to address an important issue in feminist theory and practice and by reproducing the Other in refusing to speak of my own investments in preserving silence. It is this occlusion that challenges our privilege of doing research and compels us to interrogate our subjectivities and the effects of research on us and, ultimately, on our representations of research participants.

In summary, my research experience has shown that in writing the Other, we can rewrite the self. For me, this means opening ourselves to the possibilities for personal change inherent in the process of inquiry, attending to the emotions, psychic dynamics, and issues evoked by our research, exploring the places where our research and interactions with participants have rubbed us raw and touched upon wounds and silences. This also means speaking about these subjects with colleagues to insert ourselves into the production of knowledge, describing the ways in which shifting our gaze to ourselves helps us understand the people participating in our research and the realities of their lives, and writing and speaking publicly about what we have learned about ourselves through our research. The notion of reflexivity needs to be revisited to further explore how critical self-reflection affects what we see and hear in our research. If we pay closer attention to our own processes, we might lean toward a more truthful account of our lives, and a more compassionate and insightful account of the people whose lives we are researching.

Chapter 7

Silences, Gaps, and Absences: Understanding How Differences Matter

In this chapter, I discuss some of the themes, issues, tensions, and dilemmas that emerged in my conversations with key informants in this study. Of the fourteen key informants, whom I will call respondents, the majority had worked in more than one area of the antiviolence struggle, including feminist organizing and education, shelters and second-stage housing, antiracist education, coalition building, social action, and community-based organizations. My discussion of themes and issues from these interviews will focus on barriers to survivors' processes of conscientization and participation in collective action, and on issues within the transition house movement that affect these processes. At the beginning and end of each subsection within this chapter, I present the voices of survivors who participated in this study. The interweaving of survivors' and respondents' voices will highlight the connections between the issues and tensions raised by both groups of women.

In this chapter, I use "workers" to refer to all women working in the transition house movement, both paid and unpaid. Workers may also be survivors, feminists, and/or professionals. Although we speak of these categories of workers as if they were mutually exclusive, we need to remember that they are not. To speak of them as separate categories hides the multiplicity of voices in which we often speak and, furthermore, suggests that we have little or no common ground for working together. All fourteen respondents in this study identified as feminists, and four of these women identified as survivors. Two respondents identified as feminist social workers. In my interviews with respondents, they spoke generally about all women in the antiviolence movement. Where respondents specifically referred to professionals, either in the movement or as government or agency employees, I clarify this in the text.

SPACES FOR COLLECTIVE ANALYSIS OF EXPERIENCE AND OPPORTUNITIES FOR COLLECTIVE ACTION

Paola: They have in Chile this analogy: instead of giving you fish, why don't I give you the thread, and I teach you how to fish. . . . In this society we lack the community concept. I belong to this group and as a member of this group, this is what I can contribute, but other people can contribute also. . . . It's hard to recognize, and I think a lot of feminists don't want to recognize that they have this problem of still wanting to feed into the traditional concept of woman, of me solving everybody else's problems. Many feminists haven't moved away from that. . . . I think it's so much easier to say I don't have all the answers, I am only a piece of the whole process. That's what's missing in this society, this concept of belonging.

Several respondents concurred that survivors would benefit from more spaces in which they could collectively analyze their experiences of violence and oppression. Without these spaces, it was unlikely that they would have sufficient opportunities to theorize about their experience, nurture insights and knowledge, and make explicit connections between the personal and the social. Having the time and freedom to name things in "politically actionable terms" (Bannerji, 1995, p. 21) was seen as critical in a society where domination, oppression, and lies are the norm. However, building community and creating space for thought and critique were even more difficult to achieve given cutbacks to shelters and services for abused women, the emphasis on "case management and units of service," the growing neosexism within the social services arena, and the fact that the state does not fund feminist organizing, education, and political action. Although public policy defines woman abuse as a social issue, it has ultimately been addressed through predominantly individualized solutions. Ana Elena, a social worker who facilitates individualized feminist educational groups with Spanish-speaking women of Latin American origin, summed up the importance of spaces for women to voice their subjugated knowledge:

> The lack of opportunities for Spanish-speaking women, in particular, to get together and talk about it makes it very, very difficult for each woman to connect different oppressions. . . . From experiences in their countries women know about classism. They might experience sexism in degree also, but it's something we don't talk about. We don't acknowledge it; we don't know what it is; we just leave it and experience it. . . . If you don't have the information to think about what you're feeling and how that works for you in your life, you're not connecting anything. That's the process, but I also think it's a challenge for women to get involved because they don't have the language. They experience the oppression but they have no way of sharing that and of pulling together, and that to me is a basic piece of what the work we do in this community should be. . . . I think that we need the space and the time to do that work because it's a lot of work and it hits you hard. It's realizing that women—just because of being a woman—are seen as a disadvantage. It affects who I am and how I am. But when women come here they are more busy about when their food is going to come, what housing is going to look like, and they don't have time to be doing that work right then, and they are not even given the opportunity to do that.

Ana Elena raises the question of what constitutes respectful, collaborative ways of working with survivors. Her words also suggest that we do not always have access to the language with which to speak about our experiences. Other forms of expression may be necessary to give voice to what we have lived. What ways of working with survivors facilitate the creation of social knowledge about themselves rather than producing knowledge about or for survivors? What kinds of relationships between survivors and workers honor survivors' experience and subjugated knowledge? Sarah, a long-time feminist educator/activist and former director of a transition house, lamented the separation that has evolved between survivors and workers in the antiviolence movement, and the scarcity of respectful ways to support survivors in their healing and politicization.

> In terms of women who are coming from the shelters or from a sexual assault center . . . and trying to do activist work afterward, there's a real lack in many cases, or at least women who are admitting that part or identifying as survivors. . . . It's where we have really fallen down because we have made that division between ourselves, it's "those women," instead of joining with them. . . . That whole notion that somehow you need to separate it and then you're more objective, what a lovely thought! . . . When we have abused women or sexually assaulted women who then join an organization without sort of dealing with their own stuff and that comes out, there is a concern there, but how do you direct that and how do you do that in an appropriate way? . . . Things can set you off really easily. You find a glove or something that was your partner's or all of a sudden you're in tears or someone's life story or circumstances [are] so similar to yours, you just want to tell them what this is all about and that's a real danger. . . . I don't think we've really come to grips with that even though many of us have really pushed the notion that women should be involved in the work and in their own healing . . . but we haven't made that jump somehow. We haven't made that transition, in an appropriate kind of way. It's almost like we fall into a paternalistic kind of approach or else we throw them out . . . saying you just cope. It's those extremes, and without those kinds of supports I think it's really irresponsible because you set them up, in a sense.

Sarah's critique of current practice raises several issues: Who claims that survivors must be healed in order to work for change and on what grounds are these claims based? Who defines when survivors have healed enough either to counsel/support other women or to engage in collective action? How are assessments made about degrees of healing and possible effects of personal healing processes on other women, women's organizations, and movement work? What kinds of learning environments would assist survivors in preparation for movement work? What investment and motivation do workers have in working in particular ways with survivors?

> **Jackie:** The attitudes, the abuses that I received from the systems that I reached out to was . . . felt to me far worse than the abuse I received from my husband, 'cause these systems were the systems that were supposed to be there to help. . . . I have conversations with people from the systems now and they like to pat me on the back and say, "You're one of the ones that made it." Well, yeah, I did make it, but I didn't make it because of the system. I made it in spite of the system. I'm feeling like they're not really getting it. How do you measure success? There are women that are living with abusive partners. Every minute that they go without the violence happening is a success. How do you measure success? How do you? Two hours without violence, two years . . . twenty years . . . Success isn't going out and contributing to society. Yeah, what is success?

POLITICAL AND ETHICAL COMMITMENTS AND HEALING

> **Eleanor:** For as strong as I am in my political endeavors, I still have difficulty confronting my abusive partner. . . . For all the action that I take, do you think I can find the strength to tell this man to fuck off? . . . I'm finding it very, very difficult and because I'm now in the political circles, I'm not comfortable to get counseling on this [for fear the community will find out] . . . . I think that's going to undermine my effectiveness. Oh! Survivor! Healing process! Damn it all! I knew this was going to happen sooner or later.

Respondents who expressed concern about survivors' healing identified three areas for discussion: (1) that survivors who have not worked through their experiences may, especially if they counsel other women, transfer their issues onto them, thus hindering their growth; (2) that survivors may become involved in women's organizations with the mission of rescuing women and children; and

(3) some survivors who engage in collective action require a degree of support that is unlikely to be met through such involvement. Carol, an activist, feminist counselor, and former director of a shelter, felt that it was important to ask, "For whom are we doing the work, for ourselves or for others?" However, Judy, a feminist educator, activist, and support group facilitator, suggested that sorting out reasons and motivations for why women choose to do this work is complex and cannot be neatly categorized as helping oneself versus helping others.

> I think it's sometimes safer to say, "I want to help other women." It's a safer place to start from, too, because I don't believe anybody that ever walks through the door of a shelter or second-stage [housing] or any feminist agency that says "I want to volunteer to help women" aren't there because they know deep down, even if they're not saying it, that they're going to get something . . . that it's going to help themselves, like there's something connecting. . . . I know I personally benefit from speaking out about what is fundamentally wrong, about social injustices that are going on, so I don't separate it.

Judy reported that some professionals with whom she worked expressed the view that survivors should not be attending conferences where they would be exposed to the politics and current debates in the antiviolence movement. Although their reasons for saying this were unclear, perhaps survivors' exposure to the larger movement was perceived as a threat to healing. These professionals appeared to see healing primarily as an outcome rather than a process. What is the relation between healing and political action? How has healing become a prerequisite to political and ethical commitments to create a more just world? How did political and ethical commitments come to be judged by the degree to which they promote individual healing (Kitzinger, 1993)? Why has healing been constructed as a therapeutic, individualized process and collective action as a politicized, collective process that is often viewed as unrelated to healing? How do we know when we are healed? Clearly, this issue merits further debate within the transition house movement to interrogate the meaning of healing and its possible relation to political action, and to design strategies that could address current concerns.

The second concern was that survivors become involved in women's organizations to save other women and children rather than work for a socially just world. In her experience working with survivors, Katarina, an activist, group facilitator, and community worker, observed that women's desire to help other women may reproduce socially constructed roles for women. Adopted with little critical reflection, these roles may have limiting consequences for oneself and others.

> The way it sometimes works for some women is that when . . . they've made some connections for themselves . . . they want to give back . . . get involved . . . organize and do action, but their motivation is around helping other women or saving other women or saving children. . . . She now has this horrible responsibility because she's figured out this huge secret that other women and children don't know, but everybody's in danger. Sometimes the motivation isn't about changing a world whose systemic structures are really screwed up, it's about saving other women or saving children, and sometimes I think that's a piece that we still need to do some work on, a part of being selfless, a martyr, and helping and giving as opposed to the part that "This is wrong, and this is why it's wrong, and I have to work to change the world because it's wrong." . . . It's really easy to do the work for someone else, to help because there's a real sense of satisfaction of walking home every day thinking, "I helped these people."

Helping is a culturally and socially constructed process and activity closely linked with gender. While the desire to help others is a healthy and laudable part of community life, helping individual women and working for social change need not be viewed as dichotomous or mutually exclusive activities. Nevertheless, Katarina points to the need for educational environments in which to articulate these issues and make explicit the connections between the provision of services to women and larger social arrangements. Although many survivors may not choose to identify as feminists, a social analysis that integrates critical thought and feelings of compassion for others' suffering is necessary to design effective strategies for social change.

BARRIERS TO BUILDING COMMUNITIES OF HEALING, ACTION, AND CHANGE

> **Heather:** That's what I'm trying to do with [the women's action group], but it's very hard to get . . . you know, women come through the systems and they come through their divorces and their lives are hell and they're drained and they're exhausted. They want change. They want to get involved, and then it's like we have a whole different life here and then we have new routines. You know, it's really hard to get everybody together.

Respondents identified a range of obstacles to women coming together to build community and talk about their lives. In dominant society, a primary social barrier concerns the paucity of life lessons about how to communicate, make friends, accept one another, and talk about our views, feelings, and differences. Moreover, a conspiracy of silence exists against talking about realities like abuse and poverty that affect our lives. In addition, for women to build community and heal within it often requires that they overcome misogynist, racist, and other social lessons that they have learned. Elizabeth, a feminist therapist and activist, emphasized the importance of building community but also of recognizing women's fear of trusting other women and the reality that they have been hurt, betrayed, or abused by women in their lives.

> It's important to build that community . . . but there are a great many women who are absolutely terrified of women and they also have the experience of male violence, so then their whole struggle to find safety or . . . trust in that is really, really a huge struggle, and women haven't always experienced women as good people. When you talk about the silence of violence, the whole silence of women's violence against other women is a huge topic still. . . . Early 1990s, I know that at many of the violence-focused conferences, it was very much the beginning

stages of women naming the violence from other women and there's tremendous pain about that. . . . I mean it's very, very, very, very confusing.

In healing from violence and oppression in communities of women, issues of trust and betrayal surface for survivors. Sometimes survivors are devastated when they are hurt or betrayed in their new relationships with women, who may be fellow residents of shelters, second-stage housing, or members of support groups or community centers. If women have lost the social support system that they had before they spoke out about abuse, these experiences of hurt and betrayal can almost be more shattering than their initial loss. Katarina and Carol observed two patterns affecting survivors' continued participation in women's organizations.

> **Katarina:** When a woman has experienced a lot of violence in her life, has gone to a shelter, a rape crisis center, has gotten that support, that nurturing, sometimes what happens is that they replace the family they lost with the family of feminism, and I think that sometimes doesn't get voiced real clear in terms of, "I've lost my identity with my partner, my family, my home, my social connections, but I have found this new wonderful place, and I can volunteer and I've got friends and we can talk about real neat things, and I replace that world with this world."

> **Carol:** That's part of the journey, too. You think, "I've found a new family" and when I say family I mean a group of people who love each other, who care for each other in mutual respect. Part of my journey is, "well, we're all women so naturally it's going to be wonderful," and of course . . . part of the consciousness . . . is that is just simply not the case.

Homophobia is also a barrier to women's participation. Myths about feminists and woman-centered women as man haters come to the fore as if, as Katarina said, "loving women had anything to do with hating men." Yet respondents drew attention to the deep bonds and lasting relationships that survivors develop with other women in the process of rebuilding their lives. These connections, at once profound and transformative, happen on a deep level, and survivors take significant risks to make them happen. These barriers to building trusting relationships and community need to be openly acknowledged and discussed.

Paola: That's such a challenge to the whole method, [the belief that] as long as we are with women we are safe. I don't think it's true. I've learned that through my work in organizations . . . a lot of times you cannot really trust people that you work with to the extent that you would like to. I work with women, white women and many other women from our communities who, whenever it touches their own personal interests, they turn their backs and they're going to protect themselves . . . so that's probably the hardest part for me working here. There was a difference working in Chile. In Chile I knew that if . . . one of my friends got arrested, I knew he was gonna do the best to protect us, protect me . . . because there was this whole concept of we have to help each other. Here it's "as long as you don't touch my pocket or . . . my life, you can count on me, but whenever you come any closer to threaten me in any way, you can forget it.". . . The concept of solidarity that people have in this country is so screwed up. . . . I think you really need the spirit of coming together. . . . We sort of spread everybody with our understanding of knowledge, of issues with no real substance to it, no real, real, real understanding, no real life to it.

CONSTRUCTING AVENUES
OF ACTION FOR SURVIVORS

Jackie: At that time I wanted to do volunteer work . . . go into the shelter and work with the women. It was over a year since I had been in the shelter and they swayed me. "Look, I don't really think this is the place that you needed to be." . . . They had a policy that you had to be out of the shelter for at least a year and my year was up. I think it may have been that being a volunteer I would have access to files, maybe my own files. I don't know. If that was to happen to somebody else right now, I would tell them to find out. I actually think it was the volunteer coordinator at that time—I would assume [she] really felt that there was no place for survivors.

Several respondents named the polarization of service provision versus strategies and action for social change, which is entrenched in the work and structures of the antiviolence movement, as an obstacle to survivors' engagement in collective action. For some shelters and related services, service provision is no longer contextualized in the women's movement nor is it viewed as a manifestation of resistance to racist patriarchy. Organizing for services to the exclusion of organizing for power prompts questioning about the kind of social change that service provision can create. For Jane, a feminist social worker, advocate, and activist, the split between activism and service provision had significant implications for survivors, limiting the avenues through which they could work for change.

> I'm not saying in order to do political action there aren't women who need to heal. . . . There are, and I absolutely support counseling for women, but I also support the fact that women should be given this as an alternative over here, and they're not told about something else they can do. . . . They're told, "You can get this for your housing. . . . You can go to counseling," but they're not told, "You can go to this rally. . . . You can write your MPP." And what you find is that when you tell women those things, there's resistance, not from the women, but there's resistance to the people that are wanting to do both of those things, and I've experienced that directly and that comes from the therapeutic angle.

Jane identified therapeutic ideology as a major factor creating the polarization of service provision and collective struggle, and shaping current practices with abused women. Katarina reported that staff at some services did not refer women to specific feminist services because they feared that women (clients) would be forced into participating in political activities. For many feminists and activists in the transition house movement, the appropriation of woman abuse by therapeutic ideology has resulted in social problem management. Robin, a former shelter worker and long-time political activist in social justice movements, observed that the artificial dichotomy between women's lived experience of violence and its politicization has reproduced an institutionalized model of working with abused women that excludes possibilities of other subjectivities and actions:

> Propagandizing women with politics, that comes up all the time . . . that politicizing the issue was the feminist agenda being foisted on vulnerable women. . . . This really irrational separation of politicization of violence against women from the experience of violence that women were coming and talking to you about, it left advocates in a no-win situation. . . . The minute you talk about anything other than her personal interaction with this person who abused her, then anything outside of that, of course, is politics. . . . That doesn't happen to the family systems theorists. They don't get accused of introducing all this extraneous, irrelevant information into this personal interaction between these two people. It only happens to feminists who talk about the world. It's a way of producing . . . the institutionalization and the therapeutic model. . . . I don't think I've ever met an abused woman who didn't want to know what was going on, or who just wanted to talk about "I'm really scared . . . or I'm really sad . . . and I'm really disappointed my relationship didn't turn out the way I hoped it would turn out." I've never met an abused woman who didn't want the answer to the question "why?" and "why me?"

All interventions are valued based, context specific, culturally rooted, and based in assumptions that must be critically examined to determine who and what they exclude and/or marginalize. Are groups of women excluded by a particular political stance and set of interventions?

Modes of intervention such as therapy and counseling may be accessed more comfortably by certain groups of women than others. Vicky, an antiracism educator, community worker, and instructor at a community college, refutes the assumption that all women feel comfortable partaking of individual therapy or counseling:

Healing, certainly for me and for many women [African-Caribbean women] I work with, has . . . a strong spirituality piece. . . . I don't think our community functions very well healing in isolation. We heal with human touch and connection and connecting with God, Goddess, whatever. . . . That becomes a real source of strength for women. It becomes a place where their heart[s] can heal in joy because it's a place where they can put it all out, just the same way as you would with a therapist. . . . Often I think that plays out even more when people are connected in the group. For me, the healing is not just only in the support groups, but it's women going to places where they feel they can connect with people from their own groups and whether that is church, whether it's a cultural function, there's just that whole validation that takes place, for one thing. Healing also looks different for women of color, especially if they're dealing with systemic discrimination, 'cause often in pulling themselves away from abuse, there [have] to be transformations as well, taking place in other areas.

Although survivors may benefit from a range of possibilities for action, the dilemmas and risks that participation in collective action pose for women must also be recognized. For Ana Elena and Liliana, working with and for women affected how they were perceived by members of their community. Liliana, a community worker and group facilitator with women of Spanish-speaking Latin American origin, described her balancing act:

Many people see us different, completely different, and they even feel different when relating to us, even family. . . . You are or you're not part of the family sometimes—you don't fit. That's what I'm saying with the community. Sometimes I behave different with a group of friends than when I behave with my family or at work because I have to accommodate to different situations. You know what I mean? It is a struggle—it's like juggling. You have to do that to be accepted in the community. Otherwise you're going against the community all the time and there are some things that I actually want them to accept [nonviolence], so I behave the same way here that I do there but there are some other things that I still have to accommodate.

Ana Elena and Liliana suggested that if women are unsure of how to negotiate their changing relationships with their community and fear that they may lose it, they may be reluctant to take part in antiviolence work. For Isabel, a shelter and community outreach worker, shelter policies such as requiring that women remain in a shelter while their partners attend counseling programs for abusive men reinforce tensions between survivors, advocates, and their communities.

Vicky also pointed out that participation in specific forms of collective action may not be comfortable or safe for women and may not be considered as a possibility. Survivors also may not have the literacy skills or self-confidence to feel able to take part.

> If you're talking about social action where you do a demonstration, many women feel very vulnerable, and I even find myself, too, feeling a little uncomfortable sometimes. They feel that they might be targeted because they're a lot more visible. . . . It might be used against them, and I think that comes from when you live in a society where you don't always feel welcome, when you often feel like the outlaw, to do those kinds of things makes you feel that you're even putting yourself even more at a distance and really becoming even more of an outlaw. The other thing is that men and women of color come from societies where war—I mean, there's serious ramifications for protesting and social political action. . . . From a class perspective you're assuming that women have all of the skills . . . and many women don't. Where literacy might be a problem, they don't— even skills of feeling the freedom of being able to speak openly in public. Many women don't have that kind of self-confidence. They're sort of embarrassed about accents and sounding different. I mean, I'm not saying this is all women . . . but what I'm saying is that if we are going to look across the board and realize—and white women of working-class . . . background may not feel comfortable as well, too, with those forms of doing things, so it's not just women of color or black women.

If we think of the population of women who most often use shelters and second-stage housing, they are generally poorer and less formally educated than women who do not resort to shelters but draw on other resources. This population may feel inadequately prepared or uncertain about how they can participate. Sarah identified apprehension as a significant barrier for survivors wanting to join the work against violence toward women and children.

> A lot of women want to do political work, but they're really unnerved about it and unsure, so part of that is about, well, you've got to learn about . . . where it comes from, why it's here, what the debates are, what the problems are with different things, and that sort of critical awareness doesn't have to do with just book learning. . . . We talk a lot about [how] it's okay to make mistakes and then if anybody does . . . [we say] how could you make this mistake? . . . I think that's one of the things that is really important that we talk about and yet we fail to do it . . . for ourselves and . . . for other women in a conscious way, particularly in working with . . . women who are wanting to give back some of the support that they got in a longer-term way. We really need to do it [give support and constructive feedback] there . . . not in the crisis moment, it's not the time to criticize what people have done. . . . That's the time when you do something else and sort of try to see the stages as opposed to pretending that we're all one . . . we're all equal, and we're the same, and isn't that wonderful, and it's just not true. And we do a disservice to everybody when we think that way.

Networks of support are needed for survivors in this learning journey. Engaging in collective action can perhaps best be viewed as a process in which differences in ways of understanding and responding to woman abuse, as well as differences in power and knowledge among women, need to be acknowledged and addressed. If these differences were openly articulated and used as learning moments, both survivors and workers might benefit from mutual political and personal learning.

CLASS RELATIONS

Eleanor: I'm one of the few parents left who feels that an appropriate spanking on a covered bum [to discipline a child] is the very farthest outside boundary that a parent can tolerate after all the other nonphysical disciplines and approaches have been applied. . . . What's going to happen if we get a law passed that you're no longer allowed to use any form of physical discipline? . . . I'm so deathly afraid that the women are going to get caught in the middle again with this. . . . Where's the support mechanisms? . . . I'm a victim of child abuse, but we need safety nets . . . support systems, and who's worried about designing these? . . . I don't see where women are going to be given the support mechanisms that they need to deal with their children. My children acted out—I was hit . . . called a bitch . . . told to fuck off. . . . I kept going to staff and I would say, you want me not to hit the children, then you better give me some other skills . . . but they didn't tell you what you could do . . . . You can't help the children if you're not helping the parent at the very same time. It has to be a unilateral, horizontal movement forward. . . . Think of the number of women who are going to be further victimized if this bill passes! Further oppression . . . let's heap one more on . . . this movement to the far right to protect children at all costs by the same voices who say we must protect women at all costs.

Class very much shaped relations between survivors and workers in the transition house movement. Many respondents concurred that while there was a lot of rhetoric about class, it was rarely addressed in any clear, definitive way, either in terms of the production of knowledge about woman abuse and strategies for change, the privilege of staff (for example, in shelters), or the dynamics of the broader antiviolence movement. Class relations were rendered invisible and taboo. Five respondents who identified as coming from working-class backgrounds stated that class perspectives were marginalized both in the workplace and in the movement. The paucity of understanding that many workers with middle-class outlooks have about the lives of survivors (clients) was a theme running through these respondents' comments. Class shaped workers' perceptions of the ways in which survivors responded to abuse. Robin suggested that working-class women are often viewed as not really knowing or understanding the realities in which they live:

> Lots of abused women who are never involved in social change actions come to the shelter and say, "What are you doing about this stuff? They're doing this at Family Court. I can't get any welfare. What are you doing about this?" . . . Often women come in the door talking about politics. They may not use the word "feminism" but they're talking about changing the system . . . particularly women who have had a lot of experience with the system and know the system very well. . . . There's sort of this stereotyping of abused women as a bunch of crying victims at the door who don't know what to do, emotional wrecks. . . . Who's stereotyping them as a bunch of hapless, uneducated people who don't know what's going on in the world? They told us what was happening—let's not forget that.

The perception of survivors as hapless victims erases women's experiences and their importance as a source of knowledge about the operation of power and strategies for social change. It also disguises power relations between working-class women, professionals, and the systems, and obscures the realities of the social world and the decisions that significantly affect working-class women's lives. The notion that abused women are primarily hapless victims encourages them to cope with misogyny and with a misogynist world instead of changing it. Jane, a survivor of working-class origin, linked class relations and the professionalization of shelter staff, pointing to the effects of class privilege coupled with professional education. Although it is well-intentioned, she emphasized that professional training often does not encourage social workers to both grasp the nature of oppression and explicitly identify their own beliefs and values about all kinds of things, for example, the concept of good mothering.

> It's not like because I have a [social work degree] I'm not going to be an abused woman one day. It doesn't protect me. The difficulty I have with social workers is there's . . . this total

distance between this person and this person. . . . I think, "Wow, what's that? It's just like some sort of facade, right? Like this has nothing to do with me." . . . There's no sort of education that addresses those things in social work. They will continue to put out these people—they're well-intentioned, they want to help people, but they're so privileged themselves, and you don't have to experience oppression I don't think, necessarily, to be able to support people and help people out, but you have to understand it on some level.

The power of professional language and professional norms is also implicated in the distance that has developed between survivors and workers in the transition house movement. Working-class respondents were keenly aware of the power of the language of professionals to define and control. They talked about arming themselves with the weapon of language, and learning how to effectively use this weapon to clearly articulate their positions and combat the power of professional jargon. In contrast to the early years when many women claimed survivor status, a stigma now exists about workers' and particularly professionals' identification as survivors and/or speaking out about experiences of oppression. This norm is usually implicit. Although politically and strategically there may be advantages and disadvantages to assuming or not assuming the status of survivor, the divisions that have emerged between workers and survivors, partially rooted in class relations, undervalue survivors' engagement in antiviolence work.

> **Paola:** This whole concept of professionalism, if you look at it, is more than class, is elitist. It's an elitist concept, that the feminist movement is a few women who know all the answers so we can help those poor women. And I think that's the mistake that antiviolence movement has made, is to believe that because you have some training—I'm not denying that many of the women, if not most, all of us have gone through some form of violence in one way or another, we have some experience to rely on—but . . . a lot of women seem to think that because they have some training and also have the experience, that all of a sudden they have all the answers. And instead of focusing on your experience, you're coming to me

for some help instead of me trying to focus on what's going on with you. I'm trying to give you the answers because I know better.

CONCEPTUALIZATIONS OF
AND ATTITUDES TOWARD SURVIVORS

Eleanor: That was some of the myths that I was talking about without naming them last night [at a public rally]. Oh, my goodness, if we get a survivor she's gonna bring her personal issues to the table. Pardon me? . . . If you think that of me, what do you think of us collectively as survivors? . . . I had professionals come up to me and say ridiculous things like, "You're so articulate for a survivor." What do you mean? I'm so articulate for a welfare recipient or I'm just so articulate? And I'd get others saying, "I don't really know what to expect with a survivor at the table." . . . I began to dispel more myths about the capabilities of survivors and welfare recipients.

The majority of respondents were distressed about current conceptualizations of abused women that construct them as Other. Images of what battered women were thought to be, such as uneducated or lacking in cognitive skills, were projected onto survivors by workers in the movement and by professionals in the systems. These ideas about survivors minimized their strengths, abilities, and other dimensions of human agency. Survivors in this study resisted current myths and stereotypes about who and what survivors are. Furthermore, respondents suggested that the notion of agency needs to be problematized and examined to unearth our assumptions about it.

What are the limits of survivor discourse, and what does the discourse of survivor exclude and/or marginalize? What do the experiences of movement workers and survivors tell us about the inadequacy of the discourse of survivor and survivor empowerment? What processes of power and knowledge are sanctioned through "expert needs discourses" (Fraser, 1989, p. 173) about women who have been abused? What are the connections between limiting discourses about survivors and practices that make them Other and exclude them as agents for social change?

Survivors are constructed as the Other in different ways. Isabel, who came to Canada as a refugee from El Salvador, was disturbed by conceptualizations of survivors by some staff, volunteers, and board members in the shelter where she worked. As the staff representative on the board, she observed that many board members preferred to have survivors as passive recipients of predetermined services rather than as board members and active agents interpreting their needs. She described how survivors were viewed as "handicapped" in some way, rendering them less capable of agency, and how the social practice of helping made invisible the social control functions of helping and the powerlessness of clients:

> Professionals have their jobs and they don't invest themselves. Survivors are seen by helpers as handicapped. As a refugee [and woman who had been beaten by her partner] I didn't view myself in that way. There was no time to be handicapped. Many of the Canadian ways and models of helping are not helpful in creating change, in involving women in changing social conditions. Survivors tend to see service providers as those responsible for making change—it's not something that has to do with them. We need to treat women as adults responsible for their actions, not as handicapped but as resourceful equal persons. Why does a woman who has gone through abuse fall into this antiquated way of helping? Is it our models? Many professionals are working for a job and not because they are aligned with women or social justice, and this enables them to distance themselves from "these" women, to view anything, any male violence they've suffered, as something different than what these women have suffered. Therefore they see themselves as different from "these" women.

Isabel's evaluation of such a conceptualization of survivors challenges some of the models we currently use in our work with abused women. In her study of women's postshelter experiences, Susan Gadbois (1999) highlighted some contradictions between the policies and practices of the current social service model of shelter service delivery and the stated goals or outcomes of shelter service for survivors, such as to help survivors reestablish themselves in the community. Shelter practices that situate residents in the role of "one who is helped" minimize the value of women's helping work and erode the sense of reciprocity in relationships so critical to one's sense of self-worth. Social service models that exclude women from real involvement in shelter work also need to recognize the poverty and discrimination that further prevent women from reestablishing themselves as valuable and competent members of the community after they leave the shelter (Gadbois, 1999).

Power dynamics in hierarchical organizational relations also contribute to making survivors Other. In the organization where Sarah had worked, she observed power dynamics between survivors and workers that spoke of emotional investments, unacknowledged desires, and perhaps even pain.

> What I've been noticing lately is, a lot of women who are shakers and movers, they really need . . . it's not adoration exactly, but it's like, "well, you've got it all together." That feeds them in a sense and I'm sure that can be really seductive, and in order for that to keep on happening, you need to then keep other women—it's another way of making Other—in a more victim or less powerful position. It's not a way of really joining and that's a really important little piece that we miss . . . . Any time anybody starts to talk to you about, "Oh, you're so wonderful . . . you saved my life," . . . is to really say, "Wait a second, no I didn't. I gave this insight or that insight . . . I told you where the phone was.". . . I think that's really critical. Otherwise . . . I think that a woman stops growing right away, which is a real tragedy, and you're not really doing good work.

Several respondents identified the need for workers to examine both their own investments in their positions and identities, and the issues and emotions elicited by their work. This is not an easy task, especially given the culture of professionalism, the structures within which they work, and the constant daily demands upon workers who are doing the best they can with inadequate resources. According to Isabel, staff in the feminist shelter where she worked were to "be professionals and come to work, and then go home and find ways to deal with the impact of the work, and never talk about it or about the fact that we have been abused ourselves." These implicit expectations raise important questions about caring, professional-ism, and self-care.

Heather: There's a certain point where we say, okay, enough is enough. Forget our safety if someone else is involved be-cause it's scary. Like the vigil in town here—apparently there was one letter from a male and the whole vigil was rerouted . . . damn it. . . . No, we'll go the right route. That would have been fine for community women, and community women did take it a step farther and go to the main park, but see, agency women have to step back because [of] their jobs or are not permitted to [speak out] because of their job positions. Community women can. We have the freedom and choice . . . but then there's no money. . . . So let's just oppress it on one hand—who the hell's gonna listen to us anyway, because we're just women. We don't even have a job, and if we do, it's, "Well, you don't have an agency job so you can't be respected." A lot of agency women do have a lot of power. They do allow for those doors to open for us community women.

INVESTMENTS IN IDENTITIES
AS WORKERS/FEMINISTS/PROFESSIONALS

Heather: I don't think they [some professionals] wanna open up the can of worms. I really think that they're afraid to look at it, the dynamics of abuse and what it does to women and children. I really think that they are trying to avoid it at all costs because it's very frightful. If they really turned and looked at the damage that abuse did, they'd be astonished. I really think they're avoiding the whole process.

Several respondents believed that the nature of some investments made by workers in their identities as helpers were harmful to self and others at the same time that these investments were self-affirm-ing. Robin suggested that certain unacknowledged investments served to protect the self by countering powerlessness and despair:

Women who demand change . . . sometimes those women don't get support in the same way that women do . . . who

really need a lot of emotional support and information. . . .
Those women who are demanding change are more angry. . . .
So that's inappropriate, of course, so then they're taught how
to cope with their anger or confronted about their inappropriate behavior in the shelter because it makes a counselor feel
powerless. In a lot of ways it's much more self-fulfilling as a
counselor or a social worker or whoever might be sitting there
to take care of a woman who is in crisis or . . . despair and
make her feel better than it is to deal with someone who is
feisty and fed up and is demanding that you do something
about it. . . . And what's really sad is when you see a woman in
a therapeutic ideology-based system taught to stop being feisty
and demanding so, in fact, her resistance strategies and her
ability to advocate for herself [are] undermined by being told
that she's too angry or she's overreacting or "you're never
going to get anything by being hostile." . . . And activists know
this as well.

Robin's observations also uncover the existence of ideas about
who qualifies as a "good victim," an obviously unfair and harmful
expectation. There are implicit, and perhaps explicit, messages
about what it means to be a "good abused woman."

Linda, a community worker with a community-based organization and a survivor, cautioned that feminist therapists and professionals who assume ownership of social action efforts with survivors sometimes do so out of their own investments.

To me that's one of the debates in feminist therapy. . . . "Who
owns the meeting to do social action?" because there's a lot of
women who—like I certainly have experienced abuse in my
life and I'm here partly for it, and I'm really lucky that I've
had the experience and support to have worked out where am I
here for me and where am I here for you, and I think that gets
lost a lot with feminist therapists and the social action stuff.
You know, the need to have women stand up and feel that
you're radicalizing them is really meeting your own needs. . . .
What I've learned is that women need support and that has to
be the primary—if we throw that out then we're meeting our
needs and not their needs, and that need for support changes,

and what I've learned . . . is how to respond and how to negotiate this change.

Carol felt that some investments were a way to section off and contain pain. Workers' investment in emphasizing the positive outcomes of individual counseling with women served to distance themselves from the complexity of larger political goals concerning social change and feelings of hopelessness about creating this change. Sometimes it covered a reluctance to examine their own lives and complicity with oppressive structures and relations.

> I find, working here and also working in women's centers, abortion clinics, and on and on, that women will section their lives in such a way as they hopefully will never have to deal with reexperiencing pain and oppression, and then what happens is they lose sight of what the fight is really all about.

What are the consequences when workers' stories and emotions are left out? If they do not have a space in which to talk about them in some form, how do unacknowledged, unspoken, or repressed emotions affect our relations with survivors? Robin suggested that our own processes, for example, resistance to seeing, do affect our work with survivors:

> We're so in denial, I suppose, to use therapeutic language, about how awful it is and how much it's happening ourselves that some of us don't want to believe it is happening, and often what we'll do is focus on one nice guy who seemed to be supportive over at the Crown attorney's office or something, to convince [a client] that it's not all bad.

For workers, there is a contradiction here. Speaking of the relation between psychiatric survivors/consumers and mental health professionals, Kathryn Church (1995) argues that, "The difficulty is the degree to which such workers themselves are decontextualized. Right now, we are not making significant subjective/objective connections in our own lives. How can we possibly expect to make them for Others?" (pp. 127-128). If one of the tasks of workers is to help women make connections between subjective experience and current social arrangements, then this task will be hindered by the fragmentation that they themselves experience. Church suggests that the formation and reformation of professional identities is crucial in constructing new relations between survivors and professionals if we are to reform both identities and policies, subjectivities and social relations.

> **Eleanor:** At this conference [on woman abuse] there were lawyers . . . judges . . . Children's Aid people . . . Family Court mediators. . . . I was taking notes on what they were saying and I would stand up and . . . address it. . . . It took someone like me to stand up and start it, because I think others are in a position, because they get money from governments to support their agencies and programs, so they feel I'm safe. What have I got to lose—they're going to pull my welfare check?

WORK STRUCTURES AND PROCESSES

Victoria: The us and them attitudes, the holier-than-thou, it's the systems speaking so eloquently and so beautifully, and nobody wanting to offend anybody, because God forbid that someone might have to go home with an issue and work on it. We might have to be able to take one minute tiny little pseudo step up the stair to share what's going on down here—that's what really upsets me. . . . The other thing that's part of this war is the language. Well, the language we use is so much a part of the pitfall that we find ourselves caught up in, just to communicate our ideas, just to get beyond the barrier of communication itself. . . . I think they tolerate us because in order to do this work we have to be tolerated.

Workers in the transition house movement operate within a range of structures and processes that are not of their own making. Funding constraints, limited resources, structures of accountability to government, organizational policies and boundaries, and nonparticipatory modes of decision making all shape our interactions with survivors. Nowhere was the dissatisfaction about relations between survivors and workers/feminists/professionals, particularly "system-bound professionals" (Quinby, 1995, p. 278), greater than in what respondents called interagency or coordinating committees. Several respondents felt that these committees, situated within the discourse of family violence, channeled women's actions into structures and processes that would keep them occupied but very likely produce little real social or material change for abused women. Moreover, these committees often function at the local level, isolating women from the larger antiviolence struggle. Jane described her experience with an interagency committee and the context in which it functioned.

> Everybody sits around a table. They have their token abused woman because accountability is important in order to maintain control, and they all have about one vote all the way around the table, and who has the power? . . . It's all about self-preservation of the mainstream as opposed to making changes to end violence against women, so who's responsible for that? What happens is that when you don't adequately fund women's organizations, women don't talk about what's going on because they don't have time, and then what happens is that women fight with each other and they're forced to choose, right? "Well, where should we cut? Do you think we should prioritize this or this?"

Accountability is a salient issue here. What does accountability mean? To whom are workers accountable? What is the accountability of the so-called abused women's advocate to the abused women for whom they are advocating? Clearly, there are contradictions between workers'/feminists'/professionals' accountability to abused women, those most affected by woman abuse, and their accountability to mainstream agencies and status quo agendas that reproduce oppressive social relations. If, for example, shelter workers keep silent in the face of the current wave of cutbacks and neosexism in order to keep shelters open, are they being accountable to abused women? What gives them the mandate to speak and act for the women they serve?

Despite the limits to the kinds of change committees can effect, Judy observed that survivors and workers face a dilemma if they do not participate.

> The people [agency representatives] who sit at that table have said that the voice of the survivors at the table will carry the most weight . . . because it's lip service, right, until it's really put into action. . . . You sit in that committee, you're not going to change the individual mandates of those agencies or the persons that are sitting there representing them, so that's a dilemma, though, isn't it? Do you not get involved with something that might effect some change, or do you get involved and sell out a piece of who you are? And is it really change that happens?

In these structures, power differences were identified not only between survivors and workers but between feminists/activists and professionals in the systems. These committees obscure differences in social and decision-making power among members, assuming that all participants come from a similar perspective and have similar goals. Ideology and differences in power are rendered invisible under the missive of cooperation and coordination to end violence against women. Robin described how the silence on these issues prevented real engagement and discussion, and how the organization of political representation reproduced hierarchical relations and privilege:

> You're never allowed to identify that some people at the table have power and other people . . . don't, and the ones that don't should be listened to. And they're not going to be listened to, and then they get angry and then they're put down and then they go away, which is exactly what they want you to do. . . . They want to get on with doing things their way for the survivors that they think are worthy of getting their support, because they are non-trouble-making survivors. There's all kinds of lip service and pontificating about survivors and having the survivors on board to tell them what to do and to be on their advisory boards, until the survivors came in making demands and being angry . . . and then the survivors got attacked just the

way anybody else would because they were radical survivors
. . . . There's certain measurings . . . certain behaviors and
certain kinds of women who deserve our support, and they are
the kind of women that toe the line and are polite, nice women
. . . saintly women who never swear and do bad things. Other
women who break the rules or who fight back or who drink or
who are prostitutes or lesbians—they are not worthy victims
and they don't deserve our support.

These professionally dominated processes accord survivors a to-
ken voice but little real power. Survivors' speaking as well as the
conditions of their speaking are determined by larger social arrangements. Survivors, too, are often caught in a double-bind situation. As
activists they are told to speak politely and calmly in order to counter
the myths about survivors as overemotional, angry, and unstable.
Survivors who express emotion and/or display anger, an emotion that
is not tolerated publicly, are often deemed irrational and out of control. Codes of professional etiquette implicitly define "emotionality
as irrational," delegitimating "survivor knowledge repertoires"
(Church, 1995, pp. 90, 95). After survivors become frustrated at a
lack of progress and change, they may opt for asking impolitely and
behaving disruptively so that they wrest some degree of change from
those with power to grant it.

Kathryn Church (1995) suggests that survivor participation can
be understood as what Bannerji et al. (1991) call an "unsettling
relation." It evokes in professionals a range of emotions such as
silence and anger because it destabilizes their notions not only of
how they do their work but of who and what they are.

"Consumer participation" as an unsettling relation isn't (just) a
new program technique or an intellectual exercise. If there is
any room at all for it to be genuine, it will engage people
emotionally and personally; it will raise suppressed emotions
and in the process challenge professionals' identities as "know-
ers" and "doers." Professionals must not marginalize these feelings, in themselves or particularly in survivors, for the sake of
"getting on with business." (Church, 1995, p. 74)

Church cautions that the challenge for survivors is to constructively "direct their anger in ways which do not objectify professionals as 'evil others,' which move them beyond personal revenge into collective political action" (pp. 73-74). The relation between survivors and professionals needs to be understood as a social relation requiring transformation. Another key issue here concerns the silence of professional women. What are the responses of feminists/professionals to survivors' demands and anger? How do feminists/professionals make meaning of their responses to survivors' challenges about who and what they are?

Survivors must also be strong enough to withstand public censure, often from other women in the movement who disagree with their strategies and tactics. They may face other risks as well in speaking out, such as losing employment. The realities of survivor participation contradict the rhetoric of safety for survivors in coordinating committees. Rather, "safety is an illusion." Given their life experiences, some survivors found it offensive that professionals thought they could spare them from some level of discomfort in these committees. As Heather stated, "We're not here to feel comfortable. Why should they be making me feel comfortable when I know I don't make them feel comfortable. . . . I think that's a key issue." Whatever the illusion of safety, the fact that the operation of power is a complex and contradictory process has not been addressed in these committees.

> **Heather:** In certain situations they've been very strong on coming down on community women, like "you're not strong enough, you're not intelligent enough to understand the language process." I might not be able to speak it very well but I sure can understand what they're saying, and one wom[a]n had responded very emotional[ly] to a situation and they kind of viewed it as unacceptable. I think they need more community women and they really have to really look at the power and control at that table. We're there . . . to end violence and there's a lot of power and abuse and control at that table . . . that needs to stop. . . . I don't know if they have that intimidation there because they know that intimidates a community woman from speaking up, because that comes back, that egg-

shell [sense of walking on eggshells with an abusive partner].
We'll put a sense of fear into that woman because you know
that she's not going to say anything.

FUTURE DIRECTIONS AND CHALLENGES

Donna: In the last two years, I have had to look at [the feminist organizations in my community] and see that they are not
so revolutionary after all, and also the community coordinating committee isn't going to face [the fact that] they're doing
what they say they are against. Class issues are critical too. I
am concerned about [the women's organizations], concerned
about how they are becoming so conservative.

With respect to the broader antiviolence movement, respondents
identified key issues affecting the strength and inclusiveness of the
movement and survivor participation in it. These issues included
the pressure upon women's organizations to provide quality service
with few resources, difficulties in working across differences and
understanding the diverse forms of oppression women face, and
internal struggles within women's organizations about racism, heterosexism, and classism. Although many in the transition house
movement have made significant attempts to work through these
issues, further work remains to be done. Robin described some of
the struggles and contradictions present in women's organizations:

All of these sort of internal challenges where women are attempting to come to the table and say, "What about me? You
talk a good line, but when it comes right down to it, you can
use any power you've got, any chance you get to take stuff that
belongs to me and I'm not going to let it happen to me anymore." . . . Those kinds of struggles are happening every-
where, and part of institutionalization is entrenching white
women's and straight women's agendas, and they're abusing
power and institutionalization to keep out some of those challenges as well. They're using the master's tools not to dismantle the master's house but to dismantle challenges against
them, and that just strengthens the ideological power of thera-

py, of institutionalized models. . . . They'll strengthen the institutionalization and the professionalization of the service as a way of keeping out the radical, antioppressive kind of stuff when they used to use it for their own benefit.

Silence about these issues reproduces hierarchical relations. Part of the difficulty in dealing with these issues concerns the emotionality that they evoke. As well as requiring thought, this work engages us personally and emotionally. We have not always known how to deal with these emotions and use them for growth in the change process. Vicky suggested that we have not yet found ways of grappling with this emotionality:

> Work with other forms of violence, just the same way as working on wife assault or partner assault, is very emotional. . . . When we start talking about issues of power, issues of dominance, issues of systemic racism, examining those issues bring[s] up all kinds of guilt, all kinds of anger, fear, and terror, depending on which side of the spectrum you're on, and we have not found ways or models or whatever you call it to grapple with that, with emotional dimensions of the work.

In addition, Vicky suggested that the antiviolence struggle needs to include men in some way. Although the practice of engaging primarily women in antiviolence work is well-intentioned, the responsibility for change remains with women, reproducing gendered roles and absolving men of responsibility. Perhaps because women have been so occupied with the immediate needs of abused women and their children, we have not been able to build other models that can more fundamentally address the many forms of violence against women at their root sources. Vicky affirmed the need to theorize about violence against women across race, class, and gender in order to design more effective strategies for improving women's spiritual and material lives.

> As an African-Caribbean woman, I don't feel that I can talk about violence in isolation [from] issues of race. . . . We tend to just sort of compartmentalize it to just this gender thing. It's seen mostly as wife assault, domestic violence, woman abuse,

and precisely because all women, no matter where we come from, we experience that. At the same time I take a very broad definition of violence because when women come to me and tell me about the violence and describe the violence they're experiencing in their lives, specifically black women and women of color, it is not only about male violence, it is also about systemic forms of violence . . . the racism they experience, how that impacts on the kind of housing that they live in . . . their abilities to get a job . . . the quality of the job that they will get . . . the education that they have, they want, or will get . . . the kind of barriers that they experience. You know, there are all kinds of issues around language, barriers of language. . . . I can't isolate that discussion to merely look at male violence. I have to include systemic forms of violence. . . . There are really many common threads. I often say for me poverty is violence when it means that children must go hungry, when it means that people must live in substandard housing, that is a form of violence. When it means that people must live in housing that is overrun by rodents or roaches or not enough heat so that they're cold so that they get sicker, to me that is a form of violence because it impacts on a person's physical, emotional and spiritual well[-being]. . . . I think that with any form of oppression or violence, you violate somebody and, in turn, you violate yourself.

Vicky's insights return us to the task of thinking about the issues that facilitate survivors' commitment to working for change, individually and collectively. The issues that respondents have advanced can, if explored and addressed, yield rich possibilities for progressive change in survivor and worker/feminist/professional relations, in the organization of political voice, and in the reformation of the work that we all do to end violence against women.

Chapter 8

Implications and Directions
for Feminist Social Work Practice

Reflecting on what I have learned from this research, I ask what we as feminists can do in the transition house movement to revitalize our spirit and the struggle against violence toward women. I have identified four areas as sites for potential change.

RERADICALIZING OUR MOVEMENT
AND OUR WORK WITH SURVIVORS

What can be done to repoliticize shelters and women's organizations as sites of collective struggle for social change and how can survivors be actively involved in this work?

The findings of this study suggest that participants became involved in collective action after a substantial period of making sense of their experiences and rebuilding their lives. Although most participants sought counseling and therapy at some juncture to work through crises, painful emotions, and pressing issues, their process of facing pain, reworking experiences, and developing a critical understanding of what had happened/was happening to them was not time limited to a ten-week support group or a one-year residency in second-stage housing. Their comprehension of their oppression developed over time and in the company of other women, and their desire to act on their knowledge occurred simultaneously with undertaking personal change. For several participants, their desire to speak out and resist oppressive relations and structures arose when they realized, implicitly or explicitly, the *systemic* nature of violence and oppression and became angry at the injustice. Opportunities for survivors to make sense of their experience, develop a critical consciousness, be supported, and belong to community were critical to their involvement in collective action.

Although survivors do benefit from therapy, this study clearly demonstrates that they also benefit significantly from a collective analysis of experience that encourages an exploration of feelings and a critical understanding of the social world. Naming our emotions and feelings involves something more than simply "discovering" what we are feeling (Scheman, 1993). It involves giving a name to the feeling, situating it in our social world, joining feeling and behavior in a meaningful way, and noting a purposeful pattern, and this occurs "not from focusing on one's feelings but from a political redescription of one's situation" (Scheman, 1993, p. 177). Feelings are not just about an "inner self" that is divorced from an "exterior" social world. Such a stance presupposes "an elision between ideological and structural understandings of power and domination and individual, psychological understandings of power" (Mohanty, 1994, p. 156). For participants in this study, this redescription occurred in feminist/antioppressive environments such as women's support and self-help groups, educational programs and groups, feminist organizations, and other communities of learning.

An assumption of some professionals and workers in the transition house movement is that survivors' empowerment is solely an individual process, occurring through individual therapy and support. Based on participants' stories, I would argue that survivors' empowerment is also a social and collective process as well as a cultural one. Yet individual therapy is often viewed as a neutral process, whereas alternative feminist/antioppressive approaches are perceived as value-laden. However, experience is not transparent, "immediately accessible, understood and named" (Mohanty, 1992, p. 82), but is itself discursively mediated. As Linda Alcoff and Laura Gray (1993) clarify, "experience is not 'pretheoretical' nor is theory separate or separable from experience and both are always already political" (p. 283). Although women's recourse to therapy or counseling is itself a political act with social consequences, unless of course they maintain the status quo (Alcoff and Gray, 1993), women who have been abused also gain significantly from collectively placing their experience in a theoretical context and making the realm of the personal politically efficacious and transformative (hooks, 1988). A primary focus on individualized self-rehabilitation and healing fosters both the cleaving of the personal from the political and the conflation of the personal with the political. In our work with survivors, we need to challenge this approach advanced by mental health, professional, and recovery discourses that appropriate the language of transformative feminism.

To this end, I suggest that we continue to build ways of working with survivors based on genuine collaboration and power sharing. An integrated continuum of opportunities for survivor involvement in feminist/antioppressive theorizing and activism would recognize their agency, the nature and complexity of survivors' processes of conscientization, the different meanings of "survivor" for women, and their right to define their needs and wishes. This includes the choice to not question gender roles or bring about social change (Agnew, 1998). Given current funding constraints and pressures for case management and treatment-based services, this is a difficult, yet important task. For example, at the point where women leave a shelter to reestablish themselves in the community, feminist support groups could provide them with the networks of support to counter fear, isolation, and despair while struggling to survive, overcome barriers, and make sense of their lives. Such networks are important in everyday problem solving and in maintaining a sense of self as survivor, since women rebuilding their lives often do so with limited support networks (Gadbois, 1999).

Participants in this study provided many examples of the significance of these networks in their lives. Networks of support included ex-residents of second-stage housing, former members of support groups, and ongoing contact with survivors and staff at shelters and other women's services. For one participant who had moved into the community from second-stage housing, continued contact with staff and residents at second-stage housing was critical to her survival and politicization. Her court-ordered custody arrangements dictated that she participate in a supervised child access program in which her ex-partner would have visitation rights with their son. At the outset, she was given a personality test (MMPI) by a psychologist in the program and was informed that she had "a hard time dealing with crisis." The reality was that she had lost her marriage, her property, her family support, and was in danger of losing custody of her child. In talking with staff and residents at second-stage housing about her sense of what had happened, she validated her intuition that she had been defined as the "problem." She thus validated her observations about sexist bias through interpreting this event with others who could hear and support her. She refused to accept the judgment of the psychologist and ensured that her safety was paramount in making visitation arrangements, since her ex-partner had tried on different occasions to kill her. Educational support groups for women who have left shelters or second-stage housing could combine information sharing, practical assistance, emotional support, social gatherings for specific events or on commemorative dates, and collective analyses of women's experiences, including the politics of violence against women, social relations of power, and individual and collective strategies for resistance and change. Strategies for political advocacy could emerge from and build on survivors' lived experiences with abusive partners, social institutions, and their communities.

Feminist/antioppressive education and organizing programs could be offered to survivors as well as women in the community who do not identify as survivors.[1] Participants in these groups could be linked with strategies for change and avenues for collective action, whether that be a social action group, advocacy, public education, coalition work, or other political action. For example, I was familiar with a second-stage housing program that provided survivors with training to become community activists and advocates for abused women. Training and skill building for making change and familiarity with different strategies for change might better prepare some survivors to participate in the movement. This is especially important when we know, for example, that the use of particular kinds of language excludes some survivors, that the idea of participating in some forms of action is frightening, and that some women feel that they do not have the necessary skills or knowledge to participate.

A critical piece of creating environments in which survivors can express their social commitment to change involves helping women connect with one another and with avenues for action. With support from shelters and women's organizations, survivors could maintain support networks, cultivate leadership, organize political action, and/or coordinate their efforts with initiatives already in progress. Ex-resident groups and networks connected with shelters and women's organizations could link up with other feminist political struggles and social justice movements. Self-advocacy models that enable survivors' speaking and activism can be nourished with moral and concrete support. In this way, survivors can continue to be theorists of their own experience. New or revitalized models of working with survivors need to operate within a discourse of collaboration and coalition rather than a discourse of illness, recovery, and healing that excludes the possibility and necessity of political struggle. An effect of the polarization between clients and abused women as survivors, services and social change, has been the institution of a hierarchy of feminists/professionals/activists and survivors that marginalizes survivors in the work of the movement, sometimes even in feminist sites of struggle. These false dichotomies need to be examined and dismantled, and horizontal collectivity needs to be rebuilt.

At the organizational and community levels, women who have survived violence and abuse must be accorded real power in decision-making structures and processes. This needs to occur in feminist and women's organizations, and in decision-making bodies formed out of alliances between feminist organizations, state institutions, and nonfeminist community agencies. In this study survivors active in their communities were often treated as tokens in coordinating committees rather than equal participants in decision-making processes. While survivors may be included or "consulted," the power of decision often resides with others. Feminists/professionals and others invested in maintaining the status quo and/or bending to the forces of accommodation need to rethink how particular structures, processes, and rules of etiquette exclude survivor participation. Survivors' subjugated knowledge, voices, demands, and expressed emotions need to be considered as legitimate in their complexity, and not simply as a product of their status/experience as survivors. We need to analyze more closely the social relations between survivors and feminists/professionals in the systems in order to alter them, exposing the specificity and interrelatedness of both their social locations and the kinds of knowledge and experience that each group contributes. Structures and processes for survivor participation must be democratized through concrete practices to foster genuine collaboration and power sharing.

In the community where I undertook part of this research, the shelter and second-stage housing encouraged survivor participation in many aspects of their work. In second-stage housing, for example, survivors were members of the board of directors, social action efforts, political advocacy, and involved in the day-to-day support of residents, the advocacy program for residents, the volunteer program, and the advocacy training program. Some survivors were active in the local coordinating committee. Survivors pointed out that staff at the shelter and second-stage housing were instrumental in encouraging their activism. These organizations worked hard to implement and maintain policies, structures, and processes that ensured the inclusion of survivors' voices and input into both service delivery and political action. Staff were attentive to the ways in which professional language, formal educational levels, and attitudes and stereotypes about survivors impeded their participation, thus diminishing the perspectives from which to work for change.

The respect with which survivors spoke about their participation in these organizations speaks to both principles and practices. Staff and survivors sought to establish and sustain nonhierarchical and cooperative relationships, and their advances were accomplished through engagement and hard work. While we may be dismayed at the internal politics of some feminist organizations, it is often precisely because they are attempting to grapple with power inequities among women (for example, racism, ableism) that the difficulties and issues they encounter become so evident and significant. As feminist organizations continue to expand their worldview and develop a more comprehensive understanding of women's experiences of violence and abuse through interaction among diverse groups of women, new forms of social relationships will evolve.

One of the barriers to survivors' equal participation in confronting violence against women, including survivors who are staff members, is elitist attitudes and exclusionary practices toward survivors. Critical self-reflection by workers and professionals is urgent. Comments such as, "Oh, you are so articulate for a survivor!"

are manifestations of a patronizing and elitist practice, and call into question who our allies are. Feminists/professionals need to listen to the heterogeneity of survivors, including women's experiences of racism and being poor. Continued collaboration with diverse groups of survivors will deepen our understanding of oppression and its multifaceted nature.

Critical to survivors' participation in collective action, then, would be a recognition that abused women can move "beyond victim and survivor roles . . . to become advocates and activists for justice" (Stern and Leppard, 1995, pp. 171-172). A collaborative approach would respect survivors and their experience, refusing to define them only as "victims" or "Other." As Linda Alcoff and Laura Gray (1993) explain, the fact that survivors can be both witnesses of and experts on their experience, reporters of experience, and theorists of experience, will alter existing subjectivities. This study affirms that if survivors also have opportunities to politicize their personal experience, their examination of the " 'line of fault' of a disjunction or fissures in the selves . . . [may yield] possibilities of new identities and of struggle" (Bannerji, 1995, p. 29). We must continue our search for collaborative ways of working in community with survivors that acknowledge and make room for the variety of subversive ways in which women can speak out and act against violence toward women without an insistence that all follow the same homogeneous path.

REENVISIONING OUR MOVEMENT
AND WORKING TOGETHER
ACROSS DIFFERENCES

What current remedies to address violence against women need to be reexamined and where might energies best be placed in future efforts?

The shift from political action to stop violence against women to service provision for its victims has accelerated over the past ten years. Ajax Quinby (1995), an advocate in the battered women's movement, voiced her concern over what she sees as some disturbing trends in work with abused women. She suggests that the mainstreaming of the movement and the institutionalization of feminist services has led to treatment approaches in shelters that may even reduce manifestations of social inequality to psychological issues. For example, in some transition houses, workers, instead of building on strengths, mistakenly judge the crisis point where women reach out for help with abuse "as ripe for investigating past childhood traumas and examining parenting styles" (p. 278). A focus is placed on meeting individual women's "needs," particularly for safety, but what constitutes the nature of needs and in what interests do particular needs work? While women's pain may be mitigated by this emphasis on women's individual experience and the sameness of their needs, broad-based feminist demands for structural change may be eclipsed. As Chandra Mohanty (1992) points out, "this notion of the individual needs to be self-consciously historicized if as feminists we wish to go beyond the limited bourgeois ideology of individualism, especially as we attempt to understand what cross-cultural sisterhood might be made to mean" (pp. 82-83). How has an emphasis on individual needs and interventions and strategies such as criminal justice intervention reproduced misogynist, racist, and heterosexist ideological images and practices? We must critically examine whether our interventions are actually increasing women's material and emotional resources for surviving outside abusive relationships. We must renew our commitment to ways of confronting violence against women that are rooted in more inclusive, community-based approaches, long-term strategies that recognize the connectedness of different forms of oppression, and diverse forms of organizing and mobilizing at the global policy level.

Shelters and the transition house movement must take stock of the current state of its struggle for change, a necessary but difficult task given the cutbacks to shelters and related services and the daily demands of providing assistance with inadequate funding to abused women. According to survivors and key informants in this study, we must build on our work to forge new configurations of collaboration among feminists, activists, survivors, and community-based professionals (not mutually exclusive categories) that reflect the shared interests of diverse groups of women. Such configurations must include policies and structural mechanisms that ensure inclusion and power sharing. Working together across differences of "race," ethnicity, class, and other axes of oppression also requires openly analyzing and addressing differences, including power differences. Distinct groups, organizing autonomously around issues of concern to them, encompass a diversity of experiences and social locations with which to deepen our understanding of violence against women. Recognizing existing tensions in the antiviolence movement, we must continue our search for constructive ways of building on our visions for change and our diversity to confront violence against women.

As Bernice Reagon pointed out in 1983, survival is the ground for coalition. In our present climate, survival may mean sustaining the gains that the shelter movement has made and revitalizing our work for change through new theorizing and new strategizing. As Iris Young (1997) states, "unity and understanding for a new people's movement will not come from pretending that group differences do not matter, but from understanding how they do matter, and so forging an inclusive picture of our social relations" (p. 69). Such a position has the potential for solidarity, perhaps more so than the search for common oppression as grounds for legitimate action. Such solidarity requires sharing resources, strength, and resistance (hooks, 1984, 1995). We also may need to rethink the nature of some of our relationships with state institutions and nonfeminist organizations, and create new strategies for the goals and conditions of these interactions. Quinby (1995) suggests that feminists in the transition house movement may have to make hard judgments about whether to increase our distance from "system-bound professionals" (p. 278) and other influences in order to maintain autonomy over the conditions of our speaking and renew our subversive potential. Although many transition houses and feminist organizations are painfully aware of the contradictions entailed in working with the state and in resisting collusion, we are in urgent need of further theorizing about our relations with the state, particularly in the current conservative social and political climate.

The ways in which the legal, administrative, and practical contexts of feminist and mainstream social services disempower both workers and clients is another area requiring urgent attention (Callahan, 1993; Ristock and Pennell, 1996; Swift, 1998; Walker, 1990). For example, in this study, mainstream child welfare services, public and private, held women responsible for their circumstances and the care of their children, including the protection of their children from abusive men. This position hides the social conditions that set women up to be abused and to be the primary caregivers, alone and often isolated with their children. Research is desperately needed to design strategies for altering the legal, administrative, and practical contexts in which this work is done, and to find healthier ways of working with women and children who are abused and with abused women who abuse their children (Ristock and Pennell, 1996). The need for this work is evidenced in the ways in which the welfare and legal systems, fueled by a right-wing agenda, are stepping up the regulation of women, linking income support with vigilance over women's sexuality and procreation, and making it more difficult for women escaping abusive men to get custody of and access to their children (Quinby, 1995). While gender, racial, and class discrimination in the court system and mediation services has always existed, these systems are increasingly moving in the direction of "father's rights" without any accountability to women and children (Quinby, 1995).

All of us in the struggle against violence toward women must continue to critically reflect on the subversive and transformative potential of our ways of working against it. The personal can be constituted in ways that transgress and subvert, or reaffirm, the status quo (Alcoff and Gray, 1993; Armstrong, 1994; Prieur, 1995; Quinby, 1995). When healing obscures the social meaning of history and experience, "the personal as political would be translated to read the personal is the public" (Armstrong, 1994, p. 270), or "the political is personal" (Mohanty, 1994, p. 160). As Chandra Mohanty (1994) clarifies, "all politics is collapsed into the personal, and questions of individual behaviours, attitudes, and life-style stand in for political analysis of the social" (p. 160). Individual political struggles, framed as a question of individual needs, hide the conditions that produce experience.

An example from survivors' stories illustrates the importance of ongoing critical reflection about the subversive and transformative potential of our speaking and actions. Donna explained that when she first began therapy, the therapist suggested that she had simply been unable to adequately cope with her experiences of violation. Furthermore, he reduced the origin of all the difficulties she faced in her life to the fact that she had been sexually abused. It took some time before Donna discerned that she was subtly being blamed for the abuse she had suffered because the therapist did not recognize either her grandfather's actions as an abuse of power, or the social and materials conditions of her life. Directing his gaze at Donna, he saw a woman in need of therapy but not a social world in need of transformation. Reflecting on her experience, she uncovered a far more subversive way of constituting the personal. She could then speak more clearly about what interests were being served by shifting the gaze from the ideological and structural conditions engendering her experience to her purported inability to cope.

The collapsing of the political into the personal fails to acknowledge structural and ideological conditions, and obviates the need for collective voices and for political organization and action to end violence against women and the conditions that occasion it. The personal, while indeed political, must be articulated in a politics of collectivity. As Mohanty (1992) affirms, the politics of gender, "race," class, or sexual orientation cannot be reduced to the all-too-common conflation of experience, identity, and politics. In this conflation, "politics and ideology as self-conscious struggles and choices necessarily get written out of such an analysis" (p. 80). Self-conscious struggle is especially critical now in the context of right-wing agendas for women and the family, and the neoconservative tide discounting feminisms and their discourses about the oppression of women.

THE MANY VOICES OF SURVIVORS: SPEAKING ABOUT OUR LIVES

How do we speak about violence against women and about survivors of woman abuse? What might a more liberatory discourse about woman abuse and survivors look like?

First, we need to reemphasize the social realities that give rise to violence against women. Speaking narrowly about abuse or violence obscures who is exercising power over whom and the material conditions in which women experience abuse, for example, poverty, racism, lack of decent and affordable housing, custody and access issues, low wages, homelessness, subjection to scrutiny by the systems, and inadequate income for a decent quality of life. Although participants in this study suffered pain from woman abuse, incest, and rape, sources of suffering also included systemic discrimination, financial dependency, and the policies and practices of social institutions such as Family and Children's Services. Women cannot shoulder all responsibility to protect their children unless they themselves are protected. When parenting is removed from its political context, for example, poverty, substandard housing, lack of day care and collective support, and punitive welfare policies, child abuse is reduced to a problem that lies within individual women. Consequently, we need to reemphasize the context of woman abuse, detailing the links between women's subordinate social status, economic vulnerability, and experiences of violence and abuse rooted in gendered, racialized, and class-based hierarchies and other forms of socially constructed disadvantage.

Second, we need to continue to broaden discourse about violence against women to include the many ways in which women experience violence and abuse based on gender, class, "race," ethnicity, sexuality, and ability. Although significant shifts have occurred in the past decade, the shelter movement has largely been based on, and has represented, the experiences of white, heterosexual, able-bodied women and their children. Yet the violence that all women experience is shaped by dimensions of social location and identity such as ethnicity, "race," and class (Crenshaw, 1994). As Deborah Prieur (1995) asserts, we need an inclusive analysis that encompasses differences in women's experiences of abuse and oppression in the family. What are the ways in which racism and ableism work with sexism to produce different experiences for black women, aboriginal women, women with disabilities? What are the implications of a homogenizing discourse for services and modes of working with women who are abused, for organizing at the community level, and for planning strategies for change? Do strategies for confronting abuse replicate and reinforce the subordination of particular groups of women, for example, women of color? We must disrupt the homogenization of the experiences of abused women by recognizing the range of women's voices and experiences. Our ongoing elaboration of a discourse of violence against women rooted in our understanding of a "matrix of domination" (Zinn and Dill, 1996) will capture the breadth and depth of oppression and allow for the design of intervention strategies that are responsive to these interrelated patterns.

Third, we need to rethink our assumptions about survivors and the exclusions that our assumptions create. How do we see survivors' contributions to projects for change, whatever shape these may take as personal and/or social commitments to change? What are professionals and workers in transition houses and related services saying when survivors are not "healed" enough to work for change? When is it appropriate for survivors to become involved in social change efforts? Judgments about survivors' degree of healing need to be examined to uncover stereotypes and preconceptions about survivors and the power dynamics implicit in them. A more productive approach might entail mutual learning and consciousness-raising between survivors and other workers in the struggle.

Fourth, we need to consider how what we say about abuse prevents some women from identifying what is happening to them as abuse or seeking assistance. Janice Ristock points out how the heterosexism implicit in discourses about violence against women excludes lesbian women and deters them from seeking help when they have been abused by their partners (Ristock and Pennell, 1996). We need to ask ourselves if the language we use to speak about abuse and violence includes the variety of ways in which women experience abuse, define themselves and exercise agency, and identify obstacles in their lives. Do our words portray women as capable of doing the best they can in difficult circumstances or as victims requiring endless support and counseling?

Fifth, descriptions of the interlocking ideas, institutions, and practices that perpetuate our subordination also need to include representations of women's resistance to abuse and other oppressive social realities. Stories must continue to be told about survivors who, in different ways and forms, are resisters and warriors against woman abuse as "a practice of dominance" (Heberle, 1996, p. 70). Survivors' stories and storytelling about survivors must honor individual resistance as well as the necessity of political organization and action for social change.

TURNING THE GAZE ON OURSELVES
AS WORKERS, FEMINISTS, SURVIVORS,
AND PROFESSIONALS IN THE MOVEMENT

What is our complicity, as feminists, social workers, survivors, and as women who work with survivors, in maintaining the status quo?

I urge all of us who work with women who have been abused, and feminist social workers in particular, the majority of whom are white, middle-class, heterosexual women, to ask ourselves how the knowledge we hold about abused women is produced. Since social work is a gendered profession in which women form the majority of both workers and clients, I believe that my repeated plea is particularly germane (Profitt, 1996). Social work has been heavily implicated in generating an ethnocentric and fragmented discourse and practice with respect to gender issues. We must ask ourselves how we are implicated in reproducing oppressive ways of thinking about survivors, and how we maintain the status quo by working in certain ways with abused women. How does the language we use disempower and exclude survivors? What is our investment in continuing to offer ineffective or victim-blaming solutions to women? How does our work with survivors keep us from recognizing the discursive and material conditions that construct our own power/powerlessness? How do our positions of counselor or expert reproduce the Other by refusing to speak of our investment in the status quo? How can examining our own social locations and assumptions help us to continue to fight against the co-optation of progressive demands for change? What are the complexities of caring involved in our work and how do they affect our responses to abused women? Does our work with survivors reproduce gendered roles of caring and protection, encouraging women to assume the greater burden of responsibility for ending violence against women? These are difficult but key questions that feminists continue to grapple with in their search for ways to both honor women's forms of caring and redistribute caring responsibilities among men and communities.

I believe that we will forge ahead in dangerous neoconservative waters to resist dominant discourses and practices that try to dilute our feminist political analyses of violence against women and our collective actions to end it. We will remain vigilant to the difference between subversion of dominant patterns of thought and practice, and complicity with disempowering ways of thinking and acting that no longer disrupt the status quo. There is a difference between the pain of women who are abused and the pain of men who abuse women, and we must continue to make these distinctions. As mediators of ways of speaking about violence against women, we can and do make a difference. Talking about ending racism, bell hooks (1995) suggests that a politics of resistance can address the psychological trauma that black people experience, both in the past and present. I suggest that a politics of resistance for survivors of abuse can address the psychological trauma of women's experiences of abuse and violence, and that experiences of many forms of violation can be mobilized to transform power relations and subjectivities in a misogynist society. Discursive and material conditions very much matter if women survivors are to be equal participants in the struggle against violence, if we are to truly mobilize "the subversive potential of our rage" (Alcoff and Gray, 1993, p. 286). Only if we are able to engage with one another as individuals and groups in dialogue and collective struggle will we discern how our paths to liberation are interwoven and how we can collectively strengthen our resistance to the violence exercised against us.

Appendix

Participants in This Study

JUNE

June is a white woman who identifies as a radical lesbian feminist. She grew up in a working-class family in which her father worked in the manufacturing industry and her mother worked in the home. After June's partner threatened the safety of her infant daughter, she went to a shelter for the first time. After several shelter stays, she moved into second-stage housing and then into cooperative housing. There she began to explore her sexuality, coming out as a lesbian two years later. She is forty-four years of age, has one child, and survives on Family Benefits. She has previously worked as a secretary and is now a computer technician. She has been involved for five years in advocacy, social action, and training women to work on a crisis line for assaulted women.

PAOLA

Paola came to Canada from Chile shortly after her parents immigrated to Canada to escape political persecution. Of indigenous ancestry, she grew up in a poor family in a Santiago neighborhood in Chile under the dictatorship of Pinochet. Her family's involvement, particularly her mother's, in popular neighborhood organizations was a form of survival and part of the fabric of everyday life. Paola was also active in youth groups, popular organizations, and political work. The philosophy and practice of the liberation theology branch of the Catholic Church guided their work, providing some degree of protection for it under the dictatorship. Paola recalled that although her family endured difficult times, she felt sheltered and secure growing up because of her parents' protection and the fertile soil of her community, which provided her with so many learning opportunities. Nevertheless, the trauma of economic deprivation, the sense that if she has something today it may not be there tomorrow, has remained with her. Prior to coming to Canada, Paola had been living with her partner; after her arrival in Canada, she went through a period of intense mourning. During her social work studies Paola, with a group of female colleagues, learned about feminist theories, examined her experiences of incest, woman abuse, and political oppression, and deepened her analysis of class, "race," and gender. Paola is thirty-one years of age and cares for her young son. She is completing a master's degree in adult education. She describes herself as woman-centered and has been involved in consciousness raising and community organizing with women who have been abused in heterosexual and lesbian relationships.

DONNA

Donna is a white woman who grew up in a poor family with her parents and two brothers. She is forty-five years of age and has one daughter in her early twenties. Donna emphasized that many factors such as poverty, isolation, gender stereotyping, violence in her neighborhood, and religious beliefs combined to shape who she is. Her mother was physically and emotionally abusive to her. At age three, she was already trying to avoid her grandfather's sexually molesting clutches. At age nine she was sexually assaulted by her grandfather, and at age ten by a male neighbor. During high school, she turned inward and tried to forget what had happened to her. Forgetting was made more difficult by two male teachers who constantly made lascivious comments in class about girls in mini-skirts and makeup. At age twenty, Donna was raped by a man whom she was dating. When Donna was twenty-one, she gave birth to her daughter, her only child, and was stigmatized as an "unwed mother" by the small rural community in which she lived. For a time, Donna lived with a male partner in an emotionally abusive relationship and, following its breakup, was denied Family Benefits. She became increasingly depressed as she struggled to care for her daughter and worked in low-paying jobs where she was sexually harassed by male co-workers. During this time, she was diagnosed with a rare, painful form of arthritis. At age thirty-seven, she entered a major depression, was hospitalized in a psychiatric unit, attended therapy, and participated concurrently in an incest survivors' group. Members of this group later formed a sexual assault self-help action group. Donna recently completed training to be a social services worker. She has been involved for many years in speaking out in her community about violence against women, educating young women in the high schools, advocating for/with abused women, and volunteering with the local shelter and second-stage housing.

JACKIE

Jackie is a thirty-eight-year-old white woman. She grew up in a poor family in which her mother was a homemaker and her father worked at whatever employment he could find. Jackie and her four children relocated to another town eleven years ago to escape her husband's death threats. A year prior to her relocation, she had contacted Family and Children's Services (FCS) upon her daughters' disclosure that their father was touching them sexually. FCS investigated the allegations over a period of several months and referred Jackie to a therapist who, on behalf of FCS, strongly advised her to attend an incest survivors' group. As a child, Jackie had been a victim of incest. For approximately a year, Jackie lived with the tension of trying to protect her daughters as well as cope with her husband's physical and psychological abuse. When her health deteriorated, she talked with her family doctor, who referred her to the local shelter. While the FCS investigation was still underway, Jackie went to the shelter for the first time, returning home with the understanding that her husband would no longer be living there. However, he began to stalk the house at night, pressuring her to allow him to move back in. When Jackie attempted to end her relationship with him, he threatened to kill her and their children, revealing that he had made plans to do so. Fortunately, during this time her therapist suggested relocating to another town. After relocating, she continued to see a therapist to deal with her abuse by her partner, the incest she suffered as a child, and the sexual abuse of her children. While caring for her young children, she finished high school and took a course in human services. She now works with children and has for many years been speaking out about her experiences as a survivor and educating her community and professionals about woman abuse and the barriers women face in confronting abuse. She was one of the founding members of second-stage housing for women and is an advocate for changes in community responses to woman abuse.

RUTH

Ruth is an Ojibwa woman who was born on a reserve. Per the Canadian government's policy of assimilation of aboriginal peoples in the 1950s and

1960s, Ruth was removed from her community at the age of three by child welfare authorities, along with several siblings and cousins. She was placed in foster homes from ages three to nine and in one of these homes was subjected to sexual abuse for three years by her foster father. She was adopted at age nine by a farming couple of European descent. Her adoptive mother was physically and psychologically abusive to her, and Ruth was also sexually assaulted by her adoptive parents' son. At the age of thirteen, Ruth was raped by a gang of men from her community and by the father of a school friend. When Ruth met the man whom she would marry, she felt that he offered an escape from her home. Her husband, who had a severe drinking problem, became emotionally abusive to her and her children. Several separations from her partner finally culminated in a shelter stay nine years ago. Ruth and her partner both sought counseling separately to confront her partner's abuse and their personal histories. She finished high school and then entered a community college program where she studied women's issues and the language she had lost as a child. Recently, she has located her siblings and cousins. Ruth is forty-two years of age and has two grown children and several grandchildren. She became involved in advocacy work with and for abused women and encourages aboriginal women to speak out about the violence and racism they have experienced. Her dream is to have a healing center for all women.

VICTORIA

Victoria is a forty-two-year-old white woman who identifies herself as a radical feminist. She was adopted at an early age by a farming family and grew up in a financially comfortable home. Her biological mother had placed her in an orphanage from which she was adopted by a woman who had also grown up in an orphanage and who, in order to leave it, was coerced into "consenting" to be sterilized. Victoria has struggled all her life to make sense of her adoption and her feeling of never fitting in anywhere. She was physically and psychologically abused by her adoptive mother. Her father was a gentle, spiritual man who recognized her artistic and spiritual abilities, supported her, and mediated between her and her mother. She searched throughout her twenties and early thirties for a place where she would fit. At age thirty-three, she met the man who is now her ex-partner. At different times in her life she felt as if she was going mad, particularly when she was being abused by him. She has one daughter, whom she is trying to raise in a respectful and caring way. She is an artist and has been involved in a social action women's group for four years.

BARBARA

Barbara is a forty-five-year-old white woman who grew up in what she described as a strict, proper, middle-class family. One of the traumatic events in her life was a pregnancy in adolescence. Her parents banished her to a maternity home and pressured her to give up her child for adoption, which she did. Shortly afterward, she married and gave birth to a son. The man she married turned out to be extremely abusive so she left this relationship when her son was eight years old. Six months after the end of her marriage, she met her last partner, with whom she lived for several years. In her thirties, because of her partner's abuse, she began to remember incidents of sexual abuse perpetrated by her father and stepgrandfather. She later found out that everyone, including her family, knew about their abuse of other relatives and neighborhood children. She talked with a close co-worker and her family doctor about her relationship with her partner and they suggested she contact a women's center. Barbara's son is now a teenager and she works in employment equity. She is presently trying to make contact with the child she lost to adoption and she has been involved in public education and advocacy with and for victims of incest and facilitating groups for women who have survived incest.

HEATHER

Heather, a white woman thirty-seven years of age, has three children. She grew up in what she described as a chaotic family and was affected by her mother's alcoholism. She married her first husband at age sixteen, partially to escape from home. Two years into her second marriage, her partner assaulted her and left her unconscious in a pool of blood. She called the police, who charged him with assault. While she was dealing with this trauma, she was several months pregnant and had just learned that her teenage son had been sexually abused by her stepbrothers. When the charges against her husband and her stepbrothers went to trial, Heather was moving from the home of one family member to another. It was through the leader of a group for mothers of children who had been sexually abused that she found her way to second-stage housing. Heather's ordeal did not end there. Her husband tried to kill her on several occasions, and she has had several devastating encounters with Family Court, the criminal justice system, and Family Benefits. She currently survives with her two children on Family Benefits. Heather formed a women's community action group with other survivors about three years ago and is working to educate her community and to make social institutions more responsive to the needs of women and children.

ROSARIO

Rosario immigrated to Canada with her husband and young son four years ago. She is twenty-four years of age and grew up in El Salvador in a poor family. Her father died when she was nine, and at twelve she went to work with her mother. Rosario had been married for less than a year when her husband started mistreating her. After she gave birth to her first and only child, she returned to work, but her husband pressured her to quit her job. Shortly after this, she became depressed and was hospitalized in a psychiatric facility. She became involved in a housing project where she met a psychologist who encouraged her to join a women's group. She separated from her husband several times. When he applied to come to Canada, she initially refused to consider it but later decided that she would come, if only for the opportunities that might result for her son. Shortly after she came to Canada she separated from her husband. She had a difficult time looking for an apartment, with little knowledge of the English language, and feared the legal consequences of leaving her husband. Through an immigrant and settlement center, she participated in a women's group for over a year and subsequently became involved in community organizing with Spanish-speaking women of Latin American origin.

MARYANNE

Maryanne is a thirty-six-year-old white woman. Her mother was a homemaker, and her father worked at a steel plant. She has two children and currently works as a cashier. Maryanne emphasized that she learned early in life to care about "what people would think." She felt that she had to be the perfect child, and she dreaded disappointing her parents in any way. She married at age eighteen and, early in her relationship, her husband began to hit her and verbally insult her on a regular basis. She tried to kill herself, at which time her family doctor gave her "nerve pills" to help her cope. She went to a shelter twice when she was being abused by her husband and brought charges against him for assault. She and her husband were ordered by the judge to attend counseling, but after two sessions in which the therapist confronted her husband about his behavior, he refused to attend. She moved from the shelter into second-stage housing, where she lived for a year. She became involved in the women's community action group, a group of survivors working to challenge and change the way abused women are treated when they seek assistance from social institutions.

ELEANOR

Eleanor is a forty-four-year-old white woman. Eleanor's youth was affected by her father's alcoholism and violence toward her, her mother, and her sisters. She grew up with the desire to be financially independent, went to work with a company, got her own apartment, and lived independently for some time. In her late twenties, she married and had four children. She left her husband on several occasions, and finally left the relationship after thirteen years of marriage. During their relationship she had also contacted Children's Aid because she suspected that her husband was abusing her daughter. On the advice of her lawyer, she went to a shelter and later moved into second-stage housing, where she lived for a year. There she became a leader with residents, and she has been actively involved for three years in many aspects of second-stage housing and its efforts for change in the community and with professionals. She and her children are currently surviving on Family Benefits. She has also been active in an antipoverty group for women on social assistance, and in community education and advocacy for survivors of woman abuse.

Notes

Chapter 1

1. The concept of relations of ruling, developed by Dorothy Smith (1990a, 1990b), refers to how everyday experience is transformed into objectified forms of knowledge and organized ideologically through a set of practices that do the work of ruling. Ruling organizes and generates forms of knowledge out of people's everyday experience, which are then used to maintain relations of power and subordination. For analyses of social work's alliance with dominant social norms and values and its contradictory position in webs of power as both a helping profession and mode of social control, see Carniol (1995), Epstein (1994), Langan and Lee (1989), Leonard (1994), Moreau (1979, 1990), Moreau and Leonard (1989), and Mullaly (1997).

2. The term *sector popular,* or popular sector in English, is widely used in Latin America to refer to those sectors of the population most impoverished and marginalized by their lack of access to social, economic, and political power. The popular movement or *movimiento popular* comprises rural and urban groups such as small farmers or *campesinos,* unions, cooperatives, blue-collar workers, Christian-based movements, and settlement dwellers. For a description and analysis of our work with the mutual support group which was grounded in popular education philosophy and methodology, see Pérez Naranjo and Profitt (1992) and Profitt (1994).

3. In her essay "Women, Welfare, and the Politics of Need Interpretation," Nancy Fraser (1989) discusses how the social welfare system translates political issues concerning women's needs into legal, administrative, and therapeutic matters.

4. Smith and colleagues (1975) note that, paradoxically, consciousness-raising has been ill-defined but essential to all liberation movements. Evans (1979) and Sarachild (1978) note forerunners to what would come to be called consciousness-raising in women's liberation groups: the northern student movement, in their organizing efforts, used a process of "radicalization" (Evans, 1979, p. 134) and the Student Non-Violent Coordinating Committee was a political agitation and education group (Sarachild, 1978, p. 144). Other values were community, equality, and participatory democracy.

5. For a discussion of the qualities of critical consciousness, see Ira Shor (1993).

6. The term empowerment has been increasingly appropriated by neoliberal and conservative discourses. Workfare and punitive programs for single mothers

have adopted the language of empowerment to punish people, mostly women, and separate the "deserving" from the "undeserving." However, Patti Lather's (1991) usage of empowerment avoids invoking "the current fashion of individual self-assertion, upward mobility and the psychological experience of feeling powerful" (p. 3). For a critique of the latter notion of empowerment, see Fisher and Karger (1997), and for an analysis of how empowerment can promote women's subjection by linking changes in subjectivity with empowerment practices, see Cruikshank (1993, 1994) and Lessa (1996).

7. According to Robert Mullaly (1997), feminist social work and Paulo Freire's conscientization (Freire, 1994) constitute a subjectivist orientation to social change because they see consciousness-raising and personal change as essential components in social transformation.

8. Testimonio (oral and written) is a form of social action that chronicles popular struggle against the political status quo (Beverley, 1992). Originating in Latin America, it was used during the Pinochet dictatorship in Chile to register and denounce torture (Agger, 1994). Doris Sommer (1988) clarifies that in the testimonio, a woman's singularity "achieves its identity as an extension of the collective. The singular represents the plural not because it replaces or subsumes the group but because the speaker is a distinguishable part of the whole" (p. 108). An excellent example of testimonio that illustrates Sommer's point is Rigoberta Menchú's, *I Rigoberta Menchú: An Indian Woman in Guatemala* (1984).

9. Kathleen Weiler (1988) usefully contextualizes the sources of critical educational theory and feminist social and cultural theory in terms of reproduction and production theories. Production theories, such as Antonio Gramsci's, concern themselves with the ways in which people individually and collectively assert their experience and produce meaning and culture that contest or resist ideological and material forces. Agency and the production of knowledge are considered in the context of the power of structural determinants, for example, material practices, modes of power, and economic and political institutions. There is a belief in human agency and thus in the possibility of social change through praxis—action and reflection. Reproduction theory concerns itself with the processes through which existing social structures maintain and reproduce themselves.

10. My review of government documents began with Linda MacLeod's study, *Wife Battering in Canada: The Vicious Circle* (1980), and included materials from the Canadian Advisory Council on the Status of Women, the National Clearing-house on Family Violence, and the Family Violence Prevention Division, Health and Welfare Canada, particularly recent publications of the National Panel on Violence Against Women and the Statistics Canada National Survey on Violence Against Women. The national newsletter *Vis-à-Vis* serves as an important network and information resource for the transition house movement. (*Vis-à-Vis: A National Newsletter on Family Violence.* Ottawa, ON: Canadian Council on Social Development.)

Chapter 2

1. Chiswick Women's Aid in London, England, established in 1971, was the first internationally known shelter.

2. From the beginning of the battered women's movement, different feminist analyses of woman abuse, and therefore different strategies for change, existed within it, for example, Marxist, radical, and reformist feminisms (Beaudry, 1985). Walker (1990) identified grassroots activists, academic feminists, and professional feminists as among those struggling to define woman abuse in the women's movement in Ottawa and Vancouver. Micheline Beaudry (1985) suggests that in Quebec, the movement generally tended toward providing services rather than building a broad-based radical protest movement.

3. Walker (1990) examines local events in the feminist movement against woman abuse at different sites such as Ottawa and Vancouver, how these local processes were translated to the federal level, and the input of various players such as women's groups and professionals into the social problem apparatus. She sets out three stages in "the process of institutional articulation and absorption that concepts, as ways of thinking, naming, and knowing, co-ordinate and make possible" (p. 16): (1) the women's movement sought to make public the plight of beaten women; (2) the struggle within the women's movement to provide an analysis of the issue and develop strategies in relation to the state unfolded as the issue moved onto state terrain; and (3) the women's movement fought to advance a definition of the issue that captured the complex situation and needs of battered women and ensured that the social problem apparatus would respond appropriately to battered women's needs. Walker suggests that a possible fourth stage would be the reexamination of the current state of affairs in the absence of political change.

4. The state's role in progressive change for women is an important one for feminists. For feminist analyses of the battered women's movement and the Canadian state, see Findlay (1988) and Randall (1988). Sue Findlay (1988) examines the contradictions embodied in placing wife battering on the political agenda. See Currie (1990) for an analysis of the role and ability of legal rights to promote material equality, and Snider (1990) for an examination of feminist demands for change in the criminal justice system. For a different perspective, see Ursel (1994), who argues that the battered women's movement has had an important impact on the state. She suggests that the ultimate criterion in assessing the success or failure of the battered women's movement is whether abused women now have more support and options available to them than they previously had.

5. In her examination of the co-optation of the battered women's movement in the United States, Kathleen Tierney (1982) suggests that co-optation was enabled by the fact that the movement itself was built on preexisting organizations of feminists and groups in the social work, mental health, and legal professions.

6. Examples of the ways in which professionals, including feminist social workers, are caught up in the social relations of ruling include the promotion of multidisciplinary approaches with a range of professional interventions, and the

explosion of social science research dedicated to pinpointing the cause of wife battering.

7. In her study of woman abuse in Canada, Linda MacLeod (1987) found that although the majority of women who stayed in transition houses were under the age of thirty-five, women of other ages were also sheltered. Although poorer women used transition houses, a small percentage of women who came to shelters were from middle and upper income levels. In addition, many women who called crisis lines for telephone counseling, information, and advice came from middle- and upper-income levels.

Chapter 4

1. Ronnie Janoff-Bulman and Christine Timko (1987) work within a framework of trauma and traumatic-negative events. According to Judith Herman (1992), traumatic events overwhelm a person's capacity to adapt, and evoke feelings of helplessness, fear, and loss of control. In contrast to the American Psychiatric Association's definition of traumatic events as falling outside the range of ordinary experience, Herman points out that violence against women can hardly be described in this way because rape and sexual and domestic violence are common experiences for many women. Although June's experience would most certainly be defined as a traumatic event, it also requires political contextualization in unequal social relations, an analysis that Janoff-Bulman and Timko fail to undertake. Despite this limitation, their material is useful in understanding how people deal with painful and traumatic experiences.

Chapter 5

1. For a discussion of the multiple issues and multilayered, routinized forms of domination that converge in the lives of women of color who are confronting abuse in intimate relationships, see Crenshaw (1994). Kimberlé Crenshaw urges us to recognize that women's subordination cannot be located primarily in the psychological effects of male domination but rather in the socioeconomic factors and the structural and political aspects that disempower women of color.

2. Cain (1993) describes this relation between ways of being/experiences and language as an unthought relationship. An unthought relationship captures the idea that not all relationships in which people live are expressible in discourse. The notion of an unthought relationship is useful in making sense of feminist work that exposes, for the first time, "the relationship in which women are placed, while yet claiming to know that the relationship preceded the exposure which 'brought it to light' " (p. 74). Examples are sexual harassment and Kelly's (1988) research on sexual violence. According to Cain, "formulating the unthought is an extremely dangerous and political business" (p. 75).

3. Although bell hooks (1988, 1990, 1993, 1994) defines self-recovery as a political process, within the helping professions, the term recovery derives from

the disease model of alcoholism situated in a discourse of therapeutism (Armstrong, 1994, p. 209). hooks (1990) is alert, however, to the ways in which discursive practices and the production of knowledge can be appropriated and transmuted into a "message that neither subverts nor liberates" (p. 163). As Louise Armstrong (1994), Cecilia Kitzinger (1993), and Susan Stefan (1994) argue, within a therapeutic discourse, women are encouraged to "heal," creating "an illusion of power where the social reality is otherwise" (Armstrong, 1994, p. 210). Therapeutic ideology convinces women that the goal of feeling "safe" is both desirable and possible (Armstrong, 1994; Hutchinson and McDaniel, 1986; Kitzinger, 1993; Mann, 1987; Stefan, 1994). Surely the goal of a safe world is a laudable and desirable one for women, children, and men but hardly one that can be obtained by convincing women they are safe if they feel safe.

4. For critiques of the ethnocentric, white, middle-class bias of some feminist theories, see Alarcón (1990), hooks (1984), and Spelman (1988).

5. Teresa de Lauretis discusses the deconstruction of identity in the context of Biddy Martin and Chandra Mohanty's (1986) reading of Minnie Bruce Pratt's essay "Identity: Skin Blood Heart."

Chapter 8

1. One example is a program for survivors that operates in Duluth, Minnesota. Focusing on personal and social change, it supports survivors in creating and carrying out social change strategies. *In Our Best Interest: A Process of Personal and Social Change,* by Ellen Pence, with contributions by Bonnie Mann, Mary Margaret Flynn, Yolanda Bako, Anne Marshall, Jan Martin, Shirley Oberg, and Nancy Burns (1987). Duluth, Minnesota: Minnesota Program Development Inc.

References

Acker, J., Barry, K., and Esseveld, J. (1991). Objectivity and truth. In M.M. Fonow and J. Cook (Eds.), *Beyond methodology: Feminist scholarship as lived research* (pp. 133-153). Bloomington, IN: Indiana University Press.

Agger, I. (1994). *The blue room. Trauma and testimony among refugee women. A psycho-social exploration*. London: Zed.

Agnew, V. (1998). *In search of a safe place: Abused women and culturally sensitive services*. Toronto: University of Toronto Press.

Alarcón, N. (1990). The theoretical subject(s) of *This Bridge Called My Back* and Anglo-American feminism. In G. Anzaldúa (Ed.), *Making face, making soul. Haciendo caras. Creative and critical perspectives by women of color* (pp. 356-369). San Francisco: Aunt Lute Books.

Alcoff, L. and Gray, L. (1993). Survivor discourse: Transgression or recuperation? *Signs, 18*(2), 260-290.

Alcorn Jr., M.W. (1994). The subject of discourse: Reading Lacan through (and beyond) poststructuralist contexts. In M. Bracher, M.W. Alcorn Jr., R.J. Corthell, and F. Massardier-Kenney (Eds.), *Lacanian theory of discourse: Subject, structure, and society* (pp. 19-45). New York: New York University Press.

Andrew, K., Barnsley, J., Ellis, M., Lewis, D., and Wasserlein, F. (1986). Feminist manifesto. *Resources for Feminist Research/Documentation sur la Recherche Feministe, 15*(1), 46-47.

Anzaldúa, G. (1990). Haciendo caras, una entrada. In G. Anzaldúa (Ed.), *Making face, making soul. Haciendo caras. Creative and critical perspectives by women of color* (pp. xv-xxviii). San Francisco: Aunt Lute Books.

Armstrong, L. (1994). *Rocking the cradle of sexual politics: What happened when women said incest*. Reading, MA: Addison-Wesley.

Bannerji, H. (1995). *Thinking through: Essays on feminism, Marxism, and anti-racism*. Toronto: Women's Press.

Bannerji, H., Carty, L., Dehli, K., Heald, S., and McKenna, K. (1991). *Unsettling relations: The university as a site of feminist struggles*. Toronto: Women's Press.

Barry, K. (1984). *Female sexual slavery*. New York: New York University Press.

Bartky, S. (1990). *Femininity and domination: Studies in the phenomenology of oppression*. New York: Routledge.

Beaudry, M. (1985). *Battered women* (L. Huston and M. Heap, Trans.). Montreal: Black Rose Books.

Beverley, J. (1992). The margin at the center: On *testimonio* (testimonial narrative). In S. Smith and J. Watson (Eds.), *De/colonizing the subject* (pp. 91-114). Minneapolis: University of Minnesota Press.

Blum, H.P. (1985). Foreword. In H.P. Blum (Ed.), *Defense and resistance: Historical perspectives and current concepts* (pp. 5-15). New York: International Universities Press.

Bowker, L.H., Arbitell, M., and McFaren, R.J. (1988). On the relationship between wife beating and child abuse. In K. Yllö and M. Bograd (Eds.), *Feminist perspectives on wife abuse* (pp. 158-174). London: Sage.

Breines, W. and Gordon, L. (1983). The new scholarship on family violence. *Signs, 8*(3), 490-531.

Briskin, L. (1990). *Feminist pedagogy: Teaching and learning liberation.* Feminist Perspectives Paper No. 19. Ottawa: CRIAW/ICREF.

Brittan, A. and Maynard, M. (1984). *Sexism, racism and oppression.* Oxford, UK: Basil Blackwell.

Brock, D. (1993). Talkin' bout a revelation. Feminist popular discourse on sexual abuse. In L. Carty (Ed.), *And still we rise: Feminist political mobilizing in contemporary Canada* (pp. 109-116). Toronto: Women's Press.

Brown, E.B. (1992). What has happened here?: The politics of difference in women's history and feminist politics. *Feminist Studies, 18*(2), 295-312.

Brown, P.A. and Dickey, C. (1992). Critical reflection in groups with abused women. *Affilia, 7*(3), 57-71.

Butler, S. (1995). Feminism and the politics of hope. Lecture at St. Jerome's College, University of Waterloo, March 10.

Cain, M. (1993). Foucault, feminism and feeling: What Foucault can and cannot contribute to feminist epistemology. In C. Ramazanoğlu (Ed.), *Up against Foucault: Explorations of some tensions between Foucault and feminism* (pp. 73-96). New York: Routledge.

Callahan, M. (1993). Feminist approaches: Women recreate child welfare. In B. Wharf (Ed.), *Rethinking child welfare in Canada* (pp. 172-209). Toronto: McClelland and Stewart.

Cannon, L.W., Higginbotham, E., and Leung, M.L.A. (1991). Race and class bias in qualitative research on women. In M.M. Fonow and J. Cook (Eds.), *Beyond methodology: Feminist scholarship as lived research* (pp. 107-118). Bloomington, IN: Indiana University Press.

Carniol, B. (1995). *Case critical: Challenging social work in Canada* (Third edition). Toronto: Between the Lines.

Carty, L. (1991). Women's studies in Canada: A discourse and praxis of exclusion. *Resources for Feminist Research: Documentation sur la Recherche Feministe, 20*(3/4), 12-18.

Chaftez, J.S. and Dworkin, A.G. (1986). *Female revolt: Women's movements in world and historical perspective.* Totowa, NJ: Rowman and Allanheld.

Chanfrault-Duchet, M.-F. (1991). Narrative structures, social models, and symbolic representation in the life story. In S.B. Gluck and D. Patai (Eds.), *Women's words: The feminist practice of oral history* (pp. 77-92). New York: Routledge.

Childers, M. and Hooks, B. (1990). A conversation about race and class. In M. Hirsch and E. Fox Keller (Eds.), *Conflicts in feminism* (pp. 60-81). New York: Routledge.

Church, K. (1995). *Forbidden narratives: Critical autobiography as social science.* Australia: Gordon and Breach Publishers.

Cramer, P. (1991). *The development of defense mechanisms.* New York: Springer-Verlag.

Crenshaw, K.W. (1994). Mapping the margins: Intersectionality, identity politics, and violence against women of color. In M. Fineman and R. Mykitiuk (Eds.), *The public nature of private violence* (pp. 93-118). New York: Routledge.

Crosby, F.J., Pufall, A., Snyder, R.C., O'Connell, M., and Whalen, P. (1989). The denial of personal disadvantage among you, me, and all the other ostriches. In M. Crawford and M. Gentry (Eds.), *Gender and thought: Psychological perspectives* (pp. 79-99). New York: Springer-Verlag.

Cruikshank, B. (1993). Revolutions within: Self-government and self-esteem. *Economy and Society, 22*(3), 327-344.

Cruikshank, B. (1994). The will to empower: Technologies of citizenship and the war on poverty. *Socialist Review, 23*(4), 29-55.

Culley, M. (1985). Anger and authority in the introductory women's studies classroom. In M. Culley and C. Portuges (Eds.), *Gendered subjects: The dynamics of feminist teaching* (pp. 209-217). Boston: Routledge and Kegan Paul.

Currie, D.H. (1990). Battered women and the state: From the failure of theory to a theory of failure. *Journal of Human Justice, 1*(2), 77-96.

de Lauretis, T. (1990). Eccentric subjects: Feminist theory and historical consciousness. *Feminist Studies, 16*(1), 115-150.

DuBois, B. (1983). Passionate scholarship: Notes on values, knowing and method in feminist social science. In G. Bowles and R.D. Klein (Eds.), *Theories of women's studies* (pp. 105-116). London: Routledge and Kegan Paul.

Elliot, P. (1995). Denial and disclosure: An analysis of selective reality as resistance to feminist curriculum. *Resources for Feminist Research/Documentation sur la Recherche Feministe, 24*(1/2), 3-13.

Elliot, P. (1998). Personal communication.

Epstein, L. (1994). The therapeutic idea in contemporary society. In A.S. Chambon and A. Irving (Eds.), *Essays on postmodernism and social work* (pp. 3-18). Toronto: Canadian Scholars' Press.

Evans, S. (1979). *Personal politics: The roots of women's liberation in the civil rights movement and the new left.* New York: Alfred A. Knopf.

Fanon, F. (1967). *A dying colonialism* (H. Chevalier, Trans.). New York: Grove Press.

Findlay, P. (1994). Conscientization and social movements in Canada: The relevance of Paulo Freire's ideas in contemporary politics. In P. McLaren and C. Lankshear (Eds.), *Politics of liberation: Paths from Freire* (pp. 108-122). New York: Routledge.

Findlay, S. (1988). Feminist struggles with the Canadian state: 1966-1988. *Resources for Feminist Research/Documentation sur la Recherche Feministe, 17*(3), 5-9.

Findlay, S. (n.d.). Speaking of silence: The personal is political. Unpublished manuscript.

Fine, M. (1994). Working the hyphens: Reinventing self and other in qualitative research. In N.K. Denzin and Y.S. Lincoln (Eds.), *Handbook of qualitative research* (pp. 70-82). Thousand Oaks, CA: Sage.

Fisher, R. and Karger, H.W. (1997). *Social work and community in a private world: Getting out in public.* New York: Longman.

Flax, J. (1990). *Thinking fragments: Psychoanalysis, feminism, and postmodernism in the contemporary West.* Berkeley, CA: University of California Press.

Flax, J. (1993). *Disputed subjects: Essays on psychoanalysis, politics and philosophy.* New York: Routledge.

Fonow, M.M. and Cook, J.A. (Eds.). (1991). *Beyond methodology: Feminist scholarship as lived research.* Bloomington, IN: Indiana University Press.

Fraser, N. (1989). *Unruly practices: Power, discourse and gender in contemporary social theory.* Minneapolis: University of Minnesota Press.

Freeman, M. (1993). *Rewriting the self: History, memory, narrative.* London: Routledge.

Freire, P. (1994). *Pedagogy of the oppressed* (M. Bergman Ramos, Trans.). New York: Continuum.

Frye, M. (1983). *The politics of reality: Essays in feminist theory.* Trumansburg, NY: Crossing Press.

Fuss, D. (1989). *Essentially speaking: Feminism, nature and difference.* London: Routledge.

Gadbois, S. (1999). Women's experiences after leaving a shelter. In *Qualitative methodology: Two examples in feminist research* (pp. 3-14). London, ON: Centre for Research on Violence Against Women and Children.

Gilman, S.T. (1988). A history of the sheltering movement for battered women in Canada. *Canadian Journal of Community Mental Health, 7*(2), 9-21.

Gramsci, A. (1971). *Selections from the prison notebooks of Antonio Gramsci* (Q. Hoare and G.N. Smith, Eds. and Trans.). New York: International Publishers.

Grosz, E. (1990). Philosophy. In S. Gunew (Ed.), *Feminist knowledge: Critique and construct* (pp. 147-174). London: Routledge.

Gunew, S. and Yeatman, A. (1993). Introduction. In S. Gunew and A. Yeatman (Eds.), *Feminism and the politics of difference* (pp. xiii-xxv). Halifax, Nova Scotia: Fernwood.

Gunn, J.V. (1992). A politics of experience. Leila Khaled's *My people shall live: The autobiography of a revolutionary.* In S. Smith and J. Watson (Eds.), *De/colonizing the subject* (pp. 65-80). Minneapolis: University of Minnesota Press.

Hall, S. (1991). Ethnicity: Identity and difference. *Radical America, 23*(4), 9-20.

Harding, S. (Ed.) (1987). *Feminism and methodology: Social science issues.* Bloomington, IN: Indiana University Press.

Haug, F. et al. (1987). *Female sexualisation: A collective work of memory* (E. Carter, Trans.). London: Verso.

Heberle, R. (1996). Deconstructive strategies and the movement against sexual violence. *Hypatia, 11*(4), 63-76.

Henriques, J., Hollway, W., Urwin, C., Venn, C., and Walkerdine, V. (1984). *Changing the subject: Psychology, social relations and subjectivity*. London: Methuen.

Herman, J.L. (1992). *Trauma and recovery: The aftermath of violence—From domestic abuse to political terror*. New York: Basic Books.

Hilton, N.Z. (1989). One in ten: The struggle and disempowerment of the battered women's movement. *Canadian Journal of Family Law, 7*(2), 313-335.

Hoff, L.A. (1990). *Battered women as survivors*. London: Routledge.

Hollway, W. (1984). Gender difference and the production of subjectivity. In J. Henriques, W. Hollway, C. Urwin, C. Venn, and V. Walkerdine. *Changing the subject: Psychology, social relations and subjectivity* (pp. 227-263). London: Methuen.

hooks, b. (1984). *Feminist theory: From margin to center*. Boston: South End Press.

hooks, b. (1988). *Talking back: Thinking feminist, thinking black*. Boston: South End Press.

hooks, b. (1990). *Yearning: Race, gender, and cultural politics*. Toronto: Between the Lines.

hooks, b. (1993). *Sisters of the yam: Black women and self-recovery*. Boston: South End Press.

hooks, b. (1994). *Teaching to transgress: Education as the practice of freedom*. New York: Routledge.

hooks, b. (1995). *Killing rage: Ending racism*. New York: Henry Holt and Co.

Hooper, C.-A. (1995). Women's and their children's experiences of sexual violence: Rethinking the links. *Women's Studies International Forum, 18*(3), 349-360.

Hutchinson, C.H. and McDaniel, S.A. (1986). The social reconstruction of sexual assault by women victims: A comparison of therapeutic experiences. *Canadian Journal of Community Mental Health, 5*(2), 17-35.

Janmohamed, A.R. (1994). Some implications of Paulo Freire's border pedagogy. In H.A. Giroux and P. McLaren (Eds.), *Between borders: Pedagogy and the politics of cultural studies* (pp. 242-252). New York: Routledge.

Janoff-Bulman, R. and Timko, C. (1987). Coping with traumatic life events: The role of denial in light of people's assumptive worlds. In C.R. Snyder and C.E. Ford (Eds.), *Coping with negative life events: Clinical and social psychological perspectives* (pp. 135-159). New York: Plenum Press.

Kelly, L. (1988). *Surviving sexual violence*. Minneapolis: University of Minnesota Press.

Kincheloe, J.L. and McLaren, P.L. (1994). Rethinking critical theory and qualitative research. In N.K. Denzin and Y.S. Lincoln (Eds.), *Handbook of qualitative research* (pp. 138-157). Thousand Oaks, CA: Sage.

Kitzinger, C. (1993). Depoliticising the personal: A feminist slogan in feminist therapy. *Women's Studies International Forum, 16*(5), 487-496.

Klein, R.D. (1983). How to do what we want to do: Thoughts about feminist methodology. In G. Bowles and R.D. Klein (Eds.), *Theories of women's studies* (pp. 88-104). London: Routledge and Kegan Paul.

Langan, M. and Lee, P. (Eds.) (1989). *Radical social work today*. London: Unwin Hyman.

Lather, P. (1991). *Getting smart: Feminist research and pedagogy with/in the post-modern.* New York: Routledge.

Lazreg, M. (1990). Feminism and difference: The perils of writing as a woman on women in Algeria. In M. Hirsch and E.F. Keller (Eds.), *Conflicts in feminism* (pp. 326-348). New York: Routledge.

Leonard, P. (1994). Knowledge/power and postmodernism: Implications for the practice of a critical social work education. *Canadian Social Work Education, 11*(1), 11-26.

Lessa, I. (1996). An atmosphere of change: Promoting well-being and healthy development of children. *Canadian Social Work Review, 13*(1), 109-124.

Lewis, M. (1990). Interrupting patriarchy: Politics, resistance, and transformation in the feminist classroom. *Harvard Educational Review, 60*(4), 467-488.

Lewis, M. (1993). *Without a word. Teaching beyond women's silence.* New York: Routledge.

Lorde, A. (1984). *Sister outsider.* Freedom, CA: Crossing Press.

MacLeod, L. (1980). *Wife battering in Canada: The vicious circle.* Ottawa: Canadian Advisory Council on the Status of Women.

MacLeod, L. (1987). *Battered but not beaten: Preventing wife battering in Canada.* Ottawa: Canadian Advisory Council on the Status of Women.

Mann, B. (1987). Working with battered women: Radical education or therapy. In E. Pence, with contributions by B. Mann, M.M. Flynn, Y. Bako, A. Marshall, J. Martin, S. Oberg, and N. Burns, *In our best interest: A process of personal and social change* (pp. 104-115). Duluth, MN: Minnesota Program Development.

Martin, B. and Mohanty, C.T. (1986). Feminist politics: What's home got to do with it? In T. de Lauretis (Ed.), *Feminist studies/critical studies* (pp. 191-212). Bloomington, IN: Indiana University Press.

McGrath, C. (1979). The crisis of the domestic order. *Socialist Review,* Number 43, *9*(1), 11-30.

McLaren, P. and Tadeu da Silva, T. (1993). Decentering pedagogy: Critical literacy, resistance and the politics of memory. In P. McLaren and P. Leonard (Eds.), *Paulo Freire: A critical encounter* (pp. 47-89). London: Routledge.

Menchú, R. (1984). *I Rigoberta Menchú: An Indian woman in Guatemala* (Elisabeth Burgos-Debray, ed. and introduction; Ann Wright, trans.). London: Verso. (Originally published as *Me Llamo Rigoberta Menchú y así me nació la conciencia.* Barcelona: Ed. Argos Vergara, 1983.)

Merriam, S.B. (1988). *Case study research in education: A qualitative approach.* San Francisco: Jossey-Bass.

Mies, M. (1983). Towards a methodology for feminist research. In R.D. Klein and G. Bowles (Eds.), *Theories of women's studies* (pp. 117-139). London: Routledge and Kegan Paul.

Mills, T. (1985). The assault on the self: Stages in coping with battering husbands. *Qualitative Sociology, 8*(2), 103-123.

Mohanty, C.T. (1992). Feminist encounters: Locating the politics of experience. In M. Barrett and A. Phillips (Eds.), *Destabilizing theory: Contemporary feminist debates* (pp. 74-92). Stanford, CA: Stanford University Press.

Mohanty, C.T. (1994). On race and voice: Challenges for liberal education in the 1990s. In H.A. Giroux and P. McLaren (Eds.), *Between borders: Pedagogy and the politics of cultural studies* (pp. 145-166). New York: Routledge.

Mohanty, C.T., Russo, A., and Torres, L. (Eds.) (1991). *Third world women and the politics of feminism.* Bloomington, IN: Indiana University Press.

Moreau, M. (1979). A structural approach to social work practice. *Canadian Journal of Social Work Education, 5*(1), 78-94.

Moreau, M. (1990). Empowerment through advocacy and consciousness-raising: Implications of a structural approach to social work. *Journal of Sociology and Social Welfare, 17*(2), 53-67.

Moreau, M. and Leonard, L. (1989). *Empowerment through a structural approach to social work. A report from practice.* Ecole de Service Social, Université de Montréal and School of Social Work, Carleton University, Ottawa.

Morgan, P. (1981). From battered wife to program client: The state's shaping of social problems. *Kapitalistate, (9)*, 17-39.

Mostern, K. (1994). Decolonization as learning: Practice and pedagogy in Frantz Fanon's revolutionary narrative. In H.A. Giroux and P. McLaren (Eds.), *Between Borders: Pedagogy and the politics of cultural studies* (pp. 253-271). New York: Routledge.

Mullaly, R. (1997). *Structural social work: Ideology, theory, and practice.* Toronto: Oxford.

Olesen, V. (1994). Feminisms and models of qualitative research. In N.K. Denzin and Y.S. Lincoln (Eds.), *Handbook of qualitative research* (pp. 158-174). Thousand Oaks, CA: Sage.

Orner, M. (1992). Interrupting the calls for student voice in "liberatory" education: A feminist poststructuralist perspective. In C. Luke and J. Gore (Eds.), *Feminisms and critical pedagogy* (pp. 74-89). New York: Routledge.

Pâquet-Deehy, A. and Robin, M. (1991). Breaking the cycle of violence for women. *The Social Worker, 59*(4), 179-183.

Patai, D. (1988). Constructing a self: A Brazilian life story. *Feminist Studies, 14*(1), 143-166.

Patton, M.Q. (1990). *Qualitative evaluation and research methods.* Newbury Park, CA: Sage.

Pence, E. and Burns, N. (1985). *In our best interest: A handbook for facilitating women's educational groups.* Duluth, MN: Women's Coalition and the Domestic Abuse Intervention Project.

Pence, E., with contributions by B. Mann, M.M. Flynn, Y. Bako, A. Marshall, J. Martin, S. Oberg, and N. Burns (1987). *In our best interest: A process of personal and social change.* Duluth, MN: Minnesota Program Development Inc.

Pence, E. and Paymar, M., with contributions by T. Ritmeester and M. Shepard. (1993). *Education groups for men who batter: The Duluth Model.* New York: Springer Publishing.

Pennell, J. (1987). Ideology at a Canadian shelter for battered women: A reconstruction. *Women's Studies International Forum, 10*(2), 113-123.

Pérez Naranjo, D. and Profitt, N.J. (1992). *Tiré el silencio afuera*. San José, Costa Rica: El Colectivo de Mujeres Pancha Carrasco.

Personal Narratives Group. (Eds.) (1989). *Interpreting women's lives: Feminist theory and personal narratives*. Bloomington, IN: Indiana University Press.

Poels, Y. and Berger, J. (1992). Groupwork with survivors of domestic violence. *Australian Social Work, 45*(4), 41-47.

Prieur, D. (1995). Patriarchy—Now you see it . . . Why we need to take another look at women's oppression in the family. In L. Timmins (Ed.), *Listening to the thunder: Advocates talk about the battered women's movement* (pp. 247-261). Vancouver: Women's Research Centre.

Profitt, N.J. (1994). Resisting violence against women in Central America: The experience of a feminist collective. *Canadian Social Work Review, 11*(1), 103-115.

Profitt, N.J. (1996). "Battered women" as "victims" and "survivors": Creating space for resistance. *Canadian Social Work Review, 13*(1), 23-38.

Quinby, A. (1995). Taking back the movement: Resisting professionalization and listening to women. In L. Timmins (Ed.), *Listening to the thunder: Advocates talk about the battered women's movement* (pp. 263-279). Vancouver: Women's Research Centre.

Radford, J. and Russell, D.E.H. (Eds.) (1992). *Femicide: The politics of woman killing*. Toronto: Maxwell Macmillan Canada.

Randall, M. (1988). Feminism and the state: Questions for theory and practice. *Resources for Feminist Research/Documentation sur la Recherche Feministe, 17*(3), 10-16.

Rangell, L. (1985). Defense and resistance in psychoanalysis and life. In H.P. Blum (Ed.), *Defense and resistance: Historical perspectives and current concepts* (pp. 147-173). New York: International Universities Press.

Reagon, B.J. (1983). Coalition politics: Turning the century. In B. Smith (Ed.), *Home girls: A black feminist anthology* (pp. 356-368). New York: Kitchen Table: Women of Color Press.

Reinharz, S. (1992). *Feminist methods in social science research*. New York: Oxford University Press.

Riessman, C.K. (1989). From victim to survivor: A woman's narrative reconstruction of marital sexual abuse. *Smith College Studies in Social Work, 59*(3), 232-251.

Ristock, J.L. (1991). Understanding violence in lesbian relationships: An examination of misogyny and homophobia. In S. Kirby, D. Daniels, K. McKenna, M. Pujol, and M. Valiquette (Eds.), *Women changing academe/les femmes changent l'academie* (pp. 113-121). Winnipeg: Sororal Publishing.

Ristock, J. and Pennell, J. (1996). *Community research as empowerment: Feminist links, postmodern interruptions*. Toronto: Oxford University Press.

Rockhill, K. (1987a). Literacy as threat/desire: Longing to be SOMEBODY. In J.S. Gaskell and A.T. McLaren (Eds.), *Women and education: A Canadian perspective* (pp. 315-331). Calgary: Detselig Enterprises.

Rockhill, K. (1987b). The chaos of subjectivity in the ordered halls of academe. *Canadian Woman Studies, 8*(4), 12-17.

Rodgers, K. (1994). Wife assault: The findings of a national survey. *Juristat, 14*(9), 1-21.

Rosaldo, R. (1993). *Culture and truth: The remaking of social analysis.* Boston: Beacon Press.

Roseneil, S. (1995). *Disarming patriarchy: Feminism and political action at Greenham.* Buckingham, UK: Open University Press.

Rushing, A.B. (1993). Surviving rape: A morning/mourning ritual. In S.M. James and A.P.A. Busia (Eds.), *Theorizing black feminisms: The visionary pragmatism of black women* (pp. 127-140). London: Routledge.

Sable, A. (1978). Facing some contradictions: My experiences as a white professor teaching minority students. In T.M. Norton and B. Ollman (Eds.), *Studies in socialist pedagogy* (pp. 335-350). New York: Monthly Review Press.

Sarachild, K. (1978). Consciousness-raising: A radical weapon. In Redstockings of the Women's Liberation Movement (Eds.), *Feminist revolution* (pp. 144-150) (Abridged edition). New York: Random House.

Schechter, S. (1982). *Women and male violence: The visions and the struggles of the battered women's movement.* Boston: South End Press.

Scheman, N. (1993). *Engenderings: Constructions of knowledge, authority, and privilege.* New York: Routledge.

Schuster, M.R. and Van Dyne, S.R. (1985). In M.R. Schuster and S.R. Van Dyne (Eds.), *Women's place in the academy: Transforming the liberal arts curriculum* (pp. 161-171). Totowa, NJ: Rowman and Allanheld.

Scott, J. (1992). Experience. In J. Butler and J. Scott (Eds.), *Feminists theorize the political* (pp. 22-40). New York: Routledge.

Shor, I. (1993). Education is politics: Paulo Freire's critical pedagogy. In P. McLaren and P. Leonard (Eds.), *Paulo Freire: A critical encounter* (pp. 25-35). New York: Routledge.

Simon, B.L. (1990). Rethinking empowerment. *Journal of Progressive Human Services, 1*(1), 27-39.

Smith, D. (1990a). *The conceptual practices of power: A feminist sociology of knowledge.* Boston: Northeastern University Press.

Smith, D. (1990b). *Texts, facts, and femininity: Exploring the relations of ruling.* London: Routledge.

Smith, P. (1988). *Discerning the subject.* Minneapolis: University of Minnesota Press.

Smith, W., Alschuler, A., Moreno, C., and Tasiquano, E. (1975). Critical consciousness. *Meforum: Journal of Educational Diversity and Innovation, 2*(1), 12-18.

Snider, L. (1990). The potential of the criminal justice system to promote feminist concerns. *Studies in Law, Politics, and Society, 10*, 143-172.

Sommer, D. (1988). "Not just a personal story": Women's *testimonios* and the plural self. In B. Brodzki and C. Schenck (Eds.), *Life/lines: Theorizing women's autobiography* (pp. 107-130). Ithaca, NY: Cornell University Press.

Spelman, E.V. (1988). *Inessential woman: Problems of exclusion in feminist thought.* Boston: Beacon Press.

Stanley, L. (1990). Feminist praxis and the academic mode of production. In L. Stanley (Ed.), *Feminist praxis: Research, theory and epistemology in feminist sociology* (pp. 3-19). London: Routledge.

Stanley, L. and Wise, S. (1993). *Breaking out again: Feminist ontology and epistemology.* London: Routledge.

Stefan, S. (1994). The protection racket: Rape trauma syndrome, psychiatric labelling, and law. *Northwestern University Law Review, 88*(4), 1271-1345.

Stern, J. and Leppard, D. (1995). Breaking in: Ex-residents organizing in Nova Scotia. In L. Timmins (Ed.), *Listening to the thunder: Advocates talk about the battered women's movement* (pp. 147-172). Vancouver: Women's Research Centre.

Sternbach, N.S., Navarro-Aranguren, M., Chuchryk, P., and Alvarez, S.E. (1992). Feminisms in Latin America: From Bogotá to San Bernardo. *Signs, 17*(2), 393-434.

Swift, K. (1998). Contradictions in child welfare: Neglect and repsonsibility. In C.T. Baines, P.M. Evans, and S.M. Neysmith (Eds.), *Women's caring: Feminist perspectives on social welfare* (pp. 160-187). Toronto: Oxford University Press.

Tatum, B.D. (1992). Talking about race, learning about racism: The application of racial identity development theory in the classroom. *Harvard Educational Review, 62*(1), 1-24.

Tierney, K. (1982). The battered women movement and the creation of the wife beating problem. *Social Problems, 29*(3), 207-219.

Timmins, L. (Ed.) (1995). *Listening to the thunder: Advocates talk about the battered women's movement.* Vancouver: Women's Research Centre.

Ursel, J. (1994). Eliminating violence against women: Reform or co-optation in state institutions. In L. Samuelson (Ed.), *Power and resistance: Critical thinking about Canadian social issues* (pp. 71-92). Halifax, Nova Scotia: Fernwood.

Vancouver Custody and Access Support and Advocacy Association. (1995). The mediation wheel: The broken promise of justice in the courts for women and children. In L. Timmins (Ed.), *Listening to the thunder: Advocates talk about the battered women's movement* (pp. 127-130). Vancouver: Women's Research Centre.

Walker, G. (1990). *Family violence and the women's movement: The conceptual politics of struggle.* Toronto: University of Toronto.

Walker, G. (1995). Violence and the relations of ruling: Lessons from the battered women's movement. In M. Campbell and A. Manicom (Eds.), *Knowledge, experience, and ruling relations: Studies in the social organization of knowledge* (pp. 65-79). Toronto: University of Toronto Press.

Walkerdine, V. (1985). On the regulation of speaking and silence: Subjectivity, class and gender in contemporary schooling. In C. Steedman, C. Urwin, and V. Walkerdine (Eds.), *Language, gender and childhood* (pp. 203-241). London: Routledge and Kegan Paul.

Wallerstein, R.S. (1985). In H.P. Blum (Ed.), *Defense and resistance: Historical perspectives and current concepts* (pp. 201-225). New York: International Universities Press.

Weedon, C. (1987). *Feminist practice and poststructuralist theory.* Oxford, UK: Basil Blackwell.

Weiler, K. (1988). *Women teaching for change: Gender, class, and power.* South Hadley, MA: Bergin and Garvey.

Wendell, S. (1993). Oppression and victimization: Choice and responsibility. In D. Shogan (Ed.), *A reader in feminist ethics* (pp. 279-305). Toronto: Canadian Scholars' Press.

Wood, G.G. and Middleman, R.R. (1992). Groups to empower battered women. *Affilia, 7*(4), 82-95.

Young, I.M. (1992). Five faces of oppression. In T.E. Wartenberg (Ed.), *Rethinking power* (pp. 174-195). Albany, NY: State University of New York.

Young, I. (1997). The complexities of coalition. *Dissent, 44*(Winter), 64-69.

Zinn, M.B. and Dill, B.T. (1996). Theorizing difference from multiracial feminism. *Feminist Studies, 22*(2), 321-331.

Index

HAWORTH Social Work Practice in Action
Carlton E. Munson, PhD, Senior Editor

WOMEN SURVIVORS, PSYCHOLOGICAL TRAUMA, AND THE POLITICS OF RESISTANCE by Norma Jean Profitt. (2000). "A compelling argument on the importance of political and collective action as a means of resisting oppression. Should be read by survivors, service providers, and activists in the violence-against-women movement." *Gloria Geller, PhD, Faculty of Social Work, University of Regina, Saskatchewan, Canada*

THE MENTAL HEALTH DIAGNOSTIC DESK REFERENCE: VISUAL GUIDES AND MORE FOR LEARNING TO USE THE DIAGNOSTIC AND STATISTICAL MANUAL (DSM-IV) by Carlton E. Munson. (2000). "A carefully organized and user-friendly book for the beginning student and less-experienced practitioner of social work, clinical psychology, or psychiatric nursing . . . . It will be a valuable addition to the literature on clinical assessment of mental disorders." *Jerrold R. Brandell, PhD, BCD, Professor, School of Social Work, Wayne State University, Detroit, Michigan and Founding Editor,* Psychoanalytic Social Work

HUMAN SERVICES AND THE AFROCENTRIC PARADIGM by Jerome H. Schiele. (2000). "Represents a milestone in applying the Afrocentric paradigm to human services generally, and social work specifically. . . . A highly valuable resource." *Bogart R. Leashore, PhD, Dean and Professor, Hunter College School of Social Work, New York, New York*

SOCIAL WORK: SEEKING RELEVANCY IN THE TWENTY-FIRST CENTURY by Roland Meinert, John T. Pardeck and Larry Kreuger. (2000). "Highly recommended. A thought-provoking work that asks the difficult questions and challenges the status quo. A great book for graduate students as well as experienced social workers and educators." *Francis K. O. Yuen, DSW, ACSE, Associate Professor, Division of Social Work, California State University, Sacramento*

SOCIAL WORK PRACTICE IN HOME HEALTH CARE by Ruth Ann Goode. (2000). "Dr. Goode presents both a lucid scenario and a formulated protocol to bring health care services into the home setting. . . . This is a must have volume that will be a reference to be consulted many times." *Marcia B. Steinhauer, PhD, Coordinator and Associate Professor, Human Services Administration Program, Rider University, Lawrenceville, New Jersey*

FORENSIC SOCIAL WORK: LEGAL ASPECTS OF PROFESSIONAL PRACTICE, SECOND EDITION by Robert L. Barker and Douglas M. Branson. (2000). "The authors combine their expertise to create this informative guide to address legal practice issues facing social workers." *Newsletter of the National Organization of Forensic Social Work*

SOCIAL WORK IN THE HEALTH FIELD: A CARE PERSPECTIVE by Lois A. Fort Cowles. (1999). "Makes an important contribution to the field by locating the practice of social work in health care within an organizational and social context." *Goldie Kadushin, PhD, Associate Professor, School of Social Welfare, University of Wisconsin, Milwaukee*

SMART BUT STUCK: WHAT EVERY THERAPIST NEEDS TO KNOW ABOUT LEARNING DISABILITIES AND IMPRISONED INTELLIGENCE by Myrna Orenstein. (1999). "A trailblazing effort that creates an entirely novel way of talking and thinking about learning disabilities. There is simply nothing like it in the field." *Fred M. Levin, MD, Training Supervising Analyst, Chicago Institute for Psychoanalysis; Assistant Professor of Clinical Psychiatry, Northwestern University, School of Medicine, Chicago, IL*

CLINICAL WORK AND SOCIAL ACTION: AN INTEGRATIVE APPROACH by Jerome Sachs and Fred Newdom. (1999). "Just in time for the new millennium come Sachs and Newdom with a wholly fresh look at social work. . . . A much-needed uniting of social work values, theories, and practice for action." *Josephine Nieves, MSW, PhD, Executive Director, National Association of Social Workers*

SOCIAL WORK PRACTICE IN THE MILITARY by James G. Daley. (1999). "A significant and worthwhile book with provocative and stimulating ideas. It deserves to be read by a wide audience in social work education and practice as well as by decision makers in the military." *H. Wayne Johnson, MSW, Professor, University of Iowa, School of Social Work, Iowa City, Iowa*

GROUP WORK: SKILLS AND STRATEGIES FOR EFFECTIVE INTERVENTIONS, SECOND EDITION by Sondra Brandler and Camille P. Roman. (1999). "A clear, basic description of what group work requires, including what skills and techniques group workers need to be effective." *Hospital and Community Psychiatry* (from the first edition)

TEENAGE RUNAWAYS: BROKEN HEARTS AND "BAD ATTITUDES" by Laurie Schaffner (1999). "Skillfully combines the authentic voice of the juvenile runaway with the principles of social science research."

CELEBRATING DIVERSITY: COEXISTING IN A MULTICULTURAL SOCIETY by Benyamin Chetkow-Yanoov. (1999). "Makes a valuable contribution to peace theory and practice." *Ian Harris, EdD, Executive Secretary, Peace Education Committee, International Peace Research Association*

SOCIAL WELFARE POLICY ANALYSIS AND CHOICES by Hobart A. Burch. (1999). "Will become the landmark text in its field for many decades to come." *Sheldon Rahan, DSW, Founding Dean and Emeritus Professor of Social Policy and Social Administration. Faculty of Social Work, Wilfrid Laurier University, Canada*

SOCIAL WORK PRACTICE: A SYSTEMS APPROACH, SECOND EDITION by Benyamin Chetkow-Yannov. (1999). "Highly recommended as a primary text for any and all introductory social work courses." *Ram A. Cnaan, PhD, Associate Professor, School of Social Work, University of Pennsylvania*

CRITICAL SOCIAL WELFARE ISSUES: TOOLS FOR SOCIAL WORK AND HEALTH CARE PROFESSIONALS edited by Arthur J. Katz, Abraham Lurie, and Carlos M. Vidal. (1997). "Offers hopeful agendas for change, while navigating the societal challenges facing those in the human services today." *Book News Inc.*

SOCIAL WORK IN HEALTH SETTINGS: PRACTICE IN CONTEXT, SECOND EDITION edited by Toba Schwaber Kerson. (1997). "A first-class document . . . It will be found among the steadier and lasting works on the social work aspects of American health care." *Hans S. Falck, PhD, Professor Emeritus and Former Chair, Health Specialization in Social Work, Virginia Commonwealth University*

PRINCIPLES OF SOCIAL WORK PRACTICE: A GENERIC PRACTICE APPROACH by Molly R. Hancock. (1997). "Hancock's discussions advocate reflection and self-awareness to create a climate for client change." *Journal of Social Work Education*

NOBODY'S CHILDREN: ORPHANS OF THE HIV EPIDEMIC by Steven F. Dansky. (1997). "Professional sound, moving, and useful for both professionals and interested readers alike." *Ellen G. Friedman, ACSW, Associate Director of Support Services, Beth Israel Medical Center, Methadone Maintenance Treatment Program*

SOCIAL WORK APPROACHES TO CONFLICT RESOLUTION: MAKING FIGHTING OBSOLETE by Benyamin Chetkow-Yanoov. (1996). "Presents an examination of the nature and cause of conflict and suggests techniques for coping with conflict." *Journal of Criminal Justice*

FEMINIST THEORIES AND SOCIAL WORK: APPROACHES AND APPLICATIONS by Christine Flynn Salunier. (1996). " An essential reference to be read repeatedly by all educators and practitioners who are eager to learn more about feminist theory and practice: *Nancy R. Hooyman, PhD, Dean and Professor, School of Social Work, University of Washington, Seattle*

THE RELATIONAL SYSTEMS MODEL FOR FAMILY THERAPY: LIVING IN THE FOUR REALITIES by Donald R. Bardill. (1996). "Engages the reader in quiet, thoughtful conversation on the timeless issue of helping families and individuals." *Christian Counseling Resource Review*

SOCIAL WORK INTERVENTION IN AN ECONOMIC CRISIS: THE RIVER COMMUNITIES PROJECT by Martha Baum and Pamela Twiss. (1996). "Sets a standard for universities in terms of the types of meaningful roles they can play in supporting and sustaining communities." *Kenneth J. Jaros, PhD, Director, Public Health Social Work Training Program, University of Pittsburgh*

FUNDAMENTALS OF COGNITIVE-BEHAVIOR THERAPY: FROM BOTH SIDES OF THE DESK by Bill Borcherdt. (1996). "Both beginning and experienced practitioners . . . will find a considerable number of valuable suggestions in Borcherdt's book." *Albert Ellis, PhD, President, Institute for Rational-Emotive Therapy, New York City*

BASIC SOCIAL POLICY AND PLANNING: STRATEGIES AND PRACTICE METHODS by Hobart A. Burch. (1996). "Burch's familiarity with his topic is evident and his book is an easy introduction to the field." *Readings*

THE CROSS-CULTURAL PRACTICE OF CLINICAL CASE MANAGEMENT IN MENTAL HEALTH edited by Peter Manoleas. (1996). "Makes a contribution by bringing together the cross-cultural and clinical case management perspectives in working with those who have serious mental illness." *Disability Studies Quarterly*

FAMILY BEYOND FAMILY: THE SURROGATE PARENT IN SCHOOLS AND OTHER COMMUNITY AGENCIES by Sanford Weinstein. (1995). "Highly recommended to anyone concerned about the welfare of our children and the breakdown of the American family." *Jerold S. Greenberg, EdD, Director of Community Service, College of Health & Human Performance, University of Maryland*

PEOPLE WITH HIV AND THOSE WHO HELP THEM: CHALLENGES, INTEGRATION, INTERVENTION by R. Dennis Shelby. (1995). "A useful and compassionate contribution to the HIV psychotherapy literature." *Public Health*

THE BLACK ELDERLY: SATISFACTION AND QUALITY OF LATER LIFE by Marguerite Coke and James A. Twaite. (1995). "Presents a model for predicting life satisfaction in this population." *Abstracts in Social Gerontology*

BUILDING ON WOMEN'S STRENGTHS: A SOCIAL WORK AGENDA FOR THE TWENTY-FIRST CENTURY edited by Liane V. Davis. (1994). "The most lucid and accessible overview of the related epistemological debates int he social work literature." *Journal of the National Association of Social Workers*

NOW DARE EVERYTHING: TALES OF HIV-RELATED PSYCHOTHERAPY by Steven F. Dansky. (1994). "A highly recommended book for anyone working with persons who are HIV positive. . . . Every library should have a copy of this book." *AIDS Book Review Journal*

INTERVENTION RESEARCH: DESIGN AND DEVELOPMENT FOR HUMAN SERVICE edited by Jack Rothman and Edwin J. Thomas. (1994). "Provides a useful framework for the further examination of methodology for each separate step of such research." *Academic Library Book Review*

CLINICAL SOCIAL WORK SUPERVISION, SECOND EDITION by Carlton E. Munson. (1993). "A useful, thorough, and articulate reference for supervisors and for 'supervisees' who are wanting to understand their supervisor or are looking for effective supervision." *Transactional Analysis Journal*

ELEMENTS OF THE HELPING PROCESS: A GUIDE FOR CLINICIANS by Raymond Fox. (1993). "Filled with helpful hints, creative interventions, and practical guidelines." *Journal of Family Psychotherapy*

IF A PARTNER HAS AIDS: GUIDE TO CLINICAL INTERVENTION FOR RELATIONSHIPS IN CRISIS by R. Dennis Shelby. (1993). " A welcome addition to existing publications about couples coping with AIDS, it offers intervention ideas and strategies to clinicians." *Contemporary Psychology*

GERONTOLOGICAL SOCIAL WORK SUPERVISION by Ann Burack-Weiss and Frances Coyle Brennan. (1991). "The creative ideas in this book will aid supervisors working with students and experienced social workers." *Senior News*

SOCIAL WORK THEORY AND PRACTICE WITH THE TERMINALLY ILL by Joan K. Parry. (1989). "Should be read by all professionals engaged in the provision of health services in hospitals, emergency rooms, and hospices." *Hector B. Garcia, PhD, Professor, San Jose State University School of Social Work*

THE CREATIVE PRACTITIONER: THEORY AND METHODS FOR THE HELPING SERVICES by Bernard Gelfand. (1988). "[Should] be widely adopted by those in the helping services. It could lead to significant positive advances by countless individuals." *Sidney J. Parnes, Trustee Chairperson for Strategic Program Development, Creative Education Foundation, Buffalo, NY*

MANAGEMENT AND INFORMATION SYSTEMS IN HUMAN SERVICES: IMPLICATIONS FOR THE DISTRIBUTION OF AUTHORITY AND DECISION MAKING by Richard K. Caputo. (1987). "A contribution to social work scholarship in that it provides conceptual frameworks that can be used in the design of management information systems." *Social Work*

DEC 03